The
Hiking Book
From Hell

Are Kalvø

The Hiking Book From Hell

TRANSLATED BY
Lucy Moffatt

GREYSTONE BOOKS
Vancouver/Berkeley/London

Greystone Books Ltd.
greystonebooks.com

Cataloguing data available from Library and Archives Canada
ISBN 978-1-77164-585-0 (pbk.)
ISBN 978-1-77164-586-7 (epub)

Editing by Derek Fairbridge
Proofreading by Alison Strobel
Cover design and composite by Jessica Sullivan and Belle Wuthrich
Cover composite illustration credits: 32 pixels, ProStockStudio,
happyholla/Shutterstock
Text design by Belle Wuthrich

Greystone Books thanks the Canada Council for the Arts,
the British Columbia Arts Council, the Province of British Columbia
through the Book Publishing Tax Credit, and the Government of
Canada for supporting our publishing activities.

This translation has been published with the financial support of NORLA.

Greystone Books gratefully acknowledges the xʷməθkʷəy̓əm (Musqueam),
Sḵwx̱wú7mesh (Squamish), and səlílwəta?ɬ (Tsleil-Waututh) peoples on
whose land our Vancouver head office is located.

CONTENTS

IN A RECENT SURVEY, almost eighty percent of people living in the same country as me, Norway, said they had gone hiking in the mountains or the forest at least once in the past twelve months.

I haven't been hiking in either the mountains or the forest for at least thirty years.

There comes a time when you have to ask yourself: Am I the one with the problem?

THAT'S
NOT IT

AT THE FARM where I grew up, there's a set of storehouse steps. Uneven stone steps that look like they've been there forever. The storehouse door is heavy and warped and difficult to open, and has to be unlocked with a rusty old key the size of a well-fed baby. The storehouse is full of what storehouses are always full of: stuff you haven't thrown away. And when you live on a farm, you never throw stuff away. Because you're so spoiled for space that you never *have* to throw stuff away. In the storehouse you'll find cooking equipment and farming implements that must once have served a purpose but now just look dangerous. You'll find old things with short names. Troughs. Looms. Pails. Churns. Sleds. Stools. Old magazines. Comics. A dollhouse that looks spooky, the way dollhouses tend to. My old twelve-inch singles from the eighties—needlessly extended versions of moderately popular hits by big-haired British artists. Electronics that lie around gathering dust until the day they suddenly find themselves back in fashion. This is where I recently unearthed a forty-year-old radio that I took home with me and which now serves as an amplifier in my living room. Not a single guest has failed to admire that radio.

And it's the same with the storehouse steps. These storehouse steps so thoroughly embody the romantic cliché of the Norwegian farm—old and homemade and uneven—that visitors tend to notice them and take a photo.

So, yes. That's the kind of place where I grew up. With a storehouse and a cowshed and troughs and looms and other old things with short names. Things that get handed down. And forest. A lot of forest. A tree house. A river whose loud, incessant rushing I never noticed until I moved away and came back to visit. A white wooden house. A bedroom with a view of a fjord. And animals. Cows, chickens, pigs. A dog that just turned up one day and never left. And always a cat.

So *that's* not it. My upbringing is full of nature, soil, animals, tradition, self-picked fruit and berries. And mountains. A lot of mountains.

An awful lot of mountains.

FROM THE STOREHOUSE STEPS you look out over the farm's fields. And beyond the fields: mountains. Drive four minutes from the farm in any direction and you hit mountains. Dramatic mountains, mountains that are tourist attractions, mountains that people travel halfway across the globe to photograph. Mountains with good hiking opportunities. And ski slopes. The Norwegian skiing championships have been held here. The Slalom World Cup has been held here. One in three ads designed to look authentically Norwegian are filmed here. Two in three ads designed to look authentically Norwegian are filmed in New Zealand. It's cheaper.

And I've done my fair share of hiking. I've spent time in the mountains. My feet are no strangers to skis. Cross-country *and* downhill. Where I grew up, that was just what you did on the weekend unless you had a damn good excuse.

So it isn't that I'm not used to the great outdoors and hiking and skiing. During my childhood, when my school had a skiing field trip, it was often held at my place. It's true. My family's farm was near the school and we had plenty of space. So the students would come to do cross-country skiing on our property. And they'd arrange ski-jumping at our place, too. Because there was a hill where I grew up that was a perfect ski-jumping hill. Do you hear that? I grew up with ski tracks and a ski-jumping hill at home.

So *that's* not it.

IN 1983—AND TO THIS DAY nobody can explain how it happened—my hometown's soccer team was that year's sensation. The team and the place are both called Stranda. Stranda played in the lowly fourth division of the Norwegian Football League and managed to make it all the way through to the third round in the Norwegian Football Cup. A highly unusual turn of events.

Along the way, Stranda knocked out a third-division team and—far more importantly—the second-division team from Ålesund, the only city in our district. They were a team with a declared ambition of breaking into the highest division, who considered themselves innately superior to us local yokels on pretty much every count. Stranda had around 3,000 inhabitants. Ålesund, 25,000. Stranda knocked them out. And in the third round, Stranda was set to meet what was then, indisputably, Norway's very finest team: Vålerenga. I'm not making this up. Vålerenga won the Norwegian championship both that year and the year after. Vålerenga are from Oslo. Stranda had three thousand inhabitants; Oslo well over half a million.

In the run-up to the match, every major Norwegian newspaper covered it, publishing photos of Stranda's best players alongside local dignitaries to show that the whole village was standing shoulder to shoulder, and interviewing stars from Vålerenga who said things like: "Stranda? Where's that?"

So it isn't that I come from a big place. It isn't that I'm used to things happening all the time.

That's not it.

BUT ON THE RARE OCCASION something actually *did* happen, we'd turn out for it. They say four thousand people watched the match between Stranda and Vålerenga.

Four thousand. In a place with three thousand inhabitants. That's a 130 percent turnout. It's equivalent to a crowd of almost 900,000 in Oslo, 8 million in Toronto, or 25 million in New York.

People came from the capital to watch the match. And people came from Ålesund to see Stranda humiliated by Norway's finest team. One of the people who came was a friend of my dad's with a comb-over. He was called The King. Don't ask. Everybody in Ålesund has names like that. The King came to visit the farm where I grew up. He most definitely noticed the storehouse steps. And he stood there gazing out across the fields. When The King went back to town and his friends asked him what Stranda was like, The King apparently declared: "There were the most enormous plains."

So it isn't that I'm used to having masses of people and masses of noise and masses of action around me. I'm used to having plenty of elbow room. Enormous plains. Silence. Storehouse steps. In a place where so little happened that when at last something *did* happen, 130 percent of the village turned out for it.

So *that's* not it.

AND IT ISN'T THAT I've got anything against physical exercise, either. I've been a promising soccer player pretty much my entire life. I've even played on the same side as some of those lads who suffered a glorious 2–0 defeat at the hands of Norway's finest team in 1983. I've been an active cross-country skier too. Not *very* active, but active all the same. I have several excellent second places to my name and a trophy to prove it. A fairly small trophy, admittedly. In fact, you wouldn't believe how small this trophy is. Imagine a shot glass. It's about half that size. But I have that trophy lying around somewhere. Probably in the storehouse.

⟁

AND IT ISN'T THAT I don't like walking. Quite the opposite. Walking is one of the things I like doing best. I walk every day, and I walk long distances. So *that's* not it.

But I walk the *wrong* way. What I like best is walking to places where there are people. Preferably waiters. I like walking around in the streets of the city center. Just milling about with no particular place in mind. There weren't a lot of people doing that kind of thing in my hometown when I was growing up. Back there, you got your driver's license the second you hit eighteen and from that day forward, you did your best never to leave your car. If people saw a grown person walking around the center of the village, they'd all think: *Wow, has he lost his license?*

Or: *Is there a new teacher at the secondary school?*

Walking was not something you did in the center of our village.

Getting into a car, driving four minutes to the foot of a mountain, walking up this mountain then back down again, getting back into the same car, and driving home? Absolutely normal.

Walking around the center aimlessly? Local eccentric.

But I have it in me. The urge to walk—a long way.

So *that's* not it either.

⟁

THE FIRST TIME a person who knows me really well came to visit the farm where I grew up, she—like everybody else—noticed the old storehouse steps. She looked at the steps. Then she said to me:

"You used to sit there gazing into the distance and thinking: *this isn't where I'm supposed to be.*"

⟁

THAT'S WHAT IT IS.

BECAUSE THAT *WAS* what I thought as I sat on these steps in my youth. And I sat there pretty often. I was one of them, I'm afraid. One of those people who sit and gaze into the distance, trying to look deep. But I didn't think about nature. I never thought how beautiful it all was. How grateful you should be to be able to live this way, active and at one with nature.

No. What I thought was: *this isn't where I'm supposed to be.*

That wasn't the only thing I thought, of course. I wasn't crazy. I was a sensitive young soul. I also thought massively pompous things that I'll never admit to having thought no matter how much you ask me, so screw that, okay?

But I did think that, too. That this wasn't where I was supposed to be. Even though my life was good in every possible way.

And it isn't an original thing to think, of course. I'm well aware of that. All of us who come from small places and descend to writing books later in life tell the same story of the longing to leave. This is horribly unoriginal. And most of the friends I grew up with who moved away felt exactly the same.

We moved to cities. We studied. We went to the pub. We discussed things we had no clue about late into the night. We absorbed culture we didn't actually like. We walked around the streets of the city center. We got ourselves new friends, new tastes, another round. Generally speaking, we kept busy. I thought then—and still do now—that most of the best things life has to offer me involve people, preferably lots of people, and lots of noise. And that if somebody's gone to all the trouble of inventing things like walls and ceilings and hotel bars, it's downright ungrateful to live in tents. We moved to the city, used the city, liked the city, and didn't look back. Loads of us were like that.

BUT.

Most people don't stay like that for the rest of their lives.

It passes. That's the thing. When you finish your studies or whatever else you use as an excuse to move to a city; when you become an adult, settle down, slow the pace. Something happens then. You find other values.

And you suddenly realize you absolutely love nature.

This has happened to almost everybody I know. Just not me.

I'VE LOST SO MANY friends to nature in the past few years. Good people. Bright people. Funny people who used to love going to the pub to shoot the breeze. What are they up to now? They get up early, take a picture of some ski tracks, post it on Facebook and Instagram, and write: "Nice day outdoors!"

These are people I once considered good friends. And witty.

"Nice day outdoors!" That's the best they can manage now.

This happens to a lot of people at a certain point in life. You start to lose your sense of humor. And your hair. The two things often coincide. In fact I'm starting to worry that maybe our humor's stored in our hair.

You lose your sense of humor and your hair, and you start going on mountain hikes. All of these things happen just when you reach that point in life where bouncers long ago stopped asking for your ID and long ago started asking if you're quite sure this is your kind of place.

A lot of life changes happen at that age.

You start going to the gym in the hopes of looking as good as you possibly can in the absence of both hair *and* humor. And yes, I know there are people who say they don't exercise to look good and that exercise is its own reward. Fine. But if exercise didn't have any impact on our health or physique we wouldn't do it, would we? No doctor has ever said to a patient: "You have a month left to live," and had that patient reply: "Right then, I'll start exercising. That's what I'll do with my last four weeks. I'll spend my last four weeks on this planet dressed in Lycra, in an overlit gym with other people dressed in Lycra who I don't know and who stink of sweat and we'll all stare straight ahead listening to music we don't like played far too loudly as we cycle on bikes that don't go anywhere."

You don't necessarily stop going out when you reach this age, but you do start going to places where there isn't too much noise. Or bouncers. Or people. Because when you get to this age, you start to enjoy meeting your friends to talk. About unbelievably dull stuff. Because that happens at this age too. If men this age give evasive answers when our girlfriends ask what we actually did on our latest guys' trip it isn't because we did something unmentionable or can't remember what we did. It's because we can't bear to admit that we sat in a pub in London for three days talking about how much paid time off we're owed.

Or worse still, about working out. Or nature.

You see, it isn't just that everybody suddenly starts wandering around in nature. They won't stop talking about it, either. And they talk about it without a trace of humor. People who were once bright and resourceful now take it upon themselves, in all seriousness, to make pronouncements like:

"The silence in the mountains is quite unlike any other."

No, it isn't. Actually, it's exactly like any other silence. Except that it probably isn't totally silent when it's silent in the mountains. So the silence in the mountains is probably more like wind. Or rain. Or mosquitoes.

"If you make an early start, you get all of nature to yourself."

I see. Well, that's a bit selfish, isn't it?

"The mountains fill me with a very special kind of peace."

Good for you. Why are you telling me this?

"It's only when you come face to face with nature that you realize how small you are."

Okay, if it's only when you come face to face with nature that you realize how small you are, your ego's just too big.

If you really need to realize how small your own problems are, think of Aleppo. Not Norwegian mountains.

"I've started collecting peaks now. I already have enough material things."

We both know perfectly well that you haven't stopped collecting material things. You just bought yourself a seven-hundred-dollar juicer. You're collecting peaks *as well*.

"This vacation, we're hiking from cabin to cabin in the mountains."

That isn't a vacation. Hiking from cabin to cabin in the mountains is, at best, a form of vacation consisting exclusively of the two most boring aspects of being on vacation: packing and transport.

BUT THAT'S WHAT people get up to in Norway. Hiking from cabin to cabin, for days on end, the sweat and sense of humor oozing out of their pores.

THEY HIKE TO CABINS with names like Pyttbua and Tjennhuken and Gaukhei and Krækkja. Some of these names can be translated, as Puddleshack or Tarnhook or Cuckoo Moor. Some of them simply can't be translated. They're old Nordic names that only fourth-generation Norwegians could hope to pronounce and nobody on earth could hope to spell.

AND I'M NOT making this up, okay? These are actual names of actual cabins in the Norwegian mountains. Cabins where people spend their vacations. Really. Fokstugu, Styggemannshytta, Myggheim— Snowdrift Croft, Ugly Man's Cabin, Gnatland. Gnatland!!

JUST HOW WIDESPREAD is this? How many friends do I have left who haven't chosen nature over a social life full of silly banter and laughter? I recently decided to set to work systematically. I hunted them all down on social media: old classmates, old university friends, old teachers and lecturers, colleagues and bosses. They all live very different lives nowadays. They live in the north, south, east, and west. They're gay and straight. They're single and coupled-up and married and somewhere in between. They have no children or two children or five children, with two or three or four different partners. They're architects and engineers, artisans and factory workers, authors and teachers; they run corner stores and sell furniture.

But all, and I mean *all* of them, have pictures of mountains.

Maybe they're standing on the mountain. Maybe bare-chested. One of them was also bare-bottomed—I'd rather not talk about that. Maybe they're standing in front of the mountain. Maybe they've just taken a picture of it. But all, absolutely all of them, have a picture of at least one mountain.

I don't know anybody who doesn't have a picture of a mountain on Facebook.

WHEN DID THIS HAPPEN? Did I miss a meeting? Who kidnapped all my friends? And replaced them with a bunch of grinning outdoors enthusiasts? Who are content to be snapped, thumbs-up, wearing silly hats in the wilderness? And actually look as if they're enjoying it?

I know single people who complain about losing touch with old friends when they pair off. And I understand that. But at least they lose their friends to the greatest thing of all: love. I lose my friends to a lump of rock.

And when it comes to those single friends of mine, just imagine what they're up against. A few of them use apps to search for that special someone. At first glance the choice looks overwhelming, but if you rule out everybody who's obviously stark raving mad, and then everybody with a photo of themselves on a mountain, there are only three people left. In the entire country. And all three of them are probably your exes.

⚠

I'VE ALWAYS TRUSTED STATISTICS more than myself. So I checked. And this isn't just some feeling I have. And it doesn't just apply to my friends. And it doesn't just apply to people my age, the ones in the death-fearing bracket between forty and fifty. More detailed and, perhaps, disturbing statistics follow later in the book, but let me say this straight off: it's safe to say there's been an explosive increase in outdoor activity in my lifetime. And it's spreading. Young people go walking in the mountains of their own free will. Pensioners hike in field and forest. Everybody's wandering about in nature. Just now, as I write this, autumn break is nearly upon us in Norway—because we have that, of course—and I take a moment to look at some online news. And there I read that, according to a brand-new study, seven in ten people plan to spend their fall vacation out in nature. And that's just the average. The figure is even higher for the forty to fifty-nine age group—my age group.

It's as if I left briefly and came back to find the whole country in the throes of a collective midlife crisis. And not one of those crazy, dangerous midlife crises they make films about either, with wild parties, sudden break-ups, and ill-advised drug abuse. Not the kind of crisis where you wake up with four front teeth missing in a city you don't remember traveling to. No, what we're talking about here is a thoroughly sensible and wholesome midlife crisis that enjoys the full and warm support of the health authorities.

It's as if common sense has won. And you can see it on several fronts.

Young pop stars who could once be relied upon to say predictably irresponsible and provocative things in interviews now say things that are just as predictably responsible and non-provocative in interviews. Role model? Mom and Dad. Leisure interests? Going to the gym.

Even reality TV is going the sensible route. Reality TV: the very definition of moral dissolution twenty years ago. When it started, reality TV was all about people drinking as much as possible and having as much sex as possible in a month. Just like Ramadan then, only in reverse. Now reality shows and docusoaps are increasingly about moving to the countryside, living the old-fashioned way, and solving tasks in groups. Norway's longest-running reality concept, which has been sold to lots of other countries too is, of course, a competition about . . . ?

That's right. Hiking. In nature.

They're everywhere. Sensible people in sensible clothes. Healthy people taking pictures of mountains. People who say: "Good shoes are the be-all and end-all" without a hint of humor.

UNLESS YOU'RE A PSYCHOPATH, you start to wonder in the end. Am I the one with the problem? Why don't I feel drawn to nature like everybody else? Why don't I long for the silence unlike any other? After all, I grew up with storehouse steps and animals and forests and troughs and looms. And mountains. An awful lot of mountains. And, as I said, I had a great life there.

What's wrong with me—a person who grew up in a spot with almost limitless space and access to nature but whose fondest memory is the one day in the history of the village when several thousand people were gathered in a pretty tiny place?

Could it just be that I'm not adult enough? Is this something that comes with age? Will I wake up one day in the near future and sense that everything has changed? That the only thing I want to do—no, *have* to do!—today is go to a high place, bare my bottom, and take a photo? And then write: #free?

▲

SOMEBODY ONCE SAID you should try everything in life once apart from incest and Morris dancing. Like every other quotable quote, it's debatable who actually said it first. And like every other quotable quote, this one is neither true nor good. Of course there are plenty of things in life you shouldn't even try once. Suicide, to take the most obvious example. But if instead of saying "everything" you restrict yourself to "everything that's legal and that the people you like enjoy doing," there's something to it. It doesn't have quite the same stylish ring to it, of course, but that just makes the message more attractive. A message about being curious and letting yourself get swept up.

In my adult years, at least, I like to see myself as the kind of person who lets himself get swept up, who's interested in what people are interested in. The most boring thing I can think of is people who automatically and on spurious grounds write off anything that lots of other people are interested in. If lots of people do something and talk about something, it makes me feel like finding out what it's all about; I want to understand why so many people are interested in it and—ideally—let myself get swept up too. That's why I listen to music nobody else my age listens to. That's why I sometimes keep track of competitions I don't entirely understand. And that's why I suddenly ended up on vacation in Iceland in the summer of 2016. I'm not remotely Icelandic. I don't know anybody from Iceland. I have no relationship to Iceland beyond the regular stuff. I know they talk funny and have hot springs, and I also used to listen to Björk during a period of my youth when I didn't know any better. But then in 2016, Iceland's soccer team was that year's sensation in the European championship. They went through. They knocked out England. And suddenly, Iceland was in the quarterfinals. Iceland, where it's pretty much always winter and the massed population is the same size as a quarter of a London borough. And there was a group of us sitting in a sports bar in Norway watching the images from Reykjavík, where close to the entire population of Iceland was standing in the middle of the city watching the matches together on a big screen. And they were singing and cheering. There was only one thing for it. We ordered tickets then and there, traveled to Reykjavík, and watched the quarterfinals with close to the entire population of Iceland. It was fantastic.

And okay, I know this is a bit boastful and not everybody has the time or the cash to take off for Iceland just like that. On the other hand, you clearly have the time to head for a mountaintop whenever the rain holds off. And all that cash you spent on your hiking gear would buy you several trips to Iceland.

▲

OF COURSE, I see there's a pattern here. There's a direct line from the day when my local team met Norway's finest team in the national soccer championship. But this isn't about soccer. It's about people. About letting yourself get swept up.

I like to let myself get swept up.

Life's just much more fun that way.

But my attitude toward outdoor life is very deep-seated. Outdoor life is definitely something a lot of people are involved in. So I should—if I'm going to live up to what I've been saying about myself here—let myself get swept up in this too.

But it's very deep-seated.

▲

HERE'S A LITTLE STORY to help you really understand just how little I am, have been, wish to be, or see myself as, an outdoorsman.

Not so long ago, I suffered a knee injury. As a result, I had to use crutches for a few weeks. It can be pretty good fun stomping around the streets on crutches. You get a ton of sympathy. People smile at you. People give you encouraging nods. But after a while, I started to see something else in the looks and smiles of the people I met. Was it indulgence? A kind of recognition? Several of the people I met nodded and gave me a look that said, "I know."

That's when the penny dropped. This is what people see: a man in his forties on crutches. Knee injury. This is what they think: *he overstretched himself on a trip to the mountains.* Typical climbing accident, they think.

Oh no! They think I'm one of them.

I felt an overpowering need to explain myself. In every social situation, I would explain lightning fast what had really happened— too loudly, in too much detail, and often without anybody asking. IT HAPPENED AT A PARTY, I would yell. I WAS DANCING! IT WAS THREE THIRTY IN THE MORNING. IT HAPPENED AT A PARTY! IT'S A DANCING INJURY. NOT A SPORTS INJURY. NOT A HIKING INJURY! IT HAPPENED AT A PARTY! A PARTY!

DO YOU GET IT?

No?

Okay. Let me have another go at explaining to you just how little of an outdoorsman I am. This is the sum total of outdoor activity I have pursued in my life, in seven points.

1. I went on some cabin trips in my youth. About five in total. Very little outdoor activity was involved. I'll say no more. That way you can imagine for yourself how crazy my teenage years must have been.

2. I've also been on a few cabin trips as an adult. Around four. In all cases, a car was driven almost right up to the cabin. In all cases, more plastic bags than backpacks were involved. And there was no hiking.

3. I've worn skis once since graduating high school thirty years ago. It was on one of the cabin trips described in point 2, when abnormally large amounts of snow meant we had to park a hundred yards away from the cabin and take the last stretch on skis. On this occasion, too, more plastic bags than backpacks were involved. Which is much more complicated when you have ski poles.

4. The past two summers, one week of my vacation has been spent in a rented cabin on the coast. I like the coast. My sole stipulation for this cabin was that it must be within walking distance of at least two restaurants. We found one within walking distance of three. It was absolutely lovely.

5. Of course I went on some walks in my youth. Because the mountains were there, right beside us, like constant grounds for guilt, like a constant reminder you could be doing something more sensible with your time than playing foosball and shooting the breeze with your buddies.

I actually managed to resist this tremendous pressure from The Mountains pretty often. But when there was a school excursion, you had to go along. There were parts of the curriculum you could be excused from on religious grounds or because you had a different first language or because you had special challenges when it came to numbers or letters. But hiking was compulsory no matter what. If it happened today, I'd undoubtedly take the case to an international court, but in those days that option simply didn't occur to us. My most abiding memory of these trips now is of the extremely intricate alert system. The thing is, it was always uncertain right up to the last minute whether the excursion would happen at all, because in the corner of the world where I grew up, the sun may be shining on the green meadows in the center but it can still be the depths of winter a mere three hundred yards away. The alert system worked like this: early enough in the morning that it was strictly speaking still night, the teacher would place a phone call to the pupil who sat at the front desk of the window row to say whether there'd be an excursion or not. That pupil would call the pupil who sat behind them, who would ring the next pupil back and so on until, in theory at least, the whole class had got the message. The system was highly vulnerable. All it took was for one family to sleep through the ringing phone, and that did happen—after all, it was the middle of the night. And somebody would always forget who the next person was, or they just didn't like the person behind them and were reluctant to ring her. Or two of them would get chatting about something totally different and forget what they were actually supposed to say. It's a miracle we ever got to go on these excursions at all.

6. I spent a year in the army when I was eighteen because that's what you had to do in Norway in those days, unless there was a viable case for exemption or it was fundamentally against your personal convictions or you really didn't feel like it and were extremely good at lying. I met only one of these requirements (I didn't feel like it), but that wasn't enough.

In the army, of course, we went out into the forest with backpacks now and then, because that's obviously what you're meant to do if you're attacked by an enemy. And I slept in a tent. I've never done that since.

I remember these army trips a bit like the way I remember the school excursions. First and foremost, there was a lot of hassle. Packing, ski-waxing, unpacking, setting up, taking down, organizing. I remember the school excursions as ninety percent hassle and ten percent hiking. The army trips I remember as ninety percent hassle and ten percent sleeping. In cold tents that took a day to set up.

7. A couple of years ago I was in Svalbard. I was there for work, of course, to entertain those poor freezing wretches in the farthest-flung outpost of society. But since we'd traveled all that way, a bunch of us stayed on a few days extra to do the stuff you do in Svalbard. We went dogsledding, for example. We probably had an overly romantic image of what this involved. We pictured ourselves sitting under heavy furs drinking wine as the huskies hurtled along. This was not how it turned out. After being ferried to a building a bit like a prison camp by a dour man with a rifle in his car, we were stuffed into thermal suits and informed that not only would we be the mushers, we would also have to harness the dogs. And the sled dogs, they're wolfish creatures that stand there slavering and howling and nearly ripping up the chains that restrain them. Somebody who was on that trip, a person who knows me really well (maybe you remember her from earlier in the chapter—she was the one who imagined me on the storehouse steps as a kid), says she saw a totally new side of me that day. I hurled myself into the task of harnessing the dogs with rugged determination. I treated the animals with tough, resolute affection, barked orders at the others, and got the job done super fast. Like some kind of primal man.

There are several things to be said about this. For example: it isn't that I can't handle nature or solving macho tasks at temperatures well below freezing. I can. I can handle all that perfectly well.

It's just that I don't like it.

And the reason why I approached this task with such manly vigor was not because it gave me a buzz to get in touch with my inner Man of Nature; it wasn't that it made me feel truly alive to use my body as the cold nipped and the dogs barked. No. The reason was that I'd realized the sooner we got this job done, the sooner we'd get to the pub.

And let there be no doubt whatsoever about this: it was much more fun telling people about the dogsledding trip at the pub than it was actually being on the dogsledding trip. Snow I've seen before. Dogs too. And uncoordinated people in big quilted snowsuits. I live right next door to a kindergarten.

So there you have me. That's what I'm like. And fewer and fewer of my friends are like that. They've chosen nature.

And that's what I have to do too. I have to face down my own resistance, all my fear of hassle, all my fear of losing my sense of humor. I have to venture out into nature and find out what it is they're going on about, the whole lot of them.

After all, I'm the kind of person who lets himself get swept up.

And maybe out there in nature they get up to stuff they haven't told the rest of us about. Maybe they have the craziest of times out there. Maybe I'm actually missing out on something.

I have to go to the mountain. And to the forest. Maybe I'll find salvation there. Maybe I'll feel everything fall into place. Maybe I'll understand at last how small I am.

And if all this should fail, I hope at least to find those old friends of mine again, bring them back home with me, shower them off, put them in some proper clothes, and take them out to the pub.

BUT FIRST OF ALL, I have to try and get a better grasp of what this is actually about.

AND THEN I HAVE TO ring the person sitting behind me and tell her there's going to be an excursion.

THINGS
I DON'T
UNDERSTAND

I THINK I UNDERSTAND many things. There are lots of things I don't like. But I usually manage to understand them if I make a bit of an effort. And if I'm the only person in the room. But there are three things in the world I really struggle to understand. Religion. Hard drugs. And outdoor life.

And these three things do have a lot in common. They're a bit too heavy on the quest for personal satisfaction, a bit too light on humor, and a bit too heavy on people who are a bit too into talking about their interests. And if you don't know your limits or when to stop? Fatal.

Okay, let's forget about hard drugs. Which is generally sound advice. But I've now made a pretty serious attempt to understand a bit more about outdoor life and the appeal of nature. I've read, talked to people, Googled, watched films, and I've tried to talk to some of the many friends I've lost to nature. They weren't especially easy to get ahold of as most of them had their hands full drying their socks and trying to decide whether to post #lovetheoutdoors or #lovelife-outside on Instagram, or whether to let rip, go totally crazy, and just post both. But I did get ahold of them. And I've understood a bit. And it's quite impossible not to notice how much outdoor life and religion have in common.

Try this, for example: flick through a few of the thousands of coffee-table books published every year about the good life out in nature. Then go through the past year on the Facebook and/or Instagram feed of one of your mountain-loving friends. Lastly, Google "evangelical Christianity." In all three places, you'll find exactly the same thing: loads of pictures of suspiciously happy people with their arms raised to heaven.

Perhaps this is something deeply human. Maybe it's a reflex. But whatever the cause, it seems quite impossible to be pictured on a mountaintop without your arms raised to heaven.

Of course all those coffee-table books and social media posts aren't just about arms raised to heaven. But pretty much all the pictures, in the books and on the internet, have a distinct whiff of the born-again about them. It's their boundless happiness. It's the way they're close to losing it. It's the thumbs-ups. It's the people in wet clothes with their arms around each other. It's the children—cheerful despite the cold because they've bundled up, and happy because they've found a sense of achievement and learned to fashion food and cabins and toy cars from spruce sprigs and raindrops.

And there's also something of the born-again about those lost friends of mine I've discussed this with. They possess, for example, the same missionary fervor you see in born-agains.

Okay, let's be a bit kinder. Let's call it missionary *enthusiasm*.

No, actually. Let's call it missionary *fervor*.

They're desperate to convince the rest of us. And they do it in two ways. Either by telling us that in nature you can experience something you can't experience anywhere else. Or—and this is much odder—by telling us that in nature you can experience exactly the same thing you can experience anywhere else. And this is where all the mountain folk start to seem a bit too much like those people who went to Christian summer camp in their youth and tried to convince the rest of us that you could have just as wild a time there as in Ibiza. Like teenagers who've just discovered some secret, born-again mountain folk will tell you about all the goings-on at these tourist cabins in the mountains. You remember those cabins, right? Tarnhook and Puddleshack and Gnatland and Ugly Man's Cabin and Crow's Croft and Asscat? Those cabins. Don't go thinking it's dull at those cabins, the born-agains say, with a wink. No way, José! Cabins? The bigger cabins are actually more like hotels. And they're happening places. There's wine and food, and—and here they'll often pause briefly and cast a glance around them before continuing—yes, hookups. Yeah, there are plenty of hookups at these cabins. The mountains? The world's biggest pick-up joint. Yes, sirree.

So what they're saying is that if you walk uphill for six or seven hours in the rain, you'll reach a place where, with luck, you can experience exactly the same things you can experience anywhere in any city on any evening. Just that in the city, you're spared the experience of having a slightly scary teacher from Germany in high-tech thermals stare at you relentlessly. And in a city, if you get bored or don't get lucky, you can just go somewhere else. Or home. You can't do that in the mountains because the nearest cabin is thirty miles away. And it's called Gobspittlegland.

Unsurprisingly, this missionary fervor is most evident on the internet. And missioneering is, of course, just an old-fashioned word for what we now refer to as boasting. Nobody goes out into nature without making sure other people get to hear about it. As many people as possible. With as many hashtags as possible. So many people post so many pictures with so many hashtags that the internet's almost full up. And this is where they seem most religious. Because here on the internet, as with people who've seen the light in other ways, you won't see much moderation, or much nuance. There isn't much "I've started something new here and I don't know how interesting it is for other people." No, here it's all about boasting, without an iota of shame: Look at this! Look what I've discovered. This is the best thing ever! This is the way the truth and the life! #thegreatoutdoors #getoutdoors #lovetheoutdoors #myplayground #lovelifeoutside #mountainsarecalling #ilovenorway #dontsitindoorslikeastupididiot #standingonamountaintopwithyourarmsraisedtoheavenandabarebottomisthewaytohappiness

And people have revelations out there. People turn to nature in search of answers. When Jonas Gahr Støre agreed to become leader of Norway's largest political party, the Labor Party—thereby, in practice, also agreeing to take on the battle to become prime minister—he told a press conference he'd made the decision during a mountain hike. Absolutely alone.

And a lot of people nod approvingly when they read that kind of thing. But I think: Really? You decided you wanted to become prime minister alone in the mountains? Shouldn't you have talked it over with somebody instead? An adult, for example? Or your family?

But politicians who want to show how strong and down-to-earth they are—and they certainly want to do that—seek out nature. Even Angela Merkel is routinely pictured with a walking staff, heading to the mountains in the summertime. Although she's clearly not keen. Vladimir Putin regularly issues pictures of himself out in nature, with a fishing rod or on horseback, bare-chested. And they probably hope we'll think of them as authentic folk who are in touch with nature.

If I saw one of my political leaders bare-chested on horseback, I wouldn't think, *What a strong leader. He's the one I'll vote for.* I'd think, *What the hell are you doing?! Get some clothes on and go govern the country, you idiot.*

The past three or four US elections have shown us that the cliché of the American dream is actually true, although not always exactly as we learned about it. Anybody at all really *can* become president of the United States: reality TV billionaires and people with Hussein as a middle name can make it to the top in the United States. Even women can make it almost all the way. But no matter who you are, you still have to believe in God. You're liable to get into trouble if you refuse to say "God Bless America" because you don't believe God exists and think deep down that religion is pretty silly. In the Nordic countries, it's a different story. Here, we've had atheist prime ministers, and the general rule is that you face a greater risk of ridicule as a political leader if you *are* religious. And the people most likely to be Norway's future ministers and prime ministers include committed Christians, the religiously indifferent, atheists, and a couple of middling Muslims. However, you may well have difficulty mustering support in Scandinavia if you publicly declare that you don't understand the point of going for a hike, or that cabins are for losers.

Could it simply be that, in our times, nature has taken over the place previously occupied by religion? Plenty of different surveys suggest that people in Scandinavia are among the least religious in the world. Is it true, as certain religious people claim, that we need something in our lives that is greater than ourselves, that is constant in changing times—something that reason cannot explain? If so, it may be worth noting that everything in the sentence I've just written could just as easily be applied to a god or a mountain. Pretty smart.

And if, once more, we seek out the born-again mountain folk on social media, it's striking how casually they throw around phrases that start with "God's own." And how close to the limits of the absurd this can be taken. Peaks can be described as "The Lord's own spear tip," "God's own potato peeler," "The Lord's own waffle iron."

So the question is: Has nature taken the place of religion? If you're willing to stake your life on statistics and have even the slightest desire to make smart theories add up, one might mention that religion was much more strongly positioned thirty to forty years ago, while outdoor life has taken off as a popular activity—that's right—in the past thirty to forty years.

Have my friends simply gone and gotten religious?

No.

As I said, I've spoken to them and asked them what's made them start wandering around in nature. And they all tend to talk about keeping fit. Some suddenly discovered they'd gone pear-shaped. Some saw pictures of themselves at an office party and realized they had a belly. Something they should have realized long before. Some think wandering in nature is a more pleasant way of keeping fit and offers much better views than many other ways of keeping fit. And one of my friends firmly believes he can testify that walking down mountainsides gives you a really great butt.

All well and good. But most people also think there's something about nature they can't quite put into words. A feeling they claim you actually have to experience. Something... inexplicable. Several describe reaching the top of a mountain as a victory, a powerful experience. And looking down from the top gives them a really special feeling, incomparable to anything else. And it's definitely more than just a matter of looking at something beautiful. One of my friends (the one who said that thing about his butt in case you're wondering) also claims views make him horny. That may not be religious, but it certainly is inexplicable.

You also find it in books about hiking. Not the thing about being horny, I mean. All the rest. Because the people who write about nature often become quasi-religious too. Or have difficulty finding words.

Briton William Cecil Slingsby is said to have been the first man to scale around fifty Norwegian peaks. In 1904, he published the classic book, *Norway: The Northern Playground*, which he opts to begin with an alternative creation story where the Norwegian mountains come into being during a battle between God and Satan. God wanted Norway to be livable and lovely. Typical God. Satan wanted it to be bleak, inaccessible, and full of rocks. It ended up like a sort of mixture.

Henrik Ibsen himself put it more simply: "Up here on the fells must be freedom and God: Men do but grope in the valley."

Pretty insulting to people who don't go hiking, of course, but that's Ibsen in a nutshell.

More recently, there's a bit less God and a lot more freedom to be found in hiking literature. But freedom for what? Or more precisely: freedom *from* what?

The Norwegian adventurer Erling Kagge writes: "Whenever I am unable to walk, climb or sail away from the world, I have learned to shut it out."

Freedom from the world, pure and simple. Nothing less.

Sigri Sandberg is a Norwegian journalist and author who has written a great deal about nature and mountains. In an interview she says she has to protect herself when she's in crowded places because people radiate so much, and this is a major reason why she goes out into nature and seeks silence: to get away from all the human noise.

Freedom from the world and people, then. These aren't trivial.

There's always somebody who has to take things that bit further. Briton Thomas Thwaites is one of them. He decided a few years back that he wanted to live like a goat in the Alps. He wrote about both the idea and its execution in his book, *GoatMan: How I Took a Holiday From Being Human*. This project is, of course, extremely weird on all counts. But his reasons for attempting such a fundamental return to nature aren't all that different from what Kagge and Sandberg say and write:

"Wouldn't it be nice to just switch off that particularly human ability for a couple of weeks? To live totally in the moment, with no worries about what you've done, what you're doing, or what you should do? Wouldn't it be nice to escape the constraints and expectations of not just society, your culture, your personal history but your very biology? To escape the inevitable worries of personhood?"

The short answer to this long question is, of course, "No."

The slightly longer answer is that what he's really asking is whether it wouldn't be nice to escape responsibility for your own actions and for functioning alongside other human beings. Well, maybe, but we have words for that sort of behavior. Self-centered, for example. Irresponsible. Escapist. Childish.

Or goat-like, obviously.

This attitude recurs in almost everything people write about experiencing nature nowadays. The idea of logging off, shutting things out. Nature is a place where you get away from interruptions, disturbances, problems, noise. Or life, as it is also known.

IF YOU TURN TO FICTION, it tells you a quite different story about nature. There are plenty of novels, TV series, and films about people keen to leave behind a stressful life and live at one with nature. I've lost count a bit over the course of my life, but I don't think I'm far off in estimating that the fates of the characters who want to live at one with nature are distributed more or less as follows:

Ten percent of them spend the rest of their life doing things wrong while the locals laugh at them.

Ninety percent of them are killed.

And of course you can say that fiction always seeks out drama. But I've also read non-fiction books along the same lines. One modern classic in the wilderness literature genre is American Jon Krakauer's book *Into the Wild*. In it, he tells the true story of a student who decides to abandon everything and live a true and authentic life out in nature. He starves to death.

△

RIGHT, LET'S TRY and sum up what we've got so far.

It's a bit rough and tough out in nature. People starve to death. And this may well appeal to some of us who don't live especially rough and tough lives on a day-to-day basis, in our middle-management jobs in private-public organizations. So perhaps that explains some of the appeal. And then there's the physical exertion, the exercise, the great butt, the escape from the pear shape. And the experience of nature, the fresh air, the arousing view.

And then there's all the rest, too: the slightly inexplicable part, which isn't religious though it's a bit like it, and which could perhaps be summed up as a desire to stop time, switch off the noise, shut out the world, find breathing space and time for reflection. We live stressful lives in hectic times and so we have a greater need than in any previous age simply to be alone and quiet.

And that might sound like an attractive and understandable need.

If it weren't for the fact that this description of the lives we now live is totally wrong. In fact, it's the opposite of right.

We only seriously started seeking out nature as a means of stopping time and switching off the noise in the past thirty to forty years. What else has happened in the same period? Well. Here are a few things.

Since 1970 people have gained an average of one extra hour of leisure time per day. And we spend less of our leisure time than we previously did in the company of others.

In 1980, ten percent of people in Norway didn't have a bathroom or shower. In 2015, nearly forty percent of all Norway's inhabitants lived in homes with two or more bathrooms. And a lot fewer people live in these homes than before. Families are smaller. Nearly forty percent of all households in Norway consist of one person. What's more, these constantly shrinking households have more and more homes. A quarter of us own a holiday home. Forty percent have access to a holiday home. And the number of Norwegians who own homes abroad has increased eightfold since the start of the millennium alone.

So what has actually happened in the period during which we've apparently developed such a tremendous need for more time to be alone in a large space is that we have acquired more time and more space that we share with fewer people. We have never before had so much time and so much space to be so quiet and so alone.

The explosion in outdoor living is not a reaction against our times. The explosion in outdoor living is a classic example of those that have a lot wanting more. A couple of generations ago, when people actually worked long, hard days and came home to enormous families in tiny homes, when people *really* might have needed breathing space and peace, almost nobody used to wander around in the mountains just for the fun of it. This was something we took up in earnest only once we had more leisure time, more homes, and small families. Perhaps outdoorsy people aren't born-again after all. Perhaps they're just demanding. You have three homes in two countries and suffer constant nagging guilt about not using them enough, and on top of that you want to have *nature itself* all to yourself?

You can, of course, object that people aren't longing for even more when they're drawn to nature; they're longing for something else. Something you can't find in your fancy homes and enormous holiday cottages. There are, as anybody who's ever listened to pop music knows, a good few things money can't buy. Love, among others. And happiness.

And happiness is, after all, something we know a bit about. The UN regularly ranks the world's best countries to live in and the world's happiest people. As a rule, these are very unremarkable lists which show that, on average, people in wealthy, fully functioning, peaceful democracies are better off than poor, starving people in war zones. The Nordic countries almost always rank high up on these lists. Of course. But the mountains certainly aren't the reason why people are happy and thriving.

If they were, how would you explain the fact that Denmark is always high up in these rankings? Denmark's tallest mountain is around twenty inches high. Most Danes have never been higher than a barstool.

Of course, something else has also happened in our times that I haven't mentioned so far. In many respects we have distanced ourselves from nature—on an everyday basis, that is. A lot fewer people live off and in nature now than in the olden days. Maybe that's another reason why we talk about nature in such exotic terms if we happen to be asked about it. Why we become religious. Or horny. Or say that we can't quite explain what nature does to us. You don't say things like that if nature is an absolute given in your life, all the time, every day.

And maybe that's also why we have an even greater need nowadays to demonstrate that we're still a bit rugged and primal despite all the evidence to the contrary. Those lost friends of mine who collect peaks—and there are a good few of them—often talk about "bagging" this or that peak. Not going up it. Bagging it. Pretty macho. We may be living in an age when everybody under twenty-five has a diagnosis and we adults need psychological support to cope with corporate restructurings. But damn it all! We'll bag that mountain.

Spending time in nature—indeed, walking, moving, using our bodies—isn't part of everyday life for all that many of us nowadays. Instead it has become something we seek out and spend time doing intentionally, and more often than not dress up for, in our spare time.

When we exercise, when we're at our cabins. And there's a sharp divide between the one and the other.

I mentioned that when I was young the only people who wandered around the streets in the center of my hometown were the eccentrics. Nowadays, more people walk the streets there. But they walk quickly and they wear shoes and workout pants in glaring colors to make it perfectly clear that they aren't just wandering around aimlessly. They're keeping fit.

I once saw a really athletic guy who shuffled. It was clear he'd come straight from the gym. Gym bag in hand. Extremely well built. And there he was, shuffling along. Dragging his feet. Bench press a few hundred pounds at the gym? That he could do. But pick up his feet on his way out? He just couldn't be bothered.

That shuffling bodybuilder strikes me as a pretty good, and perhaps rather sad, image of our times.

My maternal grandfather, who ran the farm where I grew up during the time I lived there, was in many ways a man of nature. I think he knew, in the most self-evident way, everything there is to know about nature and animals. He lived on the farm. He'd dress up for special occasions. Otherwise he went around in overalls.

He never went wandering in the forest for no good reason. He never went for a walk just for the sake of walking. He didn't lift things just for the sake of lifting things. He never put on a brightly colored fleece, headed for the nearest mountaintop, raised his arms to heaven, and then came home again. If Instagram had existed in his day, he would never have written #lovetheoutdoors.

Now and then my grandfather would sit on those storehouse steps I talked about before, smoking a pipe and stroking the cat. I don't believe for an instant that he sat there thinking how small he felt.

And it's probably still true that people who live or have grown up in small places, with nature right on their doorstep, are less inclined to pompous declarations about stopping time and finding breathing space. Well, at least that's what we like to think.

City folk go out into nature to find inner peace. Country folk go out into nature to shoot things.

City folk watch reality TV shows where people compete to live the old-fashioned way because it's good entertainment that can teach you something. Country folk watch that kind of thing to have a good laugh at the city folk who don't know one end of an ax from the other.

City folk well up at the sight of a lamb. Country folks' mouths start to water.

ALL OF US who can boast of a rural upbringing have this tendency. We like to brag about our unromantic relationship to nature. But in most cases, all that's left of it is probably rhetoric. Let's be honest: we wouldn't survive very long absolutely alone in nature without a phone. Besides, what would be the point of spending time out in nature without a phone?

Wandering in nature for no reason other than that it's lovely is something both city and country folk do nowadays. Possibly because country folk and city folk live more similar lives now than previously. But historically, this sort of experience of nature was a typically urban phenomenon.

People living in a Nordic country, may—in fits of ahistorical chauvinism—find it easy to assume that this business of hiking in the mountains for days on end is a distinctly Nordic activity, down-to-earth and ancient. The truth is that it was imported from abroad, it's snobbish, and it's pretty new.

The tradition of hiking draws its inspiration from England, where it was the upper classes who engaged in this kind of activity. They were probably the only people who had time for it. Funnily enough, the first recorded use of the word "boredom" in the English language

dates from around the same period that better-off Englishmen seriously started traveling to Norway to hike in the mountains. There
were also people in the mountains before then, of course, but they
were mostly people who had some business there, so they don't
count. Much of the writing of William Cecil Slingsby—the man I
mentioned earlier, who did all that climbing of Norwegian peaks
150 years back—suggests that the local farmers didn't really understand the point of what he was doing. And why should they have?
The mountains were their workplace. It would be like today's HR
heads and executive officers spending their vacation time wandering
around open-plan offices.

And when a bunch of people sat down to found an association to
promote the experience of nature in Norway, it wasn't exactly the
farmers who were behind it then, either. The Norwegian Trekking
Association runs many of these tourist cabins people hike to. You
remember those cabins, right? Spitestile and Ugly Man's Cabin and
Stray Cat Hill and Quicksand? The organization was established
in 1868. In Oslo. By people with upper-class names. They were
directors and colonels, or had titles like Consul, Bailiff, Assessor, or
similar honorifics that you only otherwise find among people whose
common trait is that they were all made up by Henrik Ibsen.

In other words, it wasn't exactly a grassroots initiative, this. And
wandering around in nature for the fun of it is still not an especially
folksy activity. It's still the case that the more you earn and the higher
your educational level, the more likely you are to go hiking.

It's only in the past thirty to forty years that outdoor life has
started to resemble a mass movement, something almost everybody
does. That's when you can say that outdoor life switched from being
an activity for wealthy city folk to being an activity for everybody.
Or to indulge in a spot of hyperbole, it is still an activity for wealthy
city folk. It's just that in the past thirty to forty years, almost all the
inhabitants of Norway have become wealthy city folk.

Of course, that isn't entirely true. As is often the case with hyperbole. But the average salary in Norway has risen 124 percent since 1980, and that's adjusted for inflation. And eighty percent of Norway's entire population now lives in cities and small towns. And, as I mentioned earlier, fewer people—even in rural areas—now live directly from and in nature.

It's as if we've spent generations freeing ourselves from toil and reaching a point where we can live comfortably, no longer in thrall to the whims of nature; and just when we've finally reached that point, that's when we want to get back to nature. A bit like couples who long to have children more than anything else in the world and, when they finally have children, long for nothing more than to have time off from the children. So that they can have a glass of wine and talk to grown-ups. About how exhausting it is having children.

OKAY. NOW LET ME TRY to sum up what I've learned and understood: outdoors people are born-again, demanding, wealthy people who want to have great butts. In the meantime, they raise their arms to heaven and write #lovetheoutdoors without a whiff of irony.

Surely there must be something more to it. Statistics don't really provide all the answers. Nor does the literature. And my friends are normally great people. Or were, at least. There must be something I haven't understood.

I have to go out and experience it.

And I must take the classic approach: I must go to Jotunheimen, the very birthplace of Norwegian mountain tourism; the first area in Norway where cabin-to-cabin hiking became possible; the mountain range that took upper-class Britons' breath away; the mountains that have inspired great art; and the site of all the highest peaks in Northern Europe. I must go up Besseggen. Besseggen is a Norwegian classic. Everybody's been up Besseggen. And I will scale the highest mountain in Norway and Northern Europe, Galdhøpiggen.

In fact I will *bag* Galdhøpiggen. And then I'll check in with myself to see if I feel small. Or big. Or macho. Or happy. Or religious. Or horny.

And I'll stay at cabins with peculiar names. And meet these demanding, born-again, wealthy people.

And live at one with nature.

And starve to death, probably.

⟁

BUT FIRST I HAVE TO buy absolutely all the gear you need to take a trip like this.

INDOOR
MOUNTAINS
AND POPCORN
ON THE CAMPFIRE

STORES THAT SELL THINGS you have no clue about are the scariest places in the world. You pluck up your courage, you go inside, you answer yes to every question so you don't look like a total idiot, you try to joke a bit to show you're on top of things, and a quarter of an hour later, you find yourself back out on the sidewalk after spending four thousand dollars on stuff—and you have no idea what any of it is.

That's why this is one part of the whole hiking adventure I'm most dreading: getting all the gear I need. And probably lots of gear I don't need.

Before I can get even that far, I have to become a member of the Norwegian Trekking Association, the organization founded, as you may remember, 150 years back by city folk and upper-class men with Ibsen appellations, and which gives you access to many of these cabins out in Norwegian nature with names like Bacon Valley Shack and Fat Lady and Shufflebutt and Cockhill Grange and Junior Woodchuck Cabin. The association has a store right in the center of the city where I live. There you can buy all the things you'll need out in nature. You can get help planning your trip. And you can become a member and receive a master key to Sloppy Valley Shack and Crotchety Croft and Snowdrift Cottage and Foggy Realm. And that's where I am now, after spending a quarter of an hour outside plucking up my courage and gazing longingly at the café on the other side of the street where people are reading papers and talking and laughing like normal happy human beings.

Inside the outdoor store there are lots of people wearing pants with way too many pockets. Two of them are standing right beside me now, just looking at me. They have pack lunches and maps and thermos flasks. Hikers are apparently hiking even when they're at the store. After a while, I realize they want to get past me and over to a table in the corner. I smile, step aside, and wave them past with a generous sweep of my arm. They don't smile, don't thank me, but walk past, sit down, open up their pack lunches, unfold their map, and start to mumble.

It's my turn. I prepare my broadest and most winning smile (and it actually is pretty broad and winning—ask anybody who knows me) and go over to the counter.

"Hi!" I beam. "I need help."

"Yes," she replies.

I laugh out loud. Because I thought it was funny. And to show that I'm on top of things. But there's nothing to suggest she meant it as a joke.

I'm starting to wonder whether hikers might have a little trouble with normal social interactions.

I say I'd like to become a member.

First and foremost, the woman behind the counter appears to be busy. She isn't exactly drumming her fingers, but she's not far off it, either. Quite honestly, I'd expected this to be a place where you took your sweet time. I'd pictured maps being spread out and coffee being brought to the table, probably thin coffee served from a thermos; I thought I'd receive carefully considered advice and a clap on the shoulder from people who'd been everywhere in Norwegian nature, and were happy, grateful, and perhaps even a bit proud to have won yet another person over to the right side. I hadn't exactly assumed that my request for membership would merit brass bands and red carpets but I had assumed I'd be met with something other than haste. She's probably desperate to close the store early so she can leave the city as quickly as possible and get out into the forest and sit there and be quiet all on her own. It must be hell for people like that to work in the middle of the city. She's wearing hiking pants, I see, with way too many pockets. She's ready to head out into nature at closing time on the dot.

There's no room for small talk here, so I give my name and number, pay up, get my membership card, and my key to the cabins with peculiar names. I genuinely feel a bit proud. And a bit excited about having some pants with way too many pockets.

"Where will you go hiking?" she asks. Ah—here we go! Clearly you have to get the key before they'll consider you one of their own and launch into mountain chat.

"Jotunheimen," I say proudly. "Besseggen. Galdhøpiggen."

"Yes, but that's where everybody goes."

"Does that mean you'd advise against going there?"

"Oh no. As long as you don't mind walking in line."

⚐

SO: I'VE GONE WAY OUTSIDE my comfort zone and decided to do exactly what this association wants people to do. And I've decided to head for some of the classics of Norway's mountain realm. And what do I get in return? A telling-off.

⚐

I SHRUG IT OFF and leave to go and buy all the gear I need.

I've asked people what I need and it turns out that what you need to go hiking out in nature is absolutely everything you already own, prefixed by the words "hiking" or "camping." Hiking shoes, hiking pants, hiking socks, hiking underwear, hiking jacket, hiking hat, camping food, camping cutlery, camping crockery, camping towel, camping toiletries, hiking gloves, hiking sunglasses.

I start with hiking shoes. Good shoes are, in case you didn't know it, the be-all and end-all.

Outside the first sporting goods store hang three enormous posters with pictures of people raising their arms to heaven and the slogans: Outside is where it's happening. Outside is where you're free. Outside is where you're alive.

So of course it isn't very tempting to go *inside* the store. But I must.

"I need some hiking shoes," I say to a guy working in the store, unleashing my legendary winning smile. He doesn't smile back.

"Where are you planning to hike?" he asks.

"Jotunheimen. Besseggen. Galdhøpiggen."

"Yeah, but that's exactly where we advise people *not* to go."

"Why?"

"Because it's jam-packed there. You'll be walking in line."

⛰

WHAT THE HELL?!

⛰

SO FAR TODAY, two things have become pretty clear.

1. Hikers *do* appear to have a little trouble with normal social interactions.

2. You can count on a telling-off if you're thinking of going to popular spots.

And these two things may be connected. Perhaps it isn't so peculiar that mountain folk have a little trouble with normal social interactions. After all, they clearly aren't used to people at all. Because if you think it's jam-packed in Jotunheimen you have no idea what a crowd is. If you think there are too many people out in Norwegian nature, your problem is probably that you just don't like people. And maybe there's something in that. I've already learned from the literature that hikers often like to get away from the world, and see other people as noise.

Let's get this straight once and for all: no matter what measure you opt to use, there isn't a single place in Norway that is jam-packed, least of all out in nature. In Hong Kong it's pretty packed. On the Tube in London at rush hour it's pretty packed. Not out in Norwegian nature. Every single human being in the entire world would, in fact, fit in Østfold County in southeastern Norway. It's true. If everybody got around twenty square inches each, there'd be room for all of them. And Østfold accounts for just over one percent of Norway's entire surface area. *Every single human being in the world would fit into one percent of Norway!* It *isn't* jam-packed here. And it is certainly not jam-packed in Jotunheimen. Jotunheimen is enormous. If all the inhabitants of Europe headed up to Jotunheimen and each set up a one-person tent, there would still be more than 125 square miles of free space.

I rest my case.

But this disease is widespread, and not just among hikers, of course. When we're out traveling, we tend to want to get away from places where there are lots of other people like ourselves. Probably because we like to feel special. And we tend to assign extra value to places that are hard to reach. If there's a café somewhere out in nature, in a mountain cave, say, and you have to row and climb for hours on end to get there, you can bet your life on it people will claim this café sells—for example—the world's best fish soup.

Of course, this café probably doesn't. But if you've climbed and rowed for hours on end to get there, and climbed and rowed for hours on end to get back, it's naturally hard to admit you were served packet soup.

Maybe that's also the reason why so many of my friends who are devotees of nature talk in hallelujah terms about finally getting there. Whether "there" is a cabin in the forest or a mountaintop. The view is so much more beautiful when you've struggled a bit to get there, they say. Food tastes so much better after a long, grueling hike. Many people I know will argue that the view from the top of a mountain is actually lovelier if you've walked up than if you've taken a cable car.

I've had letdowns like that myself as a tourist. A pal and I go to Edinburgh every now and then. Because it's a great city, and they also have a festival there that's perfect for people like us. One time we decided to find a pub we'd read about in some obscure publication. The pub was recommended by an author and described as an authentic pub that wasn't overrun by tourists and festivalgoers. After we'd spent way too long searching, we finally found the pub. And realized at once that there's a very good reason why this pub isn't overrun by tourists and festivalgoers. It just isn't very nice there. There isn't any music. It hasn't been aired out in a generation. People sit by themselves and say nothing. Everybody turns around to look at you when you come in. The landlord says nothing either and only accepts cash. On the walls there are black-and-white pictures showing you what you'd see out of the windows if this pub had windows and if Edinburgh was in black and white. There we sat and squandered an hour of our lives as the locals stared at us.

You rarely feel more stupid than when you've worked and struggled to find your way to the only pub that's half-empty and quiet and unpleasant in a city where there's a distance of roughly four yards between every pub that's pleasant and lively and plays good music and has bar staff who crack jokes and call you "sir."

I think you'd feel just as stupid if you were to take a hike in the part of the country that's home to Norway's highest mountain but failed to go up Norway's highest mountain. And hiking veterans will undoubtedly tell you there are other mountains in the vicinity of Norway's highest mountain where you can hike *all on your own*. And that's highly likely. But then you won't have been up Norway's highest mountain, either. You'll simply have been on your own. That's something I can actually do at home.

SO I DON'T LET MYSELF be crushed by adversity. I stand firmly by my choice of route. And continue my quest to find good shoes.

One fun thing about stores that sell hiking shoes is that they've often built a pretend mountain in the store so you can take a test hike in your shoes. These mountains are maybe fifteen inches high (or really high, as they say in Denmark) and consist of a tiny uphill and a tiny downhill.

Quite honestly: if you can walk back and forth on a tiny fake mountain in a store *without* getting giggly, there's something seriously wrong with you. I was generally giggly when I tested out the shoes. And I was generally much more giggly than the people working in these stores. During my very first test hike on a mini-mountain, when I collided with a sales poster hanging from the ceiling, I grinned and said it was just like being in the mountains. The man in the store answered:

"Yes, it's important to test the shoes out properly. Good shoes are the be-all and end-all."

OKAY. HUMOR. SO FAR, we've struggled a bit in that area, hikers and me.

My clear impression after meeting a good number of people in many different settings over forty-odd years is that humor, self-deprecation, and irony are normal, widespread, and pretty popular. Things almost always go very well in social situations with a smile and a touch of humor.

But—and I've thought about this before, too—it seems there's a limit when it comes to nature. The closer we are to nature, the less likely it is that people will be able to take a joke. People can be self-deprecating as hell about their hometown. They may even talk in downright disparaging terms about the place where they live. But when it comes to the nature around it, joking is out of the question. There are an awful lot of people who believe in all seriousness that they live in the world's most beautiful spot. It's impossible for everybody who thinks that to be right, of course. But that's exactly the kind of thing you're not supposed to say to people. It makes them lose their sense of humor. People can be unreasonably proud of their archipelago or the mountains close to where they live. As if they were the ones who'd built these mountains themselves. And when you're on a visit and they show you the nature there and say "Isn't it lovely here?," it isn't a question. I'm aware it might seem like one, since the sentence is constructed as a question. But trust me, it isn't a question.

You might be sitting somewhere in natural surroundings with a person from that area, around a campfire, say—not because it's cozy to have a campfire but because without this campfire you'd either freeze to death or get eaten alive by mosquitoes or both. As you sit there you might think that perhaps you should have worn different clothes—not because you're not dressed sensibly or are cold, but because the clothes you're wearing now will smell of campfire for thirteen years, and in the circles you move in on a daily basis, nobody will interpret the fact that your clothes stink of campfire as a sign that you're an outdoorsman. They'll just think your house has burned down. As you sit there by the campfire and one of the locals says, "Don't we have a lovely place here?," you're supposed to nod. You're not supposed to answer.

And I know this. And I'm normally a polite and pleasant person. I pride myself on it, in fact. But the combination of local patriotism and humorlessness can bring out the worst in me. That combination can make me childish. And of course you guessed long ago that I did once sit just like this, at a campfire, in one of the roughly eight hundred spots in Norway that are considered the most beautiful place in the world by the people who live there, and one of the locals threw out his arms and said: "Look at the mountain. Isn't it wonderful?"

And I know, as I said, that this isn't really a question. I know that. But I answered.

"Speaking as a western Norwegian, I wouldn't call that a mountain," I said. "But it's a pretty nice knoll. I'll give you that."

It didn't go down well.

This is something I'm going to have to work on now that I'm going hiking out in nature.

AFTER THE FIRST two or three encounters, things go better on my great gear-getting day. Eventually, I even find somebody with a sense of humor in one of the stores that sells hiking gear. And you really need a sense of humor if you work in those stores.

Because there's necessary hiking gear. Have I, for example, mentioned that good shoes are the be-all and end-all? But there's also a lot of ridiculous hiking gear. Probably because almost everybody goes hiking out in nature nowadays, the entrepreneurs appear to have gone berserk trying to come up with as many hiking versions of normal things as possible—i.e., versions of normal things that take up very little space and weigh very little. You can get smart things like teensy-weensy crockery and cutlery, tiny folding cups, vacuum-packed meals, and towels that weigh a fraction of an ounce. But you can also get collapsible buckets, pocket showers, and a traveling wine carafe. You can get portable waffle irons and camping popcorn poppers you can use on campfires. If I'd looked a bit longer, I'm pretty sure I'd also have come across a vacuum-packed fridge, a portable storeroom, and foldable decking. There are so many different miniature products to use on hikes nowadays that you can actually live exactly the same way out in nature as you live at home, except that everything's a lot smaller.

The trick of shopping in specialist stores is, of course, to look for employees who don't quite seem as if they belong there. If you want to buy computer equipment, look for the ones who seem least like nerds. If you want to buy hiking gear, look for the ones who seem the least rugged and sporty.

That's how I find my favorite on this particular day. He may well be an outdoorsman, but he looks meek. He looks more like the type who'd gaze out to sea thinking about life than the type who'd head for the peaks and beat his breast. I know I've found my man when I'm about to try on a pair of hiking pants recommended by a poster containing at least ten words I don't understand and he says:

"I think they're nicest in blue."

Believe me, that isn't the kind of thing rugged people working in sports stores tend to say.

We study the pants and agree that they are a particularly delightful shade of blue.

After that, I trust every word this man says, so there's never any doubt that I'll also take the jacket he recommends. The information about this jacket on the label includes, among other things, the peculiar claim that the jacket has very good "air transport." I always imagined air transport was another term for planes, but apparently that's not true. My man laughs and agrees that this is a silly term. "All it means is that the jacket breathes," he says. Which is also ridiculous, obviously, but at least I know what that means. You can air yourself if it gets hot and/or clammy in the mountains without having to take your jacket off and put it back on again all the time. In other words, wherever you lay your hand on this jacket, you'll probably find a zipper. I'm very fond of air transport, in all areas of life.

I must have this jacket.

The problem is that the only jacket in this model they have in stock in my size is green. Very green. The shade of green shirts were for a brief period of sartorial confusion in the early nineties. You couldn't get any greener, if you get my drift.

I try on that very green jacket. Together with the extremely blue hiking pants.

"A lot of people go hiking in the mountains like that," my man says diplomatically. "But I'm not sure you want to be one of them. I'd maybe tone it down a bit."

Since I'm now totally convinced that I must have this jacket if I don't want to be wet and clammy for a week in the mountains, it's the pants that have to be toned down. I try a pair of much more discreet gray and black hiking pants and now we agree that it works. The jacket is still extremely green, but it works.

"It's important to be seen in the mountains," my man says. And I catch myself nodding. Wise words. And I wonder if I'll start saying things like that, too, after a few days out in nature.

It's important to be seen in the mountains.

Good shoes are the be-all and end-all.

The stupidest thing you can do is not break in your hiking shoes.

Things change quickly in the mountains; you have to be ready for anything.

It's good to use your body.

"I'll take it," I say, to interrupt myself. "The whole lot."

△

I FEEL A BIT UPLIFTED after doing my shopping. I've listened to advice from experienced mountain folk and, I hope, bought everything I need and not too much else. And I've found some hikers who laugh at the same things I do. Well, one at least.

It's all really starting to look brighter now. As I stand there at home looking over all the things I've bought, I feel so much better equipped than the last time I came into contact with nature.

The last time was at a music festival on Træna, which is an island off the northern coast of Norway, three hours out to sea by speedboat. There's a festival there. Because, as we saw earlier, anything that's hard to reach has greater value. To really hammer this point home, one of the concerts during this festival takes place on a neighboring island. You have to take a boat and then walk a while to get to the place where the concert's held. A bit farther up the mountainside, by the way, there's probably a café selling the world's best fish soup. While we were lying around waiting for this concert surrounded by natural beauty we spritzed ourselves with mosquito repellent—not that this appeared to make any notable impression on the mosquitoes. It was our third day at the festival and we sat there on the grass, a bit limp, with plastic bags and wine boxes scattered around us. Behind us, a man stood on a rock, with a damn straight back, wearing be-all-and-end-all shoes and pants with way too many pockets. It was obvious he really wanted to say something to us, so I smiled (winningly, of course) and nodded to him. And then we had this conversation:

△

HIM: Mosquito trouble?

ME (*Flapping one hand and spraying bug repellent with the other*): Not at all—it's fine, really.

(*Unnecessarily long pause*)

HIM: Maybe there aren't so many mosquitoes where you come from?

ME (*Suppressing the desire to point out to him that he doesn't know where we come from, and the desire to give a downright mean answer*): Oh, we've come across mosquitoes before.

HIM: Mm.

(*Unnecessarily long pause*)

HIM: It bites in the lee.

ME: Why are you talking in riddles?

(*Unnecessarily long pause*)

HIM: Out of the wind. The mosquito. If you stand up, it'll be better.

ME (*Thinking: So what you're saying is that the mosquito only attacks urban slobs who wear un-sensible shoes and sit down when they're out in nature rather than stand gazing heroically over the landscape?*): Oh yes, I know that. Just had to rest my knee. I have a knee injury, you know.

ANOTHER MEMBER OF MY PARTY: Drunken injury.

ME (*Thinking: Not now*): Hee hee.

(*Unnecessarily long pause*)

HIM: Isn't it great here?

ME (*Nodding*)

THE NEXT TIME I meet somebody like that, I'll handle it so much better. Because I'm ready now. I've read up on it. I know what awaits me. And I've got my gear in order.

And I'm in the process of becoming like those born-again, demanding, wealthy hikers who want to have great butts. Not that I give a great deal of thought to the business about my butt. Neither have I become born-again or demanding. But wealthy—that I obviously am. Because I've just added up how much all this gear has cost me. And let's get one thing clear: rustic living doesn't come cheap. I haven't opted for the most expensive stuff, either. On some items I've chosen to spend a bit more. There are some things you can't compromise on. Good shoes, for example, are the be-all and end-all. But I've also been downright sensible when it comes to some of the gear, so overall, I'd probably rank in the mid-range, from a purely financial point of view. This is what I've bought: sunglasses, a hat, woolen underwear, a thermos,[1] camping cutlery, camping crockery, camping cup, camping food, camping coffee, sleeping bag, fleece jacket, hiking jacket (green), hiking pants (with way too many pockets), waterproof pants, gloves, woolen socks, hiking shoes, backpack, map, compass, map case, first aid kit, sunblock, mosquito repellent, headlamp, battery for said lamp, sweatpants, membership of the Norwegian Trekking Association, and a key to the cabins. And then of course it isn't free to stay at these cabins, either. Or to eat and drink there. And transport costs money. All in all, I've calculated that this weeklong trip will cost me $4,700. And what would $4,700 buy you these days anyway?

That's something I've actually checked.

You can, for example, get twelve return trips to New York.

Or thirteen spontaneous weekend breaks to Iceland, hotel included.

You can get forty-four three-course dinners with good wine at a very pleasant French restaurant just down the road from here.

You can get 450 pints at my favorite pub, including tips.

You can get 115 concert tickets. Or, if I live an average-length life: three or four concerts a year for the rest of my life.

And if the Save the Children website is to be believed, you can use this sum to provide education for 160 children in poor countries for a year.

---

[1] This was an easy choice. Naturally I went for a "Thermos" brand thermos. When trademarks become language, you know the product has been made by quality-conscious experts. If there were a car brand named "Car," I'd go for that.

I won't be doing any of those things. I'm heading for the mountains to feel how small I am.

⛰

BUT FIRST, THERE'S one last thing I have to sort out. I simply can't travel alone. I have the equipment, true. But I'm pretty clueless about how to use it. I'm not sure how good I am at reading maps. I'm fairly sure I don't remember how to use a compass. There are an awful lot of odds and ends to sort out with all this hiking gear. Besides, I need somebody to talk to. I need to be able to let off steam and debrief. Not to mention that after a long day of conversations with other hikers, there's a reasonable danger I'll have stored up a good few jokes and catty remarks. All that will need to come out.

Besides, somebody has to take pictures of me raising my arms to heaven. The trip needs to be documented.

Put simply, I need to travel with somebody who has more hiking experience than me but who isn't totally born-again either, and who can put up with my sense of humor. There aren't all that many people who fit the bill. I know of only one person. On the plus side, I do know her pretty well. You know her too, actually. She was the one who imagined me as a kid on the storehouse steps. And the one who saw a new side of me when she watched my ruggedly masculine handling of the dogs on Svalbard. And she happens to live in the same apartment as me, so there's not far to go to ask.

⛰

ME: Will you come hiking with me in the mountains?

HER: Mountains? You know there aren't a lot of pubs there, right?

ME: I'll just have to cope with that. Will you come? Maybe you'll see the same side of me you saw when I dealt with those dogs?

HER: I doubt it. On Svalbard there was a pub to lure you.

ME: I need a Head of Documentation.

HER: That's the nicest thing anybody's ever said to me.

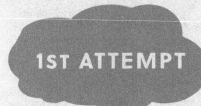

To Jotunheimen in Search of Salvation

Itinerary:

Day 1: Preparation
Day 2: Downtown Oslo–Nordmarka
Day 3: Nordmarka–Jotunheimen
Day 4: Besseggen
Day 5: Gjendesheim–Spiterstulen
Day 6: Galdhøpiggen
Day 7: Relaxed day trip and evaluation

Purpose of the trip:

- Find inner peace
- Realize how small I am
- Experience something that's
  difficult to explain
- Feel a desire to raise my arms to heaven
- Find out whether food and drink taste
  better, and whether views look better,
  if you've walked a long way
- Talk to, understand, maybe even like
  people I meet at cabins with peculiar names

LAST NIGHT OF FREEDOM

"IT'S PRETTY AMBITIOUS, this," says the Head of Documentation.

"Yes. It's important to go the whole hog. Make sure I really get to take a shot at this stuff."

"Okay, but isn't the point that you're meant to enjoy it, too?"

"I thought I'd give that a try, yes."

The Head of Documentation is looking at the itinerary I've printed out. She leafs through the descriptions of the various daily schedules. I've also printed those out. Because this is what people have told me, other than that it's important to have good shoes and that I'll find inner peace: You can't rely on technology out there in nature. You don't always have internet access, for example. That's why I've made printouts. From UT.no, a kind of net-based bible of nature where hikers share experiences and tell each other everything there is to be told about all the hikes. How long they are, how steep they are, how difficult they are, how long they take. I've also bought a plastic pouch to store all the papers in, because it can sometimes get wet out in nature. I've been smart. I'm prepared. I'm pleased with myself.

"So we'll hike to this cabin in the forest tomorrow?" says the Head of Documentation.

"Mm."

"And then we'll hike a bit the next day and catch a train and a bus to Jotunheimen?"

"Yep."

"Then we'll hike over Besseggen?"

"That's right."

"Which takes six to eight hours, it says here."

"Mm."

"And then we'll hike to this cabin by Galdhøpiggen."

"Yes."

"And then we'll hike up Galdhøpiggen."

"And down again."

"Hiking for eight hours—that's a long way, you know."

"I realize that."

"It's pretty steep in a lot of these places."

"Yes, it is."

"You have remembered your knee injury, haven't you?"

If I didn't know better, I'd swear she didn't have complete faith in me.

"It'll be fine," I say, nodding. In part to convince myself.

"Of course it'll be fine," the Head of Documentation says. And I do believe she means it.

We smile. We toast. We drink beer. We look out over the city. Tomorrow it begins. Right now, we're as far away from nature as it's possible to get in Norway.

WHEN YOU TRAVEL around in Norway, it's easy to see how close you are to nature. The closer you are to nature, the more likely it is that people will habitually walk around in hiking gear. In smaller places that are close to mountains and forests, people often wear hiking pants and good shoes even when they're at the store buying soda and potato chips. It's as if they're always ready to head out. It's as if a fifteen-minute visit to the center is just a temporary interruption in a continuous experience of nature.

Right now, we're in the eastern part of downtown Oslo, in a little patch of Norway where, in a quarter of an hour, you'll meet more foreign citizens, more gay people, more Muslims, more alcoholics, and more students than you can count on meeting in most parts of the country in an entire lifetime. This is one of the few places in Norway where it's impossible to tell when it's Easter or winter vacation. There are always just as many people on the streets, just as many in the cafés, and just as much noise in just as many languages. I've lived in this district of the city for large stretches of my adult life. I've never seen people in hiking gear here. No, actually, I did once. But I'm pretty certain that was a stag party. This is the place where Norway looks least like those coffee-table books where everybody's raising their arms to heaven.

In this part of Norway's largest city stands the Oslo Plaza, a 380-foot-tall hotel that was built in the 1980s and has, like every other Norwegian building taller than five stories, been an object of dispute and loathing.

There are few things that do more to raise the aggression level in Norwegian public debate than the building of tall things. Norwegian debate is typically characterized by decorous indifference. But if someone plans to build anything that means anybody will see something out of their living room window other than what they saw before, all hell breaks loose. You can throw up the ugliest two-story houses on the planet without anybody muscling in. But if you want to build something that's original and stylish—and tall—you'll need to set aside thirty years for bickering. Fighting against the construction of anything new and the loss of your fjord view is seen by many people in Norway as both progressive and radical. People who favored armed revolution in their youth turn out, later in life, to be mostly opposed to tall buildings. Like most others. Because although very few of us live out in nature, we do want to see it from where we live.

If you ask people what they associate with Norway, or what the nicest thing they know about in the country is, nobody's going to answer "the Oslo Plaza." For many people there's even something embarrassing about the Oslo Plaza, because if we were quite honest about it, we'd have to admit we thought this flashy building was pretty neat when it was new. This was in the days before anybody in the world thought anything from Scandinavia was cool; long before it became a matter of course that if you have a laptop and come from Bergen you're destined for pop stardom. In those days, we thought it was brilliant just to get a building that *looked like* those buildings they have in big cities in other countries. When the Plaza, then the tallest hotel in the Nordic region, opened its doors in 1990, it was the king who cut the ribbon, and people waited in line to ride the glass elevator up the outside of the building.

Now, the Plaza is no longer the tallest hotel in the Nordic region. Right beside the Plaza stands the Posthuset, which is also tall and, of course, also loathed, along with a couple of shopping malls, a traffic circle, and the bus terminal, which was voted Oslo's ugliest building in 2008. Right outside it stands a burger bar called Fiasco, which is one of the few places in Norway where you can sit at a window table, look outside, and not see the sky. I've always had a soft spot for Fiasco.

You can't get any farther away from forests and mountains in Norway than this.

And this is precisely where our trip will begin. Because of course even here there's no escape: this is where a marked hiking trail to Jotunheimen starts.

There are more than 12,400 miles of marked hiking trails in Norway. And they are mostly marked with red Ts painted on rocks. If you see a red T, you're on a hiking trail, and that means you're safe. This is something you pick up if you were raised in Norway, no matter what. There's no guarantee you'll learn to read and write, but this business about the red Ts? You'll definitely pick that up. And so one of these trails, known as the Jotunheim Trail, starts in the middle of Norway's largest city, right behind the Oslo Plaza. If you have plenty of time on your hands, you can hike all the way from here to Jotunheimen. This is a trip of over 180 miles that takes a couple of weeks.

And this is my great plan for the start of our trip. We won't hike all the way to Jotunheimen, of course. We're not crazy. And we don't have a couple of weeks. Who on earth does? But we'll hike the first leg of it. Tonight, we'll stay at the Oslo Plaza, on the thirtieth floor, with a view over the whole city. This is life, sometimes.

And then we'll hike through the city, out into the forest, and after a few hours in the forest we'll arrive at a cabin without electricity or running water. That's where we'll spend tomorrow night. This is life, sometimes. From ultimate city life to ultimate rustic life in twenty-four hours. I think this is a pretty neat plan.

And that's exactly what I say to the Head of Documentation as we sit there in the bar at the top of the Oslo Plaza, each with a beer, leafing through our itinerary. We started our expedition with a beer at Fiasco, which is ultimate city, then we took the elevator up to the thirty-fourth floor, which is equally ultimate city, only with a view. Already I sense that I have at least one thing in common with hikers. I like views. I really like sitting in a bar at the top of the Nordic region's not-quite-tallest building and seeing the city lights stretch out into the distance until there is less and less city, and less and less light, where at some point far out in the darkness lies nature. I feel vaguely optimistic and a bit poetic and take a swig of my beer. I also feel there's a childish pleasure to be had in staying at a hotel in the city where you live. I can definitely recommend it. It's a bit like playing hooky. It's one last fundamentally un-sensible action before tomorrow, when we will become sensible people who read maps kept in plastic pouches and have broken in our shoes and make sure we get enough liquids. It's late summer and rainy. I believe I'm ready.

"Isn't it a pretty neat plan?" I repeat, because I have a feeling the Head of Documentation didn't catch what I said the first time.

She nods and smiles. I know she's looking forward to this. She didn't take much convincing. She likes tasks. That said, she's clearly a bit worried about the ambition of my plan. And about my knee injury.

"I just don't want you to lose heart," she says. "After all, we don't want you developing an aversion to this. If that happens, we'll have totally failed, won't we?"

"But that's where you come in. If I start to lose heart, you have to give me a boost with your hiking experience and your good humor!"

"So I'm supposed to be the irritatingly positive person, is that what you're getting at?"

"Yes! That's exactly it."

"I'll be the one who says there's no such thing as bad weather, there are only bad clothes."

"Perhaps you don't need to be quite *that* irritatingly positive."

This is, after all, the most irritating saying in the world. It sums up everything that's irritating about irritating outdoor-fitness fanatics. There's no such thing as bad weather only bad clothes? What does that even mean? That as long as you shell out $4,700 on the right gear, anybody at all can go hiking for eight hours in shitty weather?

"I'll be the one who tells you it's the uphills that take you to the top."

Okay. Maybe the business with bad weather and bad clothes is only the second-most irritating saying in the world.

"What nobody mentions," I say, "is that it's the downhills that move you forward fastest."

"Not necessarily."

"Not necessarily what?"

"You don't necessarily get down a mountain faster, for example."

"What are you saying?"

"When I hiked up Galdhøpiggen, I took four hours to get up and four hours down."

"Is that true?"

"Mm."

This is grossly under-communicated in all the hiking literature.

"And how is the hike back down?"

"Long. And boring. And hard on the knees."

"Hm."

This is also grossly under-communicated in the literature.

"That's when I'll need to be extremely irritatingly positive, I think."

"It looks that way."

We look out over the city. We check the weather forecast one last time. We see they're forecasting pretty bad weather. The Head of Documentation is about to say something but realizes there's no need. We empty our pints.

"One more?" she asks.

"No. We need to get to bed. We've got a long day ahead of us in the morning."

"Now there's something I never thought I'd hear you say."

"It's a new era, baby. It's a new era."

TWELVE HOURS LATER, I'm standing in the rather fancy reception of the Oslo Plaza in hiking shoes, hiking pants, and one of the greenest windbreakers ever made. I'm probably the first person to walk around dressed like this in the history of this neighborhood. If anything, the jacket looks even greener here than it did in the store. On my back, I have a large and reasonably well-packed backpack. Around my neck, I have a compass and a map in a plastic pouch.

The Head of Documentation is dressed identically, although she's not green. What's more, she's had a lot of her hiking gear for a long while. You can tell she's done this before. Whereas anybody can see that everything I'm wearing and carrying bore a price tag less than twenty-four hours ago.

The Head of Documentation is taking her job of being irritatingly positive seriously and began the day by playing that irritatingly positive song about nature, "The Happy Wanderer," as we packed. In case you're fortunate enough to be unfamiliar with this classic, I can tell you it's a German hit song that has been recorded in many versions in many languages, all equally irritating. While the Norwegian lyrics have much in common with the English version, including the chorus—which must be sung at top volume—they also make the absurd declaration that "the rain is my brother."

Yes, you get it. *The rain is my brother.* Really?

Now, I'm a man who likes to let himself get swept up and I have a soft spot for weird old hits, so I sense that this irritatingly positive song actually is raising my spirits. I'm starting to look forward to going now. If only because going means doing something other than packing, which is all we've done for the past twenty-four hours. We packed for hours yesterday. We packed and unpacked and repacked and packed again. There was hiking gear scattered all over the living room floor. And the packaging! Without making too big a deal out of this I must point out that living at one with nature generates vast amounts of packaging. I'm normally an efficient packer but this could have something to do with the fact that I usually travel to places where you can just pop out and buy stuff if there's anything you've forgotten. Besides, there's an awful lot of ultra-sensible advice to think about when you're packing a backpack, to ensure that it's comfortable to carry *and* also gives you easy access to the things you need most. To sum up all this advice in a single phrase: it can't be done. As a result, your packing ends up being mediocre, so you can't find what you need when you get where you're going, which means you have to pack all over again the next day while listening to a song with an infuriatingly jolly chorus.

▲

AND THIS VERY HAPPY SONG is what I'm humming as I stand in reception. It's inescapable.

Nobody else looks like us, of course. The other people in the reception area are wearing suits or smart outfits with name badges, or they're wearing regular clothes and carrying rapidly packed bags and look tired, happy, and still slightly drunk. Several of them walk past us and turn back to take another look, wondering if they really saw what they thought they saw. Some even roll their eyes. I can't say I blame them. I'm sweating. These clothes aren't designed to be worn indoors. I open one of the sixty-eight zippers on my jacket to get the famed air transport going.

The receptionist is young and the badge on his jacket reveals that he's in training. He is as service-minded as it's only possible to be when you're in training.

"Have you enjoyed your stay with us?" he asks—a bit too loud and a bit too rehearsed—showing us his teeth. This is Receptionese for: "Why did you bring 150 pounds of luggage with you for a single night at a hotel? And is it really possible for a jacket to be quite as green as that?"

I smile my by now long-famous winning smile.

"I don't suppose you see all that many people at the hotel in outfits like this," I say to make conversation.

The receptionist is working now. This particular gambit is hardly part of the training. Our man is forced to improvise.

"No, I suppose I haven't seen so many people . . . dressed *exactly* like that."

"We're hiking along the Jotunheim Trail," I say, in explanation.

"Mm," says the receptionist. What else is he supposed to say? "Mm," incidentally, is Receptionese for "Jotunheimen? Isn't that 180 miles away? And that jacket really is extremely green."

"Did you know that the Jotunheim Trail starts right outside here?"

"No, I didn't know that." Which is Receptionese for "Should I call somebody?"

THERE IS VERY LITTLE indeed to indicate that the Jotunheim Trail begins where it's supposed to begin. On UT.no, it plainly states: "it may be appropriate to start out along the Aker River beside the Oslo Plaza. Here you will find a sign to Oset in Maridalen."

You certainly will not. And there aren't all that many people in the neighborhood behind the Oslo Plaza that it's worth asking about the route to Jotunheimen, either. In fact, I wouldn't recommend asking the few other people hanging around by the river behind the hotel anything at all unless you really fancy some drugs.

We find a lamppost that looks as if it had something screwed onto it once upon a time. We conclude that this could be where the sign had been. We share a moment's silence. Then we start walking.

We hike along the river through the city, on trails and tracks I've walked along many times before, during lunch breaks and on evening strolls. I've also walked here in the past few days to break in my hiking shoes. Which is important. Ask anybody.

We start to look out for red Ts. After all, we're walking along a hiking path. It would've been pretty neat if a red T—the very symbol of Nature—had popped up here, in the heart of Norway at its most urban. And there are more than enough rocks and brick walls to spray Ts on along the river. But we don't see any.

THERE ARE, HOWEVER, plenty of other things sprayed on the rocks and brick walls we pass. "I love sluts," it says in one place, for example.

Although it's hardly likely that the Norwegian Trekking Association is responsible for that.

Or is it? Maybe it's a sub-group? The Male Chauvinists' Trekking Club? It's actually not entirely unlikely that it exists. For people who seek out solitude and silence in nature, hikers are very keen on organizing into groups with lots of other people. The Norwegian Trekking Association has almost sixty membership organizations and loads of local groups. There are separate hiking teams and groups for young people, for children, for old people. There's a Lesbian Hiking Group. And there's a special hiking group for gay men. "For men who like men who like mountains," as their slogan puts it.

AROUND SEVEN MINUTES away from the Plaza, the Jotunheim Trail goes straight past a café where I buy coffee every morning. It's a really nice place. They know my order. There are three or four of us who often drop in early in the morning and buy the same thing. It's a little community. We say the same things to each other every day. On the rare occasions I've met one of the regulars someplace other than this café, it's been a bit like meeting a colleague or a neighbor when you're on vacation a long way from home.

This is a test. I'll go into this place where I'm a regular, in hiking gear, and I'll wear this hiking gear with pride. I'll show my people that I've become this kind of guy now. It's way more embarrassing than I could have imagined. And I've done plenty of embarrassing stuff. Ask anybody. I hold my head high, straighten my back, open three or four zippers in my jacket, and walk in.

I get off lightly. I'm usually here a bit earlier in the day, so none of my regular comrades are here now. And the woman behind the counter is pretty new, so for all she knows I could make a habit of going home after my breakfast coffee, dressing up in excessively green clothes, and then returning with baggage on my back.

Outside, the Head of Documentation takes a picture.

"The last macchiato," she says dramatically. "From now on, it's black camping coffee all the way."

"There's no such thing as bad coffee," I say. "There are only bad clothes."

It starts to rain.

"The rain is our brother," the Head of Documentation says.

And then we leave civilization.

FROM THE CITY TO THE FOREST, HOUR BY HOUR

First leg: Downtown Oslo–Tømtehytta.
On foot. Estimated time: six-and-a-half hours.

12:15: WE'VE BEEN HIKING for a quarter of an hour. We're still in the city, hiking on asphalt. The rain has eased off. The macchiato is finished. I have "The Happy Wanderer" on the brain. The mood is good.

12:45: We're still in the city but in a part of the city I'm not so familiar with. I like it. We talk about the kind of people we think live here. Suddenly we pass a place where one of us once went to a party or a meeting. Or jogged or swam. It's great hiking around in your city. Really great.

12:50: Really, really great.

13:00: We'll soon put the asphalt behind us and head off along a gravel road. We sit down on a bench for a chocolate break. It immediately starts raining again.

13:15: Around twenty seconds after turning onto the gravel road, we meet an elderly couple on their way into the city. They smile and say "Hi." People apparently start greeting strangers the second they stop walking on asphalt.

13:30: We reach Maridal Lake after exactly as much time as it's supposed to take to hike there, according to UT.no. This gives us an intense but weird sense of having done well. It's stopped raining.

13:45: We've now spent some time hiking along a cart track or something. There's more and more nature and less and less city but my focus is still wrong. I eagerly shout out things like: "Look— there's a house!" or "You can hear the cars from the road!" Must pull myself together. Focus on experiencing nature.

14:00: We come to a signpost that points away from the direction we thought we were supposed to take. We follow the signpost for a while, end up back on a highway and asphalt, consult the map, and find that there are two places with exactly the same name not so far from each other. We start to wonder whether we've already managed to lose our way in nature before, strictly speaking, we've even reached nature.

14:05: To show how good we are at being irritatingly positive, we decide this is a perfect moment to find a rock, sit down, eat lunch, drink coffee, look at the map and calmly find out where we are and where we're headed.

14:06: It starts raining again.

14:07: Note to self: Always make sure you keep your sit mat, raingear, and food close at hand in your backpack.

14:10: The Head of Documentation brews some Ethiopian camping coffee in a little bag. We eat some sandwiches. It isn't so bad despite the rain. And a quick glance at the map tells us that the trail we're supposed to hike along starts right behind us. And leads right into the forest. This is where things get serious.

14:20: We start hiking in the forest. It's more than four hours until we'll arrive at the cabin if UT.no is to be believed. And it must be.

14:25: It's raining more heavily now. I point out that you almost don't notice the rain if you're walking under the trees.

"The forest is nature's very own roof," I say. And we agree that we can hardly call ourselves outdoors people until we've learned to say stuff like that without laughing.

14:30: There's a lot less to talk about when you're surrounded by forest and nothing but forest. So we decide this is a good place to try out hiking in silence and thinking. This is when we're supposed to feel that city life and everyday existence and the noise are loosening their grip; that we're starting to see things clearly.

14:40: We've now hiked in silence and thought for ten minutes. This is what I've thought so far. "There's a tree root. There's a tree root. There's a wet patch. There's a tree root. There's a tree root."

14:43: Tree root. Tree root.

14:45: We conclude that this isn't the right landscape for silence and clear thoughts. Instead, we have a go at the Big Conversation. Several of my hiking friends say they have their best conversations while hiking: This is when they talk about the big things, because the logistical hell of everyday existence is so far away. We get started. And we do pretty well. We talk about dreams, things we've always wanted to do, places we want to travel to.

14:48: It turns out that absolutely all the places we want to travel to are places without rain or spruce forest. This conversation is downright destructive.

14:50: There's a tree root. There's a tree root. There's a wet patch. There's a slightly peculiar tree root.

14:55: We change the topic to books we want to read. I mention a new book I've heard of.

"What's it about?" the Head of Documentation asks.

"It starts with a family getting brutally murdered in a cabin in the forest outside Oslo."

14:56: Tree root. Tree root. Tree root.

15:05: We decide to focus on the most urgent matter: getting "The Happy Wanderer" out of our heads. There's only one recognized method for getting an irritating song out of your head and that's to replace it with another song. The Head of Documentation decides to teach me the lyrics to "Do-Re-Mi" from *The Sound of Music*. Don't ask me why she knows them. She knows a lot of peculiar things. I appreciate her initiative.

15:25: Now both of us know "Do-Re-Mi" from *The Sound of Music* by heart.

15:27: "Do-Re-Mi" from *The Sound of Music* is a pretty irritating song.

15:35: I think I miss "The Happy Wanderer."

15:40: We have to do something to get rid of "Do-Re-Mi" and the Head of Documentation suggests we see how many artists and bands we can think of whose first name or band name begins with A. Perhaps it's neither the clarifying silence nor the Big Conversation. But it helps pass the time.

"ABBA," I say. Of course.

"Annie Lennox," says the Head of Documentation.

"Andrews Sisters."

"A-ha."

"Adele."

It's raining pretty heavily now. There are two hours and fifty minutes to go. Around us we see trees. Nothing but trees.

15:55: It isn't going so quickly with the artists beginning with A anymore. There are long pauses for thought between each artist. It's wetter. We mostly look down to avoid stumbling or suddenly ending up knee-deep in mud. Is this the way it's supposed to be? I think. Shouldn't we be looking up? Finding things in the trees? Animals? Shouldn't there be animals here? Isn't this nature? We've been hiking for four hours and haven't seen so much as a mouse. Whereas if

I walk just ten minutes to the store in the city I often meet a cat or two. And a good few birds.

"A Flock of Seagulls!" I shout out loud.

It feels like a victory.

16:05: This business of the trail markings is more confusing than people would have you believe. Especially if you're not always keeping track because you're busy coming up with artists beginning with A. Here in the forest, there are red and blue markings on the trees. So, not red Ts on rocks, the way I learned. There can be pretty long gaps between each mark. Sometimes the red and blue trees part ways; sometimes the trees are suddenly marked with both colors. Normally we'd Google this. But of course there isn't any internet access here.

"Alphaville," says the Head of Documentation.

It's incredibly irritating that I wasn't the one who came up with Alphaville.

16:15: Suddenly there are no more markings. We can't see any trees with any colors on them. It's raining heavily now. Apparently there are no more artists in the world beginning with A. We agree that we just have to keep walking a bit in the same direction and we'll probably find more marks.

16:25: We've kept walking a bit in the same direction. We haven't found any more marks. However, we have come to a big steep hill that leads down to what is, by all appearances, a fairly enormous bog. The Head of Documentation has started saying some pretty mean things about the people who mark these routes. In other words, it's now up to me to be irritatingly positive. This is what teamwork is all about.

"Have we maybe got internet now?" I ask. And, in fact, we have.

The map function on the phone is useless. According to this map we are now in the middle of a huge area where there is nothing. Which at least means that the map matches the territory. But at any rate, we Google our way to the information that there are two types of marked routes: winter routes and summer routes. The problem with hiking winter routes in the summer is that these routes may suddenly turn out to cross a lake or—*ta-da!*—a bog or other area that cannot be crossed in summertime. And the summer routes are, logically enough, marked with the cold winter color blue. And the winter routes are, logically enough, marked with the warm color red. We know that now.

This is the kind of thing you're supposed to look into *before* you set out on a hike, is what you, the reader, are probably thinking now if you're a smart-ass hiking type. And that's exactly why I *hate* smart-ass hiking types.

16:30: We decide to be smart-asses ourselves and turn around. We have to get back to where we were. Assuming we can *find* the way back to where we were. After all, everything looks the same. There's nothing but trees here. We turn. We walk, quickly. I quietly hum "Do-Re-Mi." The Head of Documentation grimly hums "The Happy Wanderer."

17:00: We're back at the place where we lost our way. We celebrate with a chocolate.

"This way at least we got to see a bit more of the forest," says the Head of Documentation—and with that, she's back on the job of being irritatingly positive.

"There's no such thing as losing our way," I say. "There are only bad clothes."

We discuss how much time we've wasted on this. An hour? More? Two? And how much time did we waste when we maybe lost our way a bit just before our lunch break? Hard to say. We decide to put our failures behind us and press on with renewed valor. That's the kind of people we've become now. Already. Now we know we're going the right way. We have more chocolate and Ethiopian camping coffee in the backpack. And we're still stuck at A in the alphabet. We move on to B and speed up to marching pace.

"Beyoncé," says the Head of Documentation.

"Bob Marley."

"Boney M."

"Bananarama."

"Beastie Boys."

There are two hours still to go. Or three. Or more. I don't know. It rains and rains.

17:15: One of us finally asks the question I think both of us have been mulling for some time:

"When does it actually get dark?"

Right: *That's* one of those things you don't know if you don't make a habit of wandering about the forest in the evenings. I seize on the only thing I have to seize on.

"Yesterday when we arrived at the Plaza it was light. I think we got there just before eight."

"Yes. But it was pretty dark when we got to the bar."

"Yes."

In other words, it gets dark somewhere between just before eight and a bit later.

If we'd hiked without once losing our way, we should, according to UT.no, have arrived by half past six. We decide to up the tempo.

17:30: There's no experience of nature left now. We walk, a bit too quickly. We look straight down. It gets wetter and wetter. We're both probably internally calculating minutes and seconds and miles. Neither of us has said anything for a quarter of an hour. Neither of us is showing much sign of inner peace.

"Bonnie Tyler," says the Head of Documentation, with zero enthusiasm.

17:38: It's incredible how happy a signpost out in the forest can make you. As mentioned earlier, the markings aren't always easy to find and don't always leave you much the wiser. But a signpost can be trusted. That's why we both enthusiastically exclaim "Signpost!" every time we see one. This time the signpost shows us we're on the right track. How far there is left to go, however, is somewhat unclear. It only indicates the distance to a lake we know we're supposed to head for. How far it is from there to the cabin we don't know. What's more, on the map it looks as if the last stretch is mostly uphill.

"It's the uphills that take you to the top," says the Head of Documentation.

In just over two hours darkness will fall. Maybe.

17:40: Suddenly there's a jogger coming toward us. A young woman bounds lightly from tree root to tree root. Heaven knows where she came from. The only thing you can say for sure is that she must have jogged a long way and still has a long way left to go.

Now here's something I want to get off my chest for all you people who think it's pretty crowded out in Norwegian nature: This is the first human being we've met since we left the city. This is, in fact, the first living creature we've seen. And we jump. We stop her—which I think she finds a bit irritating. But we must. A person running around in here as if it were the most natural thing in the world must surely be a fount of local knowledge.

She smiles politely and jogs on the spot. We explain where we're heading. The cabin, she's never heard of, which is far from reassuring, but the lake we're heading for she knows very well. She confirms that we're on the right track. Is it far?, we ask. Not at all, she answers. It's right over there.

Then she runs off into the forest again. I bet we'll see her on a victory podium in the not-too-distant future.

18:20: Note to self: You must never, ever, ever, ever trust hideously healthy joggers in the forest who tell you that something is "right over there." People like that have no normal concept of what "right over there" means. It's like discussing distances with people who live in really sparsely populated districts. I was once in the most sparsely populated part of Norway, in the far north. Some extremely jolly locals invited us to an after-party when the pub closed. "Is it far?" we asked. "No, not far at all," the after-party host answered. "One-and-a-half hours by snowmobile."

18:25: "Signpost!" shouts the Head of Documentation. We've reached the lake. There are signs of civilization. Benches have been set up there. Somebody has barbecued there not long ago. Somebody has also barbecued on one of the benches, which is half-burnt. And at last we see a signpost bearing the name of the cabin we're heading for. It's a bit farther than we'd thought. And it is, as we'd thought, uphill. From now on, the only way is up.

19:05: We're running on sheer willpower now. I think it's starting to get dark. But that may just be the dense forest and generally crappy weather.

19:15: Fed up now. Very fed up.

19:25: The Head of Documentation is also fed up. She has temporarily abdicated her role as the irritatingly positive one. She is starting to argue in favor of razing all the forest in Oslo to the ground and building homes here. And perhaps she has a point. It may be that there is quite enough nature in this country when it's possible to hike in a forest without seeing a soul for eight hours while still in the country's largest city.

19:35: Signpost! There are two-thirds of a mile to go. And it isn't just our imagination that it's started to get dark. My head isn't anywhere near in any condition to work out how long we'll take to walk two-thirds of a mile up a wet hill with big backpacks at the end of a hike. So I do the only thing any sensible person can do in a situation like this. I start to count yards. One. Two. Three…

And to all the smart-ass hiking types reading this: Yes, we *do* have headlamps. But even so, it goes slowly enough in this gloomy, wet forest. And we're hungry. Even one hundred yards with a headlamp in the darkness is too much now. Way too much. We're going to lose it. And start dancing around in a circle, singing, "I love to go a-wandering" loudly and aggressively.

19:40: The last signpost has given the Head of Documentation a bit of a boost and she embarks on a conversation.

"Have you ever hiked in a rainforest?"

I don't say anything. Partly because I don't want to be interrupted in my yard-counting. And partly because all experience indicates that this question is merely a prelude to a story about the time she went to Panama.

"The time I went to Panama," the Head of Documentation says, "we hiked through a forest up a hill like this. There were monkeys dangling from the trees and we saw the most fantastic blue butterflies."

Really? I think. We've been hiking for seven-and-a-half hours in the rain. We've seen trees, trees, and still more trees. And a few tree roots. And that's it. We have 150 pounds of baggage on our backs and likely half a gallon of water in our shoes. It'll be dark in twenty seconds. Do you really think this is the time for a reminder that there are forests other places in the world where there's not just nice weather but interesting animal life too?

I don't say this out loud, of course.

"Five hundred yards left," I say, although it's hardly true. "And by the way: Bon Jovi!"

The Head of Documentation is impressed.

19:50: Signpost! We can just about read the signpost in the gloom. "Tømtehytta" it says. Damn it if that isn't where we're headed. It doesn't tell us how far there is left to go, which could mean it's actually right here. Out of sheer enthusiasm, the Head of Documentation starts off at a gentle run. In the wrong direction.

I manage to stop her in time. We agree that it really would be a bit silly to lose our way here. We follow the signpost and after four yards, we see the cabin.

We've hiked for pretty much exactly eight hours with a short break. My phone tells me we've hiked 16.9 miles. According to UT.no, we should have hiked 13.5.

But now we're here. At last I'll get to feel all those things everybody talks about. How good it is to get there after a long day of hard toil. How much better the food tastes. How much cozier coziness feels. How deeply and unproblematically you sleep.

19:55: Suddenly it strikes me that perhaps we won't have the cabin to ourselves. After all, this cabin is, in principle, accessible to anybody with a key; and that means, in principle, every member of the Norwegian Trekking Association—all 300,000 of them. I really hope there aren't any people here. The last thing I want now is to have to make conversation. To talk about the hike, listen to patronizing comments about how important it is to look into the business of the markings *before* the hike starts and how impossible it is to lose your way if you just know what to look for; about the importance of having good shoes and that if you know how to dress right, you really don't get your feet wet even if it rains all day long. There's no such thing as bad weather…

Eight hours in the forest and I've already started to dislike people.

20:00: There's no smoke rising from the chimney. Of course there's nobody here. It's Monday. It's late. It's raining. We've met *one* living creature the entire day, and that was a jogger who was heading away from here as fast as her legs could carry her.

20:05: These are the most irritating and unnecessary minutes in my life to date. We've finally reached the cabin. Wet and hungry and irritable. And I have to take off my backpack outside in the rain and try to find out which of the roughly six hundred smart pockets in the backpack I put the key in. As a general rule there are an awful lot of pockets involved in all forms of outdoor life.

20:06: As I search, I begin to develop a theory about how people's likeability is in reverse proportion to the number of pockets they have. Only irritatingly sensible people have way too many pockets; the kind of people who are always prepared for everything and always know how everything has to be done. The professional groupings with the most pockets are photographers and reporters working in war zones. Smart-ass, world-weary, complacent, unshaven alcoholics the lot of them.

20:08: I must have food now. Quickly.

20:11: I find the key in smart pocket number forty-three. We open up. Now we'll really enjoy ourselves, in authentic cabin style.

20:15: First of all, though, there are a hell of a lot of things to be done. That's something anybody who's ever been to a cabin knows. But still, it's astonishingly easy to forget. We have to fetch water. This means we have to find the well. And now it *is* dark. And when it's dark in a forest, it's *really* dark. I wander around with a tiny flashlight and catch sight of some small signs with even smaller symbols that are a bit difficult to see in the dark and a bit difficult to understand. They could have chosen to write "well" on the sign, in Norwegian as well as a world language or two, but they went for a symbol instead, probably out of consideration for all those English-challenged tourists from Uzbekistan these cabins in the woods are overrun with.

I don't have the patience to interpret symbols in the darkness now. I don't have the patience for anything whatsoever. I must have food. I almost walk straight past a small building in the darkness. I open the door. It proves to be the outhouse. A photo of the Norwegian royal family hangs on the wall—a must in all outhouses at all cabins in Norway, to show how amazingly great and down-to-earth and socially democratic and charming we are up here in Northern

Europe. We may have kings and queens, but we hang their portraits in the can. I hate Scandinavians. I hate people with way too many pockets. I hate the dark. I hate...

I must have food. Now!

I start to worry about the Head of Documentation. It must be worse for her. She's the kind of person who loses it if she doesn't get food in time. Maybe you think you know people who cope poorly when their blood sugar starts to fall? Forget it. This is next-level stuff.

I hear a noise behind me. Something cracking. I turn slowly and catch a brief glimpse of the Head of Documentation in the beam of my flashlight. Her long wet hair is plastered to her face. She's standing stock-still. Surrounded by trees. The trees are moving. They seem to lean forward, to stand there staring at me. Are the trees getting closer?

The Head of Documentation has something in one of her hands. An ax? A rifle?

It turns out to be a flashlight. She shines it directly on her own face. She smiles. "I'm going to fetch some wood," she says.

Food. Now.

20:23: After blindly finding water and wood we see the notice inside the cabin saying it isn't safe to drink water from the well. Yeah... no. There's still half a pint of the drinking water we brought in our bags.

Right then: food.

First we just have to find some paper to light the fire with, though; preferably paper that isn't wet and isn't the map we'll need tomorrow. Then we have to find the fire-lighting equipment. And search through half the cabin to find where they've hidden the candles. It turns out they've hidden the candles in the shed where we just went to fetch wood. So we have to go out again. And then we have to light twenty-four candles to be able to see anything whatsoever. And then we have to light the fire. And then we have to hang all our clothes up to dry. And then we have to assemble the makeshift gas stove and boil water for our food, which takes a horribly long time. Both the assembling and the boiling.

But then.

20:55: All the tasks are out of the way. At last we will sit down and eat our camping stew: just add boiling water and leave it to stand for eight minutes. Stew. Authentic, hearty cabin fare for proper people of nature.

We sit down, pour out a little of our remaining drinking water, fetch some cutlery from a drawer and prepare to dig in.

21:03: The stew has stood for the prescribed eight minutes.

The stew tastes absolutely appalling.

I mean, truly.

That's some achievement. People have been making meal-in-a-bag food for several decades. And while it may not be the kind of food that is warmly endorsed by the world's top chefs, it *is* usually food that's perfectly possible to eat. That is not, in fact, the case with this stew.

So if it's true that food tastes *better* after a long and arduous hike, then this stew really is remarkably awful food.

"Maybe our hike wasn't long enough," the Head of Documentation says.

"It would've had to be very long for this to taste okay."

"If we'd spent a few years in a prison camp being tortured it would probably have tasted really fantastic."

"In that case, I think one viable option would just be to eat good food. And preferably drop the torture."

"You may have a point."

21:15: After turning the cabin upside down, we find some meal-in-a-bag pasta left behind by some other guests. It tastes—pretty okay.

21:35: The Head of Documentation smiles slyly. She goes over to her backpack, rummages around a bit, and brings out—a hip flask!

"You brought liquor?!" I shout, a bit too loudly.

"It's all part and parcel of hiking."

She pours a small measure and passes it to me.

"You're actually supposed to take a nip when you reach the top," she says. "But we won't reach any tops before the day after tomorrow. So..."

"I knew your hiking experience would come in handy."

"There's no such thing as bad liquor. Cheers."

21:45: That's more like it. Now it's actually starting to feel like a cabin trip. And I'm reminded of the few cabin trips I've taken before, and of the fact that there's something about cabins I like. I like cabins for the same reason I like airports and hotels. You're a bit outside the world in places like that. It doesn't much matter what day it is or what country you're in. In those places, quite particular rules apply. In airports, regular people who aren't in the least bit alcoholic suddenly order a beer at eight in the morning on a Tuesday. In hotels, regular people who aren't in the least bit criminal suddenly decide to steal everything in their room that isn't bolted down. And in the cabin, we leave civilization to take care of itself. The booze is on the table. Along with the remains of the awful food. It's a bit messy everywhere. There's flickering candlelight. An intense smell of wet clothes fills the whole room. We're both sitting on the sofa, in a constant state of anxiety that the fire might go out. On the wall behind us hangs a guitar that's missing a string. This is what cabin life is all about.

There's only one thing left to do. The ultimate cabin activity: reading the cabin guest book in dim light.

21:55: A lot of people have passed through here. An awful lot. And they write and write in the guest book. I see the name of a family I know. They've written something irritatingly positive and hiker-ish.

Not "there's no such thing as bad weather," but it isn't a hell of a long way off. And for that matter, there are plenty of people who have written just that, too. And that it's good to arrive. And that food tastes so much better after a long walk. I feel a bit like writing comments in the margin but restrain myself.

And here are three couples who are traveling together. They've actually written: "What better way to disconnect from the hurly-burly of everyday life than to head for a cozy cabin free of the technological doodads of everyday life?"

Hikers truly do use a different language from the rest of us. Based on the other stuff these three couples have written, I manage to work out that they're probably in their early thirties. Hello?! Surely nobody under the age of 150 says "the hurly-burly of everyday life" or "technological doodads"? Unless they're in a sketch show.

22:40: We brush our teeth in the open air. We use the unsafe water from the well. Living on the edge.

23:00: I'm really looking forward to sleeping now.

23:30: I can't sleep. My sleeping bag is cold and the room is warm. It's totally dark. And it's dark in a totally different way than when it's dark in a house or an apartment. I seriously haven't a clue what there is an inch to my right. It could be a wall. It could be an elk. But probably not. After all, there are clearly no animals in this forest.

And it's extremely quiet.

"Is this actually safe?" the Head of Documentation says.

Right. So I've brought a woman with hiking experience along in the hope of receiving support, consolation, and backup, and now she asks, as we lie sleepless, an eight-hour walk away from civilization, whether it's *safe*?!

We talk, not for the first time, about how odd this tourist cabin system actually is. It's normally seen as a good thing in a society for people to trust one another—but there is such a thing as too much trust as well. Is it really a good idea to bed down in a remote cabin to which 300,000 other people have the key?

"It's irrelevant how many people have keys," the Head of Documentation says. "The door isn't locked."

"*What* did you just say?"

"It can't be locked from the inside."

So anybody at all could come in here. Apart from the fact, of course, that no sane human being would dream of hiking here in the middle of the night in the rain and fog.

On the other hand, of course, it isn't exactly the *sane* human beings we're worried about.

The Head of Documentation tells me she has a knife under her pillow. I think it's a joke. But I'm far from certain.

"Do you think that's why they set these cabins up in such remote locations?" she asks. "No thugs would bother to come all the way out here to make trouble, would they?"

"Good point."

"Good night, then."

"Good night."

00:10: It's truly totally insanely quiet here. The American author John Irving wrote in one of his slightly overlong novels about the most terrifying sound there is: A sound like someone trying not to make a sound. That's exactly what nature does all the time. It's totally quiet here, but at the same time, you constantly hear tiny little sounds. That maybe aren't sounds. They may just be your imagination. But they could also be raindrops. Or a branch in the wind. Or a lunatic with a master key.

00:45: I'm not used to it being quiet. Not this kind of quiet. This is probably what they're aiming for, those nature lovers who talk about getting away from all the human noise.

Something occurs to me—and this is the trip's first example of my seeing something with perfect clarity: I don't have the slightest *desire* to get away from human noise. I like human noise. In fact, I like it a great deal.

00:55: I start to think of things I like. It's better than counting sheep.

And everything I like involves sound.

People, to start with the most obvious thing.

The sound of heavy rain on an awning. I like that too. Especially when the awning is attached to a place with waiters.

Standing in the restroom in a bar and hearing the laughter of my friends on the other side of the wall. That's a sound I like.

I like the sound of tourists. Who are looking at things I see every day and talking about them in languages I don't understand.

The sound of a radio that's on someplace, though I don't know where.

The sound of a beer can being opened.

The sound of a roaring party through an open window in the summertime.

The sound of a song that starts and I know that I know this song. I mean those first three seconds of sheer anticipation, when you only know that you know the song but you can't remember which song it is and can't remember at first if you even like it.

Music. Full stop. Just think about the way a song can be the sound of a particular person. Bruce Springsteen's "The River," for example, is the sound of my brother. He's two years older than me. When we were growing up, we liked different music as a matter of principle. That's the way it is when you're brothers. If he discovered an artist before me, I couldn't like that same artist. Those were the rules. I had to find another artist and preferably one who was as close to opposite his artist as it was possible to get. My brother discovered Bruce Springsteen first. And which artist did I find who was the opposite of Bruce Springsteen? I'm honestly not sure. I'm afraid it may have been Chris de Burgh. I was extremely young in those days and didn't know any better. So "The River" is the sound of my brother. But the live version, the one with the endless intro, that's the sound of my buddy Alex who knew—and probably still knows—the whole of that endless intro by heart, complete with American accent, and this version of the song always reminds me how powerfully the sound of your favorite artist can affect you because that same Alex had the choice one summer between traveling by train through Europe with me, his best friend, and going to Oslo for the Bruce Springsteen concert. He chose Bruce. I can't say I blame him. He didn't know at the time that a few decades later Bruce Springsteen would be turning up in Norway to play concerts roughly once a fortnight. And besides, now isn't the time to see and listen to him. Or rather go ahead and do that if you want to. By all means. But that was when it meant everything. That was when he was the world's greatest. That was when it was a big event. I love big events. And big events always involve sound.

I like the sound right after big events, too. You can be sitting someplace quite unaware that something big is going on. And suddenly everything changes. Windows and doors are thrown open. People shout and cheer. Cars honk. It's impossible not to run out to see what's going on. It may be a soccer match that's just finished. A cricket match. A singing contest. It may be the announcement of a prizewinner. Or the next Olympic host. It doesn't matter. It's impossible not to get happy.

Opening the door to someplace I like. It may be my own home. It may be the home of a friend who's invited me to dinner. Or, for example, the café we went into this morning where we bought our last macchiato. Opening these doors and hearing the music and the voices and guessing who's in there. That I like.

The first laughter after something sad has happened. One of the most beautiful sounds I know.

Fits of laughter. A fantastic sound.

A concert hall or a theater or a cinema just before the show starts. When you hear a hundred conversations but can't hear what anybody's saying. Yet this sound still tells you a lot about who's there: How old they are, how drunk they are, what they're anticipating, and what kind of an evening it'll be.

Walking through a café and just picking up snippets of the conversations at the tables, and guessing what kind of people are sitting at the different tables.

"...lost it a bit in season four..." (Men, definitely, probably bearded.)

"...slept three hours last night..." (Parental leave. Undoubtedly.)

"...No. No. No. No. No..." (Friends assessing the choice on Tinder?)

"...have several exciting projects underway..." (Some person who is highly unlikely to have a single exciting project underway.)

"...owed a hell of a lot of paid time off..." (Guaranteed: men aged around forty-five with wedding rings. They have receding hairlines, drink interesting beer, and will soon leave. Because they'll be getting up early the next morning for a hike.)

01:45: But I'm not going to think about stuff like that now. I will enjoy the silence. Find peace. Sleep, preferably. It doesn't look as if it's going to happen anytime soon, though. All in all, I've experienced little of what you're supposed to experience in nature today. I haven't felt the stress loosening its grip. I haven't felt free. Or small. Or religious. I haven't had time. There have constantly been masses of things to do. I've counted yards, I've calculated hours and minutes, I've avoided tripping, I've looked for paint on trees. Generally, I've seen an awful lot of trees. Way too many trees.

02:30: I haven't experienced nature today. Not really. Today I've seen forest. And rain. Only tomorrow and the day after tomorrow will I get to experience the nature that makes people religious. That's when I'll hike without being afraid of losing my way or not arriving on time. Just hike. And enjoy. That's when I'll maybe understand all this. I have to be open. I have to be humble. I have to be really tired if I'm thinking that I have to be open and humble.

03:13: I'm just about to fall asleep now.

03:16: The Head of Documentation wakes me up. Has something happened? Has she heard something? *Does* she have a knife under her pillow?

She looks at me gravely.

"Billy Idol," she says.

FAREWELL
TO LOGISTICS

Second leg: Tømtehytta–Gjendesheim.
By foot, train, and bus. Estimated time: one day.

I LIKE TRAINS. For all the usual reasons, I think. I like the fact that they go fairly fast. They go fast enough that you arrive in reasonable time but not so fast that you can't see where you're traveling. You can watch the landscape change outside the window. Now and then you catch a glimpse into the house of a family who don't know anybody's watching them. I like the sound of the wheels on the tracks, of course. And the whistle! It has self-confidence, that train whistle. There's more room on trains than on many other means of transport. I like the fact that the people who work on trains still look as if they're in some old kids' TV series. They wander about in the middle of the computer age dressed in uniforms and caps and wave little flags and blow whistles. And then trains often have a restaurant car. This may not come as a shock to you, now that you've got to know me a bit, but I like the fact that it's possible to move through nature taking your own restaurant with you.

And then I have to admit I enjoy realizing I'm better off than a good few of the other passengers on board. And yes, I'm particularly thinking of those passengers who've been wandering about in nature, probably for days on end, and who come crashing onto the train straight from the forest, wet and filthy, with overly bulky baggage, overly fixed smiles, and overly large families. Vast backpacks and wet jackets and stepchildren and thick wool socks, all in one great tangle. Plus skis if it's winter. And poles. And everyone and everything is dripping wet. Families like that can be on the train for hours on end without sitting still for a single instant. The first few hours are spent organizing. Clothes must be changed. And preferably dried in some makeshift fashion that will infuriate the other passengers, who are preparing for important meetings in Bergen and don't need somebody else's socks dangling over their Mac. Skis and poles must be stacked. And nobody in the history of the world has ever managed to carry more than two pairs of ski poles with dignity. Good humor is on the wane, orders are issued to children as the mother looks for food and the father tries to squash a gigantic, bloated backpack into the overhead hat rack while insisting to his wife over and over again that he's got this, HE'S DEALING WITH THIS, OKAY?! And then the ticket inspector comes along and they have to abandon the overhead hat rack attempt and the food quest to spend half an hour nursing life back into the sopping wet, ice-cold smartphones that contain the app where their tickets are stored.

A lot of train passengers are irritated by people like that. Especially people for whom this train journey is their regular work commute. And I can, of course, see that hikers on trains are irritating. They make too much noise, they take up too much space, there's too much water dripping off them and they smell, and there is at all times an acute danger that at least one of them might end up losing it.

But I don't get irritated. Because I think that it must be much more irritating to be these people. And so it puts me in a good mood to imagine what would happen if I calmly went up to them and said, with a broad smile, "There's a reason why it's called a hat rack, you know."

AND THAT'S RIGHT. Now, of course, we have become those people. We started off the day by waking up way too early after way too little sleep, putting on our still wet clothes, repacking the backpacks—something we will probably do every day—spending way too much time boiling water for two cups of coffee and walking for one-and-a-half hours to a train station in the middle of the forest in northern Oslo. Somebody has graffitied "Yes to wolves" on the train station wall as if to remind us that we're still in the city despite being in the middle of the forest. At the station, we also meet a sopping wet woman who tells us she took the train out here yesterday after work and spent the night in a tent in the forest in the rain and is now going back to work. I have no comment on that.

At any rate, one-and-a-half hours in the forest is more than enough time to get sopping wet, because of course it's raining today too. So there we come, crashing onto the train, filthy, with overly bulky baggage. We're dripping wet. We don't have quite such stiff smiles as wet people on trains often have. We probably haven't spent long enough in the forest. On the other hand, there was a hint of ill humor when we lost our way right outside the cabin early today, but we got a grip on ourselves again with a spot of map reading and an excellent round of artists beginning with C.

And I can now, with a basis for my personal opinion, state that it *is* more irritating to be these wet people on the train. Once all the repacking and clothes changes are out of the way, you sit there feeling as if you're in the wrong place. You're dressed for nature and you have remnants of nature itself on your pants and shoes, everything you're wearing is too big and too dirty and too green. And too wet. And noisy! And leaves huge puddles in the aisle. It's as if you insist on taking as much of the forest as possible with you onto the train just to annoy people wearing regular shoes. And all the stuff you've brought with you gets in the way of people who are getting by with nothing but a tie and a laptop.

And we don't even have skis or poles or a big family.

And the mere thought of getting out a book or buying a cup of coffee is too much, way too much, on top of all the rest. Because it's only a couple of hours until we'll have to get off this train again. And transfer to a bus. And then it'll be the same business all over again. Repacking, changes of clothes, on with jackets that are still wet. Hassle, hassle, hassle. And then you won't want to have a book to pack away or a paper cup to dispose of as well as all the other things. At that point you have enough on your hands.

So that's why you just sit there, taking up too much room, and wait. And smell, probably.

△

"RIGHT," SAYS THE Head of Documentation. "Evaluation so far!"

"I think maybe the forest isn't the place where I'll find salvation."

"No. Not in the rain at any rate. And certainly not with stew as your reward."

"What did they *do* to that stew?!"

"I don't think we want to know."

"No."

"Do you have more faith in the mountains?"

"I do have more faith in the mountains. I like views."

"Besides, from now on, we'll be staying at cabins that serve food."

"I like that too. I like waiters. I always have. Fantastic invention."

"It'll be fine."

"It'll be fine."

"Shall we sing 'The Happy Wanderer'?"

"Let's not overdo it."

△

WHEN WE'VE GOT OFF the train and transferred to the bus, which operates on schedules that vary according to the season and the season apparently changes at around the same time as we change from the train to the bus; and when we've done our repacking and clothes change on the bus, where there's even less room than on the train although there are, at least, a couple of like-minded people on the bus since this bus drives to Jotunheimen; at that point I think it's fine to have a day like this that showcases civilization at its most irritating before we arrive at the mountains. It's good to think that all this is what we're putting behind us now. Starting tomorrow, there'll be no more unpredictable timetables and logistics. Starting tomorrow there'll be no more dense forest either. Starting tomorrow, it'll just be us and the mountains.

And now we're there.

This is Jotunheimen. The 2,174 square mile massif named by the poet Aasmund Olavsson Vinje. The home of the giants! Here lie the highest mountains in Northern Europe. Here lie the oldest marked hiking trails in Norway. Here lies a landscape that makes grown men feel small.

And here, right beside us, lies Besseggen, site of one of the most popular mountain hikes in Norway. Sixty thousand people hike it every year. This is the hike that prompts experienced mountain folk to roll their eyes and talk about long lines. The hike that is described on many websites about the Norwegian mountains as obligatory for all Norwegians. The hike that everybody you speak to has done. Here it lies. The ridge that will bring me salvation. The ridge that was Henrik Ibsen's inspiration for the famous reindeer hunt scene in *Peer Gynt*. Here it lies, mighty and looming.

Or at least people claim that here is where it lies.

And we must almost take their word for it. Because it's impossible to see anything at all in the thick fog.

It's raining too, in case you were wondering.

COMMUNAL SUPPER IN UNDERWEAR

THIS IS OUR FIRST CHANCE to test whether conditions really are so crazy at the mountain cabins, and whether it's true that the big cabins are just like hotels: This evening, we'll be staying at Gjendesheim, the cabin where many people stay before and/or after hiking over Besseggen. This is highland Norway's most visited tourist cabin, with 180 beds and twenty thousand overnight stays per year.

And there are some things that do resemble what you'd find in a hotel as soon as you come into Gjendesheim. There are people here, for example. And electricity. That alone is a gigantic step in the hotel direction after yesterday. What's more, there is a reception desk here, and they serve food.

And there, in reality, the resemblance ends.

Other than that, everything is organized to ensure that this place, offering overnight accommodation for nearly two hundred people, is as similar as possible to a small, primitive cabin. Everything that can be made of wood is made of wood. The beds are narrow and the showers few. The corridor is full of hiking shoes and the whole building smells like a mixture of sweat and soggy clothing.

THE WEATHER FORECAST for tomorrow is printed out and lying on the counter at reception. It looks gloomy.

The people working here are the kind that making hiking gear look good. Because they are, of course, in hiking gear. And they're young and cheery and open to life and actually look way too cool to be working in a wooden cabin. They should be volunteers at a festival. When fall comes and the cabin shuts down, I wouldn't be surprised if the whole lot of them headed for Australia to work at a beach bar.

We're accommodated in a four-person room. For now, it's just the two of us, which is just as well since, strictly speaking, there isn't room for four people in this four-person room, unless all four keep all their baggage up on their beds with them. There are communal restrooms in the cellar, two floors below us. And communal showers where you can shower for four minutes for ten kroner between the hour and half past the hour if you're a man and between half past the hour and the hour if you're a woman. Or was it the other way around?

By the way, here's one more similarity to a hotel. The price. You get a perfectly nice double room at a hotel for what you pay in accommodation for two in a four-person room at Gjendesheim. And at a hotel you'll often have a bathroom on the same floor and you can shower around the clock at no extra cost regardless of gender. There are several hotels around the world that promote themselves with the slogan "High standards, low budget." The Head of Documentation and I discuss whether we should pop out and check whether it says "Low standards, high budget" outside the entrance here.

And then we giggle a bit.

But then we pull ourselves together. Because now it's time to behave ourselves. Now we're supposed to be positive. Now we're supposed to blend in with the mountain folk. And right now, the mountain folk are in the fireside lounge waiting for dinner. Except for the ones who are standing in the shower having a speed-wash, anxiously wondering whether they've remembered the gender regulations right.

In the fireside lounge, there are wooden tables, wooden chairs, wooden sofas, and a wooden bookcase full of books about hiking in the mountains for anybody who needs a bit of a break from hiking in the mountains. There are several things that distinguish this fireside lounge from a hotel bar. There's no music here, for example. Although a piano stands in the corner like a kind of threat. Another thing is that everybody's talking quietly, in waiting-room voices. Still, the most obvious distinction is that everybody here is sitting around in their stocking feet, as if it were the most natural thing in the world. What's more, they all have bright red cheeks.

People are drinking red wine and checking the weather forecast on their phones. A group of sullen young men plays cards in silence. An older man converses with a younger guest who is not especially responsive. Two couples who seem to barely know each other share photos from their day's hike. All in all, a lot of phones are being passed around. A man eager for company, arms folded behind his back, interrogates one of the staff members who's just trying to clean up. A group of adult girlfriends talk—heads nodding, eyes half-empty—with an identical gang of girlfriends from another country. I'd bet they're teachers one and all. And some middle-aged men who have done some mountain hiking before are trying to make it look as if they're wandering around the fireside lounge in hiking pants and undershirts because it's practical and convenient, not because these undershirts happen to be extremely close-fitting.

So these are the mountain folk.

I do what I often do: walk through the place and pick up snippets of the conversations at the different tables.

"...six to seven hours..."

"...Oh, yes, we've been there plenty of times before..."

"...*sechs Stunden*..."

"...Oh no, it's not far..."

"...not the most challenging hike..."

"...no, no, no, it isn't at all scary..."

"...seven hours. But we took a lot of breaks..."

"...we'll go the other route, not the route everybody else takes..."

"...in line..."

"...I have some paid time off saved up..."

▲

THIS LAST COMMENT came from one of the middle-aged men in high-tech thermals, in case you're wondering.

Otherwise, absolutely every conversation in the fireside lounge is about where you hiked today, where you'll hike tomorrow, where you've hiked before, where you're thinking of hiking later, how long you took, and how easy everything is as long as you're in reasonable shape. Which is the way people often talk about their own shape if they want to boast about it in a modest way.

It's hardly surprising most hikers would rather not meet too many other people in the mountains. These are clearly people who would be incapable of coping with normal social interactions. Imagine one of these people at a dinner party. The host opens the door:

"Hello—welcome!"

"I hiked here today, you know."

"Oh, did you? Do come in."

"It took eight-and-a-half minutes."

"I see..."

"It's probably just over two-thirds of a mile, I think. A brisk walk. If you're in reasonable shape."

"Really?"

"Yes. A bit hilly. Mostly gravel road. And then it's been raining so it's a bit slippery."

"I see."

"No stress, though—a great hike."

"Lovely. But..."

"Have you hiked far today?"

"No, I've mostly stayed in cooking dinner."

"Mm. Good to get out a bit."

"Absolutely. But..."

"I was thinking of taking a different route back. Through the forest. Not so many people there."

"There probably aren't all that many people out and about here in the middle of the night anyway. But do come on in. The others are in the living room."

"The living room. Is it far?"

"Is it far? No, it's right in here."

"Eight or ten yards maybe?"

"Um...Yes, maybe."

"I'll probably take a few trips to the restroom during the evening. Try out slightly different routes. You do have restrooms up- and downstairs, right?"

"Yes..."

"I'll probably hike to both. Good to use your body a bit."

"Okay. But now you really must sit down before the food gets cold."

"Of course. By the way..."

"Yes?"

"It's okay by you if I sit in my underwear, right?"

AT GJENDESHEIM, THEY'VE realized that mountain folk could do with a bit of elementary social training: here, enforced socialization takes place during dinner.

Most of what goes on here is a bit like being at summer camp. Dinner is served at a specific time. You eat what you're served. And what you're served is probably meat. And you sit where you're told. The room is far from full, but all the guests are placed together around two long tables. We're assigned places by the window, with a view of a wall of fog. We've grasped the dress code and dressed down for dinner. So here I sit at the table, like an experienced mountain man, ready for a three-course meal, in a close-fitting undershirt and timeless, classic gray sweatpants. And indoor shoes. Most of the others are still wandering about in their stocking feet. But quite honestly, you're not obliged to let standards slide entirely just because you're staying at a cabin.

People sit at the table, greet one another. Identical conversations are conducted in different languages:

"... seven hours ..."

"... *sieben Stunden* ..."

"... *litt over seks* ..."

"... *seks og halv tres* ..."

SIX OR SEVEN MINUTES after dinner should have started, there are still five empty chairs at our table. A few people have already looked at the clock, tutted, and rolled their eyes.

Then a man of around fifty comes into the room, leading a group of five men. He's wearing a close-fitting undershirt—I think that's mandatory—and what looks suspiciously like a pair of jeans. Heavens. Civilian clothing. That's bold.

He's clearly not the kind that likes people not to notice him when he comes into a room.

"Welcome back down, folks!" he shouts, throwing out his arms. "Congratulations to all of you on surviving!"

Some people laugh nervously. Some look at the clock, tut, and roll their eyes again. His words were spontaneously translated into

English and German by well-meaning dining companions. Some smart-ass or another says that not everybody at the table hiked over Besseggen today; some will be doing it tomorrow.

I grin and think: *These five have had a pre-party.* I like that. And the five empty chairs are at our table, beside us.

We soon find ourselves in the company of what is clearly the liveliest gang in the cabin by a long margin. These five friends work together on the oil rigs and take a trip to the mountains together once a year. Last year Galdhøpiggen. This year Besseggen. That's what I call getting along with your colleagues. On the other hand, they have a lot of shore leave, those people who work in the North Sea, so maybe they have time to miss each other when they're on dry land. Once a year they also go together to a blues festival in the town where one of them lives. Those times, they stay overnight in the garden of the one who lives there in a tent that looks like a little bus. I'm shown photos of it and get the clear impression that there's not much of a focus on outdoor living on this other trip. Or blues for that matter.

We order red wine, toast each other, and bond like hell.

We show that we've embraced the local culture by asking all the questions you're supposed to ask.

They took seven hours to hike over Besseggen. And they took a few breaks. They had some beer and liquor with them. And one of them hadn't done much exercise since the previous hike a year earlier. But he stresses that he recovers his fitness levels so quickly that he generally gets back into shape during his first uphill stretch. And then he bellows with laughter.

There are many such comments this evening. And much bellowing with laughter. They're those kind of people. I like those kind of people.

We ask them if it was unpleasant hiking in the rain and fog. No, it wasn't, they say. Not at all. This jibes with everything else we've heard. Everyone you talk to who's done the Besseggen hike tells you that the ridge may look narrow and scary on the photos, but it's actually no problem, a piece of cake, plenty of room, not scary at all. Yes, of course, everybody's heard stories about people who freak out up there and have to be rescued by helicopter but they're mostly tourist nincompoops wearing Converse. The bottom line? This is easy-peasy. People hike over Besseggen with kids. People bring their dogs. Hundred-year-olds have hiked it, and people on crutches. People run across the ridge. I think I've even heard of somebody who did the hike in a wheelchair, but maybe I imagined that one.

Our new offshore friends tell us maybe they didn't see all that much up there. But they show us a few photos. And they definitely saw a *bit*, despite the fog. There are hints of a view in the distance in several of the photos.

After this, we make a definitive decision to hike over Besseggen tomorrow. We'd been thinking of leaving it for a day and taking a day trip to slightly lower-lying areas tomorrow instead if the forecast indicated zero visibility and awful weather. But now we've decided. We check the weather forecast on the phone one more time, which is what people do at these cabins when they're not talking about hours and minutes and looking at each other in underwear. Broadly speaking, all available meteorological services agree that the weather in the area of Besseggen will be awful tomorrow and will be even more awful the day after tomorrow. Of course there'll be a hike tomorrow.

We celebrate the decision by ordering more red wine.

We talk with our new friends about our trip so far. We tell them about the day we spent walking through the forest in the rain and the dreadful stew we couldn't bring ourselves to eat.

"Then you just weren't hungry enough," says one of the guys in an undershirt.

AFTER WE'RE THROUGH with all the obligatory topics of conversation and the dessert and the wine, we move to the fireplace lounge, which, in a moment of bewilderment, I refer to as the hotel bar. It's actually that cozy. We chat and laugh, talk about work and leisure, family and future, and a bunch of baloney. About where we come from and what we like. And The Eagles, actually. I don't remember why. I'll be damned if we didn't also touch on both politics and religion, which I'm pretty certain is in violation of the unwritten regulations on conversational propriety. We order beer. After a while the most frequently visited tourist cabin in highland Norway runs out of ordinary beer and we have to switch to an interesting and probably somewhat stronger local brew.

I'm thinking that cabin life is actually pretty nice. Until I realize that the reason I'm thinking that is because what's happening here right now is very much like a quite ordinary evening in any old pleasant bar. Apart from the fact that I'm wearing sweatpants. And people are wandering about in their stocking feet. And some guy is actually sitting at the fireside clipping his toenails.

Yes indeed.

We're the noisiest table in the room. Not that the competition is especially tough. Some of the others look at us with what I interpret as disapproving expressions. And soon we're the only ones in the room. The last one to go is the older chap seen conversing here earlier in the evening. Conversing is apparently his specialty. He stops by our table for some light conversation on his way out. He's been staying here for several days, alone. He hasn't hiked over Besseggen and has no plans to do so. He likes taking short hikes nearby—little rambles, is the impression I get, generally along the road. It looks as if he's found that great inner peace. Either that or he's stark raving mad. After informing us of his hiking habits, he's probably conversed himself to a standstill for the day and can now go to bed with a clear conscience. There's still a solid stretch to midnight. And everybody's gone to bed but us.

Party central.

What's most reminiscent of summer camp here is how little it takes to feel naughty. It's enough to order more than a couple of beers. It's enough to stay up until half past eleven. It's enough to laugh loudly.

Maybe we ought to be sensible and go to bed too. After all, we're going to *bag* a peak tomorrow. But I don't feel like being sensible. And this, precisely, is one of my theories about why I haven't done what everybody else I know has done and started hiking in the mountains: maybe I've used up all my good sense.

Seriously, though, hear me out: What if we all have an allotted amount of good sense to be used over the course of our lives? It almost looks that way. It's pretty common not to be sensible during your childhood, youth, and student days, for people who do that kind of thing. You swipe fruit from people's gardens and lie to your parents and smoke on the sly and steal and play hooky and throw snowballs with stones in them and ring people's doorbells and run away and drink liquor when you're thirteen and get up when you feel like it and leave the dishes in the sink and grow your hair and experiment with intoxicants and sleep around and throw stones at embassies. And then at some point in life, you realize you need to start using your good sense if you're going to use it all up before you're in your grave. And that's when people start families, get permanent jobs and cars and routines and morals and get involved in PTAS and children's soccer and extremely narrow issues that affect their local community and start going to bed at fixed times and eating healthy and hiking in forests and fields and mountains. On the whole, my life has been the reverse. I was extremely sensible as a child, embarrassingly sensible. I did what adults in authority told me to; I was good at school, I did my homework, I put up my hand and behaved well. Perhaps I simply used up all my good sense in those days?

But we ought to be sensible now. We know that, both of us, although it really doesn't come naturally to either of us. We'll be hiking for hours tomorrow, mostly uphill, most likely in rain and fog. We absolutely ought to go to bed.

And that's exactly what we do.

After one more round of an interesting and probably rather strong local brew.

And after singing a bit of The Eagles. I don't remember why.

There are hugs. And of course the oil-rig gang takes advantage of last call to buy three beers apiece so they'll probably be sitting there a while longer.

And they are very welcome to.

This business of sleeping so well at cabins in the mountains is quite simply untrue. And now I have a basis for my opinions in this field too. Everything here is, as I mentioned, made of wood. I'm not sure what kind of wood has been used but I think it is one that has been cultivated over generations to achieve maximum creaking. And if people were supposed to sleep in sleeping bags, there'd have been no need to invent duvets. They're a strange combination of too hot and too cold. And sleeping bags also make an awful lot of noise. It may be quiet outside the cabin. But goodness me it's noisy in the few square feet that are my bed.

And I actually think I'm dreading tomorrow's hike a bit. I don't quite know why. The problem with not being able to sleep is that you have to time to think about stuff like that. And it's just stupid. I should be looking forward to it. I have been looking forward to it. No more logistics, no more dense forest. Just us and the mountain. And it's easy-peasy. No problem. And it's so great afterward! Look at the oil-rig gang! How pleased and happy—and funny!—they were after *bagging* Besseggen. In less than twenty-four hours, I'll be the one coming into the dining room with red cheeks and self-confidence and ordering red wine a little too loudly.

It'll be great.

I LIE THERE, awake, sounding myself out. And what I feel is that I'd much rather be someplace else. The restroom to be precise. And that's in the basement, two floors below us. And I have to get dressed. And I have to go past the fireside lounge, where the mood is still excellent.

When I get back, I'm wide awake. I try to think of everybody I know who's done the Besseggen hike. It doesn't help. It just takes a very long time.

I try to remember the lyrics to "Do-Re-Mi." And that's when I fall asleep.

TO
THE TOP

**Third leg: Gjendesheim–Memurubu–Gjendesheim,
over Besseggen. Estimated time: various sources here.
On UT.no, some posts say seven hours, some six to eight.
The Great Norwegian Lexicon says seven.
Besseggen.net says six to eight. The cheery gang
of oil-rig workers we met yesterday say seven,
but they'd taken beer, liquor, and a pretty
unfit buddy along with them.**

THERE ARE A LOT OF important things you can forget when you're
hiking over a mountain for several hours. You're reminded of this all
the time. There are posters at Gjendesheim with long lists of all the
stuff that's sensible to take with you when you're hiking over Besseggen: water, food, change of clothes, warm and windproof clothing,
gloves, hat, headlamp.

Judging by the conversations yesterday, however, this is the worst
thing you can forget: to check the time when you start your hike.
There's little point in getting there and not knowing how long you've
taken. Then you'll find yourself sitting in your underwear in the fireside lounge with nothing to talk about.

WE'RE SUPPOSED TO take a daypack with us on the hike. Let me have a go at explaining the concept of the daypack: A daypack is to a backpack as a clutch is to a handbag—something that's easy to take out with you, has just enough space for the necessities, and matches your outfit better. Except that there are an awful lot more "necessities" on a mountain hike than at a party. And absolutely nothing in this world could match an outfit as green as mine.

So there's a lot of repacking to be done before the hike can start. Again. It's two days since we got up at the Oslo Plaza. Over these two days, I've slept a combined total of seven hours, and this is the sixth time I've repacked.

And of course we're in a hurry. Because we're supposed to catch a boat. The hike begins with a boat trip. This is exactly like being in the army again: sitting in a room that's far too small with bunk beds and trying to remember what's supposed to go where in time to get to something you don't want to do. It's also dark in the room. It's impressively dark everywhere in these cabins. Even in the cabins with electric light. And natural light. I don't know how they do it.

Considering it's supposed to be an antidote to the eternal logistical hassle of everyday life, there's an awful lot of logistical hassle in the mountains.

And just when you've filled your daypack as full as a daypack can be filled, you realize you also need to leave some space for your lunch, which you'll need to prepare and pack during breakfast. Breakfast is, by the way, the part of this cabin experience that least of all resembles a hotel. Here, they've aimed for simple, basic, cabin-like, and puritanical. Nothing is overdone. The most extravagant things you'll find are slices of cucumber that are just as dry as the slices of bread.

WHEN WE FINALLY get out and it starts to rain heavily and the fog is, of course, also even thicker than yesterday—that's when I actually feel my irritation receding. I could say it's because of the fresh mountain air, but I know what it is: it's because I'm done with the hassle. And I know I'm ready. I'm safe. I haven't forgotten anything. I can't possibly have. Because I've taken pretty much everything I own. I've brought food, drink, coffee, a change of clothes, rainwear, a hat, gloves, a helicopter.

Only joking.

But I do have a flashlight. And chocolate. And a map and a compass and a camera and a Visa card. An awful lot of this didn't fit in the daypack, so everything that can be hung around a neck is hanging around my neck beneath my jacket so it won't get wet. In other words, I no longer just look like a newbie in a jacket that's way too green. I look like a *pregnant* newbie in a jacket that's way too green.

But this green jacket will keep me dry for the rest of my life. A sensitive young man in a sports store promised as much. Besides, the jacket has air transport. And I have good hiking shoes. And I'm ready for anything. And I feel that I'm looking forward to getting started. In fact, I'd say I feel something resembling a kind of sense of freedom.

We look over to where the mountain apparently lies in the fog.

"It'll break up," I say to the Head of Documentation.

"It'll break up," she replies.

This is what people say when visibility is poor. It has certainly been said 150 times in the barely ten hours we've been at Gjendesheim alone. It'll suddenly break up, people say, both guests and the people working here. It seems like they believe it'll happen if only it's said often enough.

Of course I know it can happen. It isn't that. It happened the first time I took the Head of Documentation along on trip to the mountains (yes, I have actually done this before—I just forgot to mention it). This was in my hometown, the place with the storehouse steps. There's a mountain trip you can take there that's right up my alley.

It starts on the main road and goes via cable car up to a restaurant. And there's a fantastic view, which I wanted to show her. Or rather, there's usually a fantastic view. That precise day, in July, it snowed. And you couldn't see a thing. Zero. Nada. Inside the restaurant sat sullen tourists with oversized cameras, drowning their sorrows. We took it in good humor, because that's the kind of people we are, and ordered food. And then, when the Head of Documentation had gone to the restroom, it happened.

It broke up.

Chaos erupted in the restaurant. I ran to the ladies' restroom, tore open the door, and yelled. The tourists grabbed their cameras and stormed for the exit, knocking over pints, chairs, and nuclear families along the way.

And then everybody stood there and looked at the view that had suddenly opened itself up before us.

After fifteen seconds it was over. And again you could see nothing. In the meantime, our food had gone cold.

It was magical.

"It'll happen again," we told each other now. Because that's the kind of people we are: irritatingly positive.

And then we laugh.

And that's what we'll need to put a stop to before we can consider ourselves outdoors people.

I'M SO SELF-ASSURED and ready now that I even roll my eyes at the outfit of a Canadian couple we barely said hello to yesterday evening.

"He's wearing trainers," I say, tutting.

"And one of those rain ponchos they hand out free at music festivals. And she's wearing a normal jacket. Not a rain jacket."

"Zero air transport."

We're shocked.

"How are you today?" we say when we meet them. And smile those winning smiles, which are probably already the stuff of legend in mountain circles.

"Wet," she replies.

THE BOAT IS ALMOST EMPTY. And here's something I just want to get off my chest for all those people who babble on about there being lines in the mountains: it isn't hard to avoid them. It's just a matter of going out midweek when the weather isn't especially nice. Then I'll guarantee you an absence of lines. We see a total of ten people and one dog the entire day. Six of them we meet on the boat. There is the wet Canadian couple without air transport, two friends who aren't too eager for company and take a lot of photos, and two extremely jolly women from Utah, whom we talk to. "Your country is beautiful," one of them says instead of "Hi." I'm a bit tempted to tell her it wasn't me who made this country, but I'm well brought up, so instead we thank her politely, adding, "Sorry about the weather." They ask if the weather is often like this in Norway. We lie.

The boat goes to a place and a cabin called Memurubu. From there, we'll hike for several hours and then end up back where we started. As with so much else in life. There's hiking and hiking: The two Canadians set off up the hillside almost at a run the moment we're off the boat.

"They'll collapse," says the Head of Documentation.

The women from Utah take their sweet time. The two friends who aren't so eager for company have to take an awful lot of pictures of each other down there before starting their hike.

So now it's just us and the mountain. It's raining, but not all that heavily. And the fog isn't a problem either, at least not this far down. The ground slopes gently upward. It's easy to find your way. It's nice. We shoot the breeze. We have a quick chocolate break. We carry on. I hum "Do-Re-Mi."

And here's something I want to get off my chest for all those people who haven't tried it: hiking in the mountains in crappy weather with a mild hangover and a golden oldie earworm actually isn't all that bad.

The time passes quickly. Mostly because here, unlike in the forest, there's something going on. Suddenly the landscape changes. You go up a bit then you go down a bit. Not just straight ahead. Suddenly you see a beautiful almost green lake someplace down below. What's more, the Head of Documentation has discovered something that has given her great pleasure. She's seen the Canadians off in the distance and she is firmly convinced that we're catching up to them.

In this, the Head of Documentation and I are a bit different. I definitely think this kind of one-upmanship can have a certain entertainment value, and I could've done with some Canadians to pit ourselves against in the forest that first day, to make the hike a *bit* interesting. But the Head of Documentation is in a different league. She gets genuine pleasure out of beating other people in competitions that those other people don't even know are going on. That may be why she's done more mountain hiking than me. Me, I'm unambitious with a low competitive instinct. I know this is the kind of thing people preen about, but I actually took a personality test once that concluded as follows: not very ambitious with a low competitive instinct. I've got a piece of paper to prove it.

It's a good thing one has never had the need to try a proper job.

WE ACTUALLY DO overtake Mr. and Mrs. Canada. The Head of Documentation grins and offers a hearty "Hi."

"Your country is beautiful," he replies. This is clearly what tourists say instead of greeting you. We have a quick chat. They're a bit more talkative now. Maybe we've earned a bit of respect after catching up to them. Maybe it's just that the Head of Documentation's extremely cheery expression has a confidence-inspiring effect. Of course, they aren't to know that she's grinning because she's crushed them in a competition they don't even know is going on.

It turns out they've done a lot of mountain hiking in the past (well, what else would we talk to them about? The unstable situation in Zimbabwe?). They've done an awful lot of mountain hiking, in fact, especially in the Rocky Mountains, although they travel around the world to do mountain hiking. It seems as if that's pretty much what they do. And I know what the Head of Documentation is thinking: *And yet we still walk faster than you.*

She's welcome to.

We wave a jovial farewell and leave the experienced mountain folk behind.

"Now we're ahead of everybody who was on the boat," says the Head of Documentation.

"Now we need to remember that a hike isn't primarily a competition," I say. "It's an experience of nature. And the most important competition is the competition with yourself."

And we have yet to achieve our goal of being able to say stuff like that without starting to laugh.

▲

AND JUST THEN we see we're standing on a spot where many pictures of this hike have been taken. We are actually *in* Instagram. Only there's a bit more fog and rain than in most photographs. But not so much fog that we can't see it's nice. Or guess that it is, at least. With those two lakes on either side of the narrow mountain, someplace far below, one of which is totally green. We take a picture. And I feel as if the hiking life isn't so bad. And that maybe it pays to drink a bit too much local beer and sleep a bit too little before setting out on a mountain hike. I feel indifferent and silly.

Then we hike another twenty or thirty yards and there the trail stops. The mountain gets really pointy and goes straight up. For around four yards before everything vanishes into thick fog. What lies to the left of this pointy piece of rock that goes straight up is impossible to say. There's fog there too. To the right you can't see anything either in case you were wondering.

"Are we supposed to go up here?" The Head of Documentation says. And this is a good question. It really doesn't look like a place you'd go up unless you were a mountain climber. And a tiny little bit crazy.

"Is this the actual ridge?" I ask. Because now there's nothing here that resembles the photos anymore. Because absolutely nobody who writes books or blogs or makes websites about mountain hikes, or boasts about it on social media, takes pictures in thick fog. Nobody. This is a matter I shall take up with the powers that be if we ever get down from here.

It should of course just be a matter of following the rocks with red Ts on them. But we can't see any. Maybe that's a trace of something red we can see on a rock in the fog up ahead. But it could also just be a patch. It may be that it's just wet. Because it certainly is wet here, after all the rain. And slippery probably.

Now, if what all the moaners claimed was actually true—that you walk in line over Besseggen—this wouldn't be a problem, of course. We'd know where we were supposed to be going. And it wouldn't take a whole line of people either. If there were any people here what- soever we'd work it out. That's the great thing about people. People can talk to each other. Ask each other for advice. Help each other. Work stuff out together.

These are good things both in the mountains and in life. I'm just saying.

But there's *absolutely nobody here*!

And then it happens. It breaks up. Only *one* crack. And only for a couple of seconds. But it's just enough to show us that to our right, the mountain plunges straight down. A long way. Then we see nothing again.

Peekaboo!

△

YOU'VE GOT TO give us that, the Head of Documentation and me: we're good at making decisions that aren't especially bold but that are sensible when it matters. We turned back in the forest the day before yesterday. And now we decide to wait for the Canadians. That way at least there'll be four of us losing our way in the fog. Or tumbling down into a very green lake. Which may lie there, several hundred yards below us. Unless it's just rock there. That could well be the case too.

When Mr. and Mrs. Canada arrive, with him several yards ahead of her in classic style, he casts a swift glance at the ridge, or whatever it is, and then at the fog. And then he quickly starts to climb up the slippery wet stone. In trainers. Without a word. He vanishes into the fog almost instantly. We turn and look at his wife. She shrugs. It seems she resigned herself some years back. To the mountain, her marriage, and life.

We stand there for a while looking straight ahead. A pretty long while. It's absolutely silent.

At last we hear him shouting.

"I found a T!"

So we are supposed to go up there, then.

△

NOBODY HAS TOLD US about this. We spoke about Besseggen to friends and acquaintances, experienced mountain folk, people who work at the cabin at the foot of this mountain, people whose job it is to help others plan their mountain hikes. Nobody told us you had to climb.

Later, when I mention this to mountain folk, the mountain folk say it's not a matter of climbing but of scrambling. And that's where I feel my interest in language grinding to a halt. If you have to use both arms and legs to make your way up a rock, it's climbing. And nobody has told us about this. Everybody has told us this is a nice, easy hike that people do with kids and dogs and 150-year-old grandparents.

And perhaps it's understandable. Because most of the people we've spoken to did this hike a long while back. It's a classic, after all. One of the first things you do when you start out doing this kind of thing. So they've probably forgotten what it was like. Or suppressed it. It can happen to the best of us. And they almost certainly hiked in sunshine. There was always sunshine before.

But what about those five oil-rig guys we met yesterday, the ones we spoke to and drank with for hours on end? They had *only just* done the hike. In exactly this kind of weather.

They didn't say anything either. And we actually *asked* them. They said it was easy-peasy. A piece of cake.

We discuss this. Out of respect for personal privacy, I won't go into details, but the Head of Documentation permits herself to question the trustworthiness of one man in particular, who yesterday claimed that he hadn't had any problem at all going up here, either mental or physical. And she names names. I shall not.

BUT NOW WE must start climbing before our Canadian friend in jogging shoes makes it home to Canada again.

It certainly is climbing, what we're doing now. And it's wet and slippery. And we can't see a thing. We can't see what lies to our left or to our right but we've had a glimpse of it and we didn't like it. We can barely see what's right in front of us. And that is wet rock. What's more, I'm not totally recovered from the knee injury I suffered that time in my former life when I used to hang out with other people in nice homes with dancing and music. This means I still can't quite bend or stretch one of my knees properly. A fact I discover at this precise moment. On a slippery ridge in thick fog. With a mild hangover.

Even the Head of Documentation thinks this is a bit unpleasant. And she really isn't afraid of this kind of thing. She's been on mountaintops before. That's why she leads the main pack and finds the way. I walk behind her. And Mrs. Canada brings up the rear, in a free poncho and a bad mood.

IT TURNS OUT there are more things nobody told us about Besseggen. For example: the ridge is full of snus, that peculiarly Nordic tobacco product—pouches of moist, smokeless powder—which, in a rare case of insubordination, Sweden fought for the right to retain even though these little packets of nicotine are banned in the EU. There's snus lying about all over the place in the mountains. Tiny bags of snus that you pop beneath your upper lip. Or "diaper snus" as it was somewhat scornfully known when I was growing up, in the days when it was still common to do something as unhinged as stuffing tobacco straight into your pie hole. The terrain here is festooned with little bags of snus. A trail of pouches leads all the way up the ridge. In a way, it's reassuring. It means people have hiked here before. It means we're on the right track. Tip: If visibility is poor on Besseggen, follow the snus not the Ts.

This also puts things into perspective a bit. People who go up Mount Everest walk past the remains of human beings. We walk past the remains of snus.

Have people spat out their snus? Because they get dizzy? Or has the snus simply fallen out of people's mouths? When they scream in terror?

This is the kind of thing you think about when you're climbing/scrambling in fog along a trail of snus. With a resigned Canadian woman behind you. And a Canadian man up ahead who'll probably be back at the cabin any second now.

And then I think how stupid it would be to die here. Embarrassing. My friends will laugh at me at my funeral. I picture my best friend in a dark suit. He takes a sheet of paper out of his breast pocket, unfolds it, clears his throat and says: "He liked to surprise." Then he pauses. "And surely he never surprised us more than when he slipped on a snus pouch on a ridge 6,200 feet above sea level and plummeted into a green lake where the search party failed to find him because the color of his jacket blended in with the water." Then everybody starts to laugh.

"What are you laughing about?" asks the Head of Documentation.

Focus. Focus.

▲

IT'S STILL GOING straight up. It's impossible to know how far there is left to go because we can't see that far. Now and then, farther and farther off, we hear: "I found a T!"

"Where's the path?" Mrs. Canada shouts into the fog.

"Find your own path," the fog answers.

"I don't want to find my own path," Mrs. Canada mutters. There's a lot of life wisdom in that.

▲

I DON'T THINK this is pleasant. Or in any way positive. But we progress.

Then something happens. We meet some people! A man and a woman who are hiking in the opposite direction. Suddenly they're standing there with Mr. Canada, who waits for us, just like the teacher with the most irritating pupils on school trips.

I've touched on this before: Meeting people in the mountains? Extremely underrated. You can ask people about stuff. They can tell you stuff. These two, for example, can tell us it's only steep for a little bit longer, then it eases off and then—as one of them says—it's "flat for miles." What's more, he turns out to be from Denmark, the country where almost nobody has been higher than a barstool.

"Good luck with that," the Head of Documentation says to the Dane. She's feeling more in control now that she's found out we'll soon reach the top.

We tell them, as best we possibly can, that they have only just started out on the ridge. At least one of them loses all the color in his face and rather a lot of his vital spark. They look down, see nothing, look back at us; we nod. They lose even more of their vital spark. And their joy of hiking, I reckon. I feel like saying something encouraging but it would hardly seem credible.

They make an extremely cautious start on the downward climb, which is probably called something other than a climb, for those of you who're hung up on semantics and on being irritating.

And I wonder whether even these two, of all people, will sit in a cabin in their underwear this evening with a glass of red wine saying, "Oh, no, the hike isn't difficult at all. Sheer joy. And the fog doesn't matter! It gets a bit slippery on the rocks, of course, but that just makes it more exciting."

Judases.

Will we sit and do the same thing maybe? Does it happen to everybody?

IT CLEARLY HAPPENS to a lot of people. You become a bit more of a primal human being after hiking in the mountains. You feel a stronger and hitherto unknown need to show off.

One of the people I spoke to before we began our trip works in comedy, which means he's more than averagely demanding about this kind of stuff. He's the one who's trying to escape the pear shape, if we're going to blow his cover. When I revealed the

planned route of our trip to him, because I know he's very familiar with this neck of the woods, he called Besseggen "a kids' hike."
We're talking about a sensitive, young modern-day man with sound
cultural interests, female friends, and a well-developed sense of
humor. But put a pair of hiking boots on him and he turns into
Bear Grylls.

We heard this most recently yesterday, from the oil-rig gang.
They were on a guys' trip, with everything that implies in the way of
conversations about paid time off and the absence of an inner voice.
But even so, they bore all signs of being pleasant, sociable modern
men in touch with both their families and their own feminine side.
In precisely this setting, however, in woolen underwear and after
conquering a mountain, they become the kind of people who don't
think anything is scary or difficult, and who say you just aren't hungry enough if you can't force down your camping food.

And what did everybody in the cabin talk about last night? How
easy this hike is. How quickly it goes. And, not least, about other
hikes they've done that are much harder, although they didn't have
any problems with them either.

Here's something I've noticed before, too: the farther away from
civilization you get, the more likely it is that the people you meet
there will talk about other places they've been that are even farther
away from civilization. If you're traveling way off the beaten path in
an African country, for example, and you come to some makeshift
lodgings with an unstable electricity supply and nothing but goat on
the menu and you meet other travelers there from Europe, you can
be pretty certain they'll talk about that time they were even farther
off the beaten path and spent the night at even more makeshift lodgings without any electricity at all where they were served body parts
they didn't even know goats possessed. Or the spleen of a wildebeest
that died of natural causes.

And if you won't eat the spleen of a wildebeest that's died of natural causes then you just aren't hungry enough.

▲

IF—NO, WHEN—WE GET BACK to the cabin this evening, we'll tell it like it is. We'll be honest. I decide this then and there, as I stare at snus and climb and realize it's much farther to the top than those two we met had suggested. In other words, they started to exaggerate *straightaway*, practically speaking at the *same time* as they were hiking along the stretch they exaggerated about.

▲

BEFORE WE LEFT, I also took a look at a few internet forums where people discuss mountain hikes. This is the true dark web. This is where people who don't know any better seek advice from people who definitely do know better. How long does the hike take? Is it difficult? Is it dangerous? Is it steep? Can I take kids or a dog or grandparents or unfit people or unfit grandparents with unfit dogs?

The others reply, almost without exception: No problem.

A woman who's afraid of heights asked whether it was scary hiking over Besseggen and whether it really is a sheer drop of 1,300 feet from the ridge. Here are some of the answers she got:

"I have a pretty bad fear of heights, but I've hiked over Besseggen three times without problems."

"Besseggen is a tourist highway, so it goes without saying it can't be all that bad. I hiked over it myself when I was ten and my little brother was eight."

"Absolutely no problem. My sister and I ran up. My mother, who's on disability benefits, also got up there fine. And this idea of a sheer drop of 1,300 feet is just nonsense and exaggeration."

For the record, I've checked. It *is* a 1,300-foot drop. In other words, slightly higher than the Empire State Building.

Another person asked if it was a good idea to take his elderly, infirm father who wasn't very mountain-savvy along on the Besseggen hike. She did not receive any of the obvious answers.

Such as: "No."

Or: "It depends how much you hate your father."

Or: "What's wrong with Mallorca?"

Nope. They all answered: No problem! It'll be great!

One of the people who answered this poor wretch actually managed to write that Besseggen was neither especially difficult nor especially steep. Whether or not it's difficult to hike over Besseggen is, of course, open to debate, but since the question concerned an elderly, infirm man who wasn't very mountain-savvy, perhaps people ought to have left open the possibility that he *might* find it a bit difficult.

Saying Besseggen isn't especially steep is nothing less than an outright lie. It's like saying a circle isn't especially round.

And actually, I wouldn't put it past mountain folk to claim that.

For the record: There are good reasons for people to ask about stuff like this. I've checked that too. Between fifteen and twenty times a year, people need to be helped down from Besseggen.

I seriously considered testing where the boundaries actually lie in these discussions; what it takes for one of these people to admit that they've ever been afraid, or that there really are things that aren't so sensible to do.

I considered writing: "Hi there, hiking buddies! I have a grandmother who's paralyzed from the lower lip down. I'm thinking of taking her on a mountain trip as a hundredth birthday present. I was thinking Besseggen before lunch and Galdhøpiggen in the afternoon. Does anybody have any tips about what time of year there's most snow and wind there so I can make sure the trip's a bit more challenging?"

THEY ADMIT NOTHING. They say nothing about how things actually are. Just spend a day searching the entire internet when you have some time and see whether it says anywhere that you risk climbing alone over Besseggen on wet snus.

▲

BEFORE WE SET OFF, I bought a book of general tips and advice on outdoor life. I chose this book out of the thousands of alternatives because I leafed through it in the store and saw that it opened with the following words: "One time, not so long ago, I no longer felt like it. Going out. Being outside."

Great, I thought. *At last, a book about outdoor life written by somebody who admits it can be a pain.* Only when it was too late and our trip was already well underway did I read the next sentence in the book. "I'd been rescued by a helicopter. Airlifted out of a hurricane on a ski trip in the far north of Spitsbergen."

What the hell?!

One-and-a-half lines. That was all the author could manage before she started boasting. One-and-a-half lines. And that's more than you get in most of the books I've read where people tell you about their mountain experiences. On the rare occasions when people who describe their own mountain hikes in book form admit to having been afraid, they do so solely in order to boast that they've done things no life-loving human being ought to do.

And this mountain-boasting goes back a long way. In fact, you could say it started straightaway. William Cecil Slingsby, the Englishman who was so bored that he climbed umpteen Norwegian mountains in the late 1800s, was the first person to reach the top of Store Skagastølstind. The boasting already began with number two. Johannes Heftye was the second man to climb Store Skagastølstind in 1880 and he wrote afterward that he was astonished by how easy the trip was, and that anybody who was of sound mind and reasonably well equipped would have zero problem doing this hike. During the ensuing argument between Slingsby and Heftye, the term "lady mountain" is bandied about.

But this was long ago, in different times.

Or was it?

A friend of mine who has good cause to view herself as a feminist said something about this when we were talking about cabin-related matters in the pub. We people who write books do that kind of thing: take friends to pubs and talk to them about stuff we're thinking of writing about. We call it research.

At any rate, she told me she'd once been on a cabin trip with several female friends who also had good grounds to deem themselves feminists. And they found they were horrified when they realized they'd have to empty the outhouse pit. Because there were no men there. None of them had done it before. None of them knew how to do it. And none of them especially wanted to do it. And they had to admit, to their own surprise, that this particular task was one they saw as a job for the menfolk.

We discussed this. And we thought we identified several examples of a tendency for gender roles to be turned back a few years as soon as you get to a cabin. It suddenly—and generally without any explanation or discussion—becomes perfectly clear what the women are supposed to do and what the men are supposed to do.

I think about that conversation now. Because this is the same, of course. In nature, time is turned back to the days when men were men and only sissies admitted that anything was dangerous or difficult or scary. In this way, even modern Scandinavians with a university education have a safe space where they can show off with old-fashioned manly humor. And these are people who do nothing bolder in their everyday life than try to make their own sushi out of salmon loin.

And this doesn't just apply to the gender roles. Language is also turned back. Remember the guest book at the cabin in the forest? It seems that young people suddenly start to talk like their grandparents once they're out in nature, writing things like "the hurly-burly of everyday life" and "technological doodads."

A trip out in Norwegian nature is a trip to a Norway that no longer exists, if indeed it ever did. A Norway where men do man things and everybody's the same and everybody says "Hi" to each other and eats proper food. At the tourist cabins, you eat manly food. Steak for breakfast, lunch, and dinner. No sign of quinoa or avocado toast. Everyone is active and tough, and nobody has any difficulty getting by in nature. And there's no such thing as bad weather. And the only foreign visitors you meet are tourists who are submissively polite and praise your country absolutely all the time. What's more, the foreign visitors obviously can't afford equipment as expensive as yours so you can safely laugh at them a bit, and nobody has a problem with it. Because in the mountains, we're a bit simpler. We are ourselves, natural, and authentic.

In almost all cases, "simple, natural, and authentic" means "extremely old-fashioned." No modern-day Scandinavian with a university education and salmon loin would dream of saying they were going to a cabin at the weekend to behave in an extremely old-fashioned way. That they come into contact with something authentic and natural at the cabin, and that they appreciate the simple pleasures of nature—now those are things they very well might say.

This also goes back a long way. Another of those Englishmen who went around vacationing in Norway in the 1800s was the clergyman Richard Carter Smith. He formulated this longing for the unsullied and rustic pretty precisely. "In the cities one sees many Danish and foreign customs, ideas, and people, and certainly not of the best type. Luxury is constantly gaining ground, wealth is piling up, education is becoming better, and everything is changing. The result is that society has lost its original simplicity and genuineness without yet finding an adequate replacement for it...I hold a plain, simple mountain farmer in higher esteem than a half-educated and half-cultivated urban citizen."

I know of people who—with a few adjustments in the technical phrasing—would still endorse this today. And I also know how they will vote in the next election.

It's tenacious, this idea that only in nature are we the way we really are and really want to be. And that if we were allowed to choose without any consideration for the demands of everyday life and without being sullied by social life, luxury, education, technology, and all the artificial things we surround ourselves with, this is what we'd choose, one and all: to sit on a rock alone in nature.

The message in one of the latest yearbooks of the Norwegian Trekking Association is that we must take back time. Which, of course, means that we should spend more time in nature. So the time you spend on other things must be time somebody has taken from you: the time you spend working, inviting relatives to dinner, bowling with your buddies, getting to know people, going to concerts, taking city breaks, singing karaoke, staying up all night at a kitchen table shooting the breeze, or going on a pub crawl with your girlfriend. This is time that—had we been able to choose freely, really freely—we actually would have spent on a rock in the forest. Or on a mountaintop, arms raised to heaven. Or in our underwear in a fireside lounge, boasting about how easy we find everything.

A lot of philosophers have also thought we are closer to something authentic and see things more clearly in nature. Nietzsche put it this simply: "We are so fond of being out among Nature, because it has no opinions about us."

Maybe that's why politicians are so keen on seeking out nature. This is the only place where nobody complains. Maybe that's the key to the success of the Scandinavian countries: that we're good at running away from the problems.

Nietzsche was, incidentally, the Nazis' favorite philosopher, although we needn't make too big a deal out of that.

IN THE POST-WAR ERA, Norwegians moved to cities, acquired wealth, leisure, and cars. And private cabins. Which have become bigger and bigger and more and more numerous. The land area occupied by private cabins in Norway has more than doubled in fifty years. But fewer than half of these cabins have both electricity and running water. Every fourth cabin has neither. And more than every fourth inhabitant of Norway will probably agree that these are the *authentic* cabins. And many people say they like the work they do at their cabins. Which is quite different from the work they do on a day-to-day basis. Wood-chopping. Fence-building. Authentic work. Using your body.

And you may, of course, discuss how authentic it is to do things you no longer need to do but that people used to do before because they had to.

Or you may opt not to discuss it. Because this is just what you do out in nature. After all, nature has no opinions about us. Poses no questions. Here, we are ourselves. Here, the institute head and departmental manager can go about bare-chested smelling of sweat with axes on their shoulders and be a bit simple. There's no harm in it. Boasting about your country is something you can also do out in nature. At cabins or in the mountains, it's perfectly fine even for tolerant people with a university education to gaze out across the landscape and say: "We live in the best country in the world and nobody can say any different"—often following up with a bit of bragging about the right to roam, that legally protected right we have in Norway to wander freely in nature, and then we might brag a bit more about the fact that we don't have a special word in the Norwegian language equivalent to the English word "trespassing" because we are free, we go wherever we want, we are people of nature.

And nature has no opinions about us, so there's nobody to raise objections.

Such as: it *is* perfectly possible, with good reason and right on one's side, to claim something other than that Norway is the world's best country.

Such as: all the tourists praising Norway may just be polite people who value their lives and understand that if they say, "It's nice here but it isn't the Alps, is it?," they'll end up murdered.

Such as: we may not have a special word for "trespassing" in Norwegian, but it's still highly unpopular for people to go roaming about in strangers' gardens.

Such as: The right to roam isn't unique to Norway, although everybody in Norway believes it is. You'll find the right to roam or something like it in Sweden, Finland, Iceland, Denmark, Germany, Austria, Switzerland, and England. Norway and the Nordic region weren't even especially early adopters. Switzerland was the first, in 1907. Iceland was the first Nordic country, fifty years later.

Such as: It's easy to forget that being authentic and natural is also a trend. This has happened before. And it passes, every time. We needn't go further back than thirty-odd years to find a time when it was still cool to plan the tallest hotel in the Nordic region with an elevator on the outside. In 1985, a tourism plan was developed in Oppland, Norway's leading county for mountain tourism. The plan makes almost no mention of private cabins. In those days, people were convinced huge luxury hotels in the mountains were the future.

They really didn't see slow time and the cultivation of silence coming. They didn't see that there would come a time when luxury hotels would seem humdrum and boring, or when cooking your own meals made from ingredients you grew and picked yourself would become the foremost proof of modernity.

The idealization of nature and yearning for simplicity is nothing new. And unchanged across the ages. In 1789, the German scientist Johann Christian Fabricius wrote that in Norwegian nature, one lives "in happy solitude, far from the dissipation and burdens of newer times." They didn't use words like "doodads" in 1789, but apart from that, this could have come straight out of a guest book in 2017.

And as early as 1918, the Norwegian Trekking Association's year-book said roughly the same thing about Jotunheimen that I was told when I was planning this trip: that many will "shrug at its overly civilized character, at the mass rambles along marked paths through valleys, on ropes across the glaciers, and on the same peaks that everyone is supposed to climb."

And can you guess which century the following quotations come from?

"Don't we all dream of this? Finding a silent lake in ourselves. Shorter or longer wafts of presence."

"These hours of solitude and meditation are the only time of the day when I am completely myself, without distraction or hindrance and when I can truly say that I am what nature intended me to be."

"Outdoors, you come into quite different contact with yourself and the elements around you. You open your senses."

One of these quotations is from the philosopher Jean-Jacques Rousseau at the end of the 1700s. The other two are from an article about yoga and mindfulness in nature from 2016.

IF ANYTHING, IT'S EASY to yearn for the rustic now. Because it's easier to romanticize peasants if you don't have to be a peasant. It's easier to think that cold yet cozy and socially democratic Scandinavia is cool if you don't have to live here. And it's easier to yearn for nature if you don't have to deal with it on a daily basis.

And then you can travel to the mountains. Like a journey back in time. To a simpler, more austere age where you do basic things you don't need to do anymore, and master skills you no longer need to master. And if you cough up a sum equivalent to six or seven months of your au pair's salary, you can also buy the equipment that allows you to live in a simpler, more austere age without getting your feet wet or sweating, and you can stay overnight at places with three-course dinners and internet.

But in your stocking feet. We are, after all, people of nature.

But enough of that.

WE GET TO THE TOP. Of course we do. I've written this book, haven't I?

Pleasant it is not, but we get to the top. We reach the highest point. I know this because it says on a plaque that this is the highest point. Other than that, there is nothing to indicate that this is the highest point. Or a point at all. It's flat here. Perhaps the plaque itself is the highest point.

We promised our Canadian friends chocolate and coffee if they'd keep us company on our way up the ridge. We are people of our word. The cup is passed around. The chocolate is passed around. We congratulate each other. He probably says something about how we have a beautiful country. She looks around, sees nothing but pebbles and fog, and murmurs: "Lovely view."

Of the two, she is definitely the one more inclined to bleak humor.

After around a minute, they must press on. We say goodbye and they trot onward to the next T. This is one competition we have lost.

What's the hurry? Is there another mountain they're supposed to squeeze in before supper?

OUR LUNCH BREAK is pretty short too. It's cold and it's raining. And we can't see a thing. So we start to walk.

And it has to be said. The rest of the hike goes pretty well. It goes very well, in fact. Way too well. To put it another way: The rest of the hike is pointlessly tedious. And when I say the rest of the hike, I mean roughly half of it. It slowly descends through a kind of lunar landscape. It's possible there's a view someplace behind the fog, but I doubt it. It's mostly rock. And it goes on and on.

Nobody said anything about this either.

There's only one thing to do. We start on D.

"Dolly Parton," I say.

"So that's where we're starting, eh?"

"That's where we're starting."

"David Bowie."

"Dana International."

"Dana International?"

"Winner of the Eurovision Song Contest in 1998, from Israel."

"This could be a long hike . . ."

AND IT IS. Mountain hikes sometimes have a wretched dramatic development. They start off well and build nicely to a climax, and for a while there it's actually genuinely exciting: Will it all turn out okay? And then, when you reach the climax, you're roughly halfway. After that comes the longest, hardest, and most boring part of the hike, where there's nothing to look forward to other than the fact that it has to end sometime. It's like a crime movie where the murderer is caught after forty minutes and the next hour consists of the hero sitting at a desk in his office doing paperwork. Apart from the fact that, at least in this case, the hero is sitting indoors in a warm spot. And an average mountain hike lasts five times longer than your average feature film.

My knee doesn't like going downhill. I was prepared for this but quite honestly, here? It isn't even steep here. In a couple of days, the plan is for us to hike up Galdhøpiggen. Am I supposed to hike four hours straight up to a spot where we probably won't see a thing thanks to the fog and then hike four hours down again with this knee? And will it really ever break up? Will I ever see anything whatsoever on this trip?

We need to talk about this.

▲

"DWEEZIL ZAPPA," I SAY. This is probably the closest I come to feeling the urge to raise my arms to heaven on our hike.

▲

OR PERHAPS IT'S THIS: After a couple of hours in a very gently sloping lunar landscape we see the cabin! Far down below there. Our cabin. We've hiked for barely five hours. The oil-rig lads took seven. UT.no says six to eight. We've hiked for less than five. We see the cabin.

"That can't possibly take two hours," I say. Which is the kind of thing it's *fatal* to say.

But we see the cabin. And there, very close to the cabin, we also see two dots that are moving fast and look Canadian.

This immediately becomes a competition, a battle to beat... UT.no? The oil-rig gang? I don't know. The Canadians will be impossible to overtake. But a competition it is. The Head of Documentation gives a menacing grin and ups the tempo drastically.

I'm with her. By all means. I'm motivated and want to get this over with. We jog down. And now it's also descending faster than before. And the landscape is nicer. It helps, of course, that we can see the landscape since we're now below the fog.

What were we doing up a mountain in weather like this anyway? It's much nicer down here.

Naturally, it also helps that we overtake somebody. Not that it's much of a feat to overtake this gang—a German couple with a dog who thought they'd take a nice little hike from the cabin and are now regretting it bitterly. The dog looks unhappy, scared, and tired, and is standing stock-still on a rock. He's resting his tongue on the same rock. The owners look their dog in the eye, speak to him as if to a child, and point encouragingly to the next rock which is two inches farther on. The dog doesn't budge. I say "Hi" to them as we pass, because that's what we do in the mountains. They nod back at us grimly. The dog looks at me as if he hopes I'll carry him home.

They'll take two hours to reach the cabin.

WE, ON THE OTHER HAND, are careering toward the finish line. We grin and dance from rock to rock, advancing on the cabin, and the Head of Documentation clocks us in at five-and-a-half hours. That's half an hour below the lowest estimates on UT.no and Besseggen.net; it's one-and-a-half hours faster than the oil-rig gang; it's two-and-a-half hours faster than the upper estimates on UT.no and Besseggen.net. And we've both heard of people who've taken eleven hours. That's twice as long.

The Head of Documentation is immensely pleased.

COMMUNAL ACHIEVEMENT IN UNDERWEAR

"AND NOW," SAYS the Head of Documentation. "Now we shall go straight to the fireside lounge and have a beer."

I see no reason to protest.

I'm so fired up I think I actually will feel this time that the beer tastes better after a long hike.

THE PROBLEM IS, of course, that we finished up all the decent beer in the cabin last night along with the oil-rig lads, so the only thing to be had is low-calorie beer. And that has never tasted good. But as I sit here in front of the fire after taking off my hiking shoes, I can just about stretch to thinking that it does, after all, taste a bit better now than it normally does.

It occurs to the Head of Documentation that we forgot to drink any liquor on the top. What amateurs. So, we take a little nip now instead, along with the calorie-deficient beer. And for a second there, I really do think this isn't so bad. In fact, it's pretty okay.

But the question is, of course: Is it worth hiking, climbing, and scrambling for five-and-a-half hours in rain and fog to get a low-calorie beer to taste pretty okay when there are other places in the world where it's possible to walk for two minutes through pleasant streets to a place where you can get a beer that tastes divine?

Nature lovers often speak and write about the simple pleasures that a life in nature offers. There's a lot to be said about the pleasures of nature, but I'll be damned if they are simple.

But this is exactly how I shouldn't be thinking. You're not supposed to think too much in the mountains. You're not supposed to complicate things—just be authentic, natural, genuine. Feel yourself thinking slower and less, and, in the end, just be. Right here. Right now.

Isn't that pretty nice?

One of the people working at the cabin sees us and says, "Goodness, are you back already?"

Now the Head of Documentation at least thinks life is pretty nice.

THE PEOPLE WHO work here apparently have a short break now before supper starts. Some of them sit beside the fire with us. They're young, fit hiking types. Guess what we talk about. The conversation quickly and predictably shows us that five-and-a-half hours is pretty good but it isn't all *that* impressive either. Many of them take three hours. There's even an organized run over Besseggen. The quickest runners take just over an hour.

But a mountain hike isn't a competition, after all, as we all know.

What's more interesting is that when we tell them about our hike, most of them turn out to agree that the second half is pretty boring. The term "lunar landscape" is used by several of them. Several of them also agree that what you have to do in order to conquer the ridge amounts to "borderline climbing." And that it isn't especially pleasant to do this hike when it's wet and slippery with poor visibility.

And all this they tell us *now*!

It's as if we've become part of the club now that we've done the hike. Now we can tell it like it is, to each other, just as long as we don't tell all the others. It must stay between us.

And now they spill the beans about *everything*. We sit by the fire, sipping flavor-deficient beer, and inhaling the scent of woodsmoke and soggy socks. And this is the conversation that ensues among these young hiking types:

"The first half hour of a hike is always hellish."

"The first hour I'd say."

"And on top of that there's the hour you spend dreading it before you leave."

"Especially if it's bad weather."

"And it often is."

"Very often. And then it really isn't pleasant at all."

"I remember how much I hated hiking when I was younger."

"I was forced to go on hikes by my parents."

"And there's often only a short part of the hike that makes it all worthwhile."

"Yes, you have to put up with lots of boring bits."

"The boring bits are the ones that dominate, aren't they?"

"It's almost nothing but boring bits."

This is where I break in.

"Why do it then?" I ask.

IT GOES ABSOLUTELY QUIET in the fireside lounge. People drop what they're holding. Everybody looks at me in horror. The fire goes out. Everybody leaves. Gjendesheim closes down and people abandon the outdoor life.

Okay, so I'm exaggerating a bit now but I get the distinct feeling this is a question that doesn't get asked in this fireside lounge every day.

But they have answers. Of course. It's all about how good it is to get there. It's about the reward that follows. About using your body. And it's apparently about achievement.

"Didn't you get a sense of achievement when you reached the top?" somebody asks.

I give this a good deal of thought. The first thing I think is: Does anybody really use that term, "sense of achievement," as if it was a completely normal phrase? I mean, anybody who's neither a psychologist nor a childcare expert nor a coach nor a retired professional athlete delivering motivational speeches to corporate clients? I really do believe I've never used the word "achievement." Mostly because I don't want to go through life sounding like I'm delivering a lecture. But here the word is in frequent use. In fact, I think "achievement" is one the most frequently used words in the fireside lounge this afternoon. Right up there with "hours," "weather," and "recharging." There's an awful lot of talk about recharging in the mountains. For people who are so hung up on logging off and disconnecting, mountain folk are very worried about their batteries running out.

But there's this sense of *achievement*. Did I experience it when I'd put the ridge behind me? When I'd *bagged* the ridge?

Can't say I did, really. I was pleased to be done with it, of course, but that's what happens when you've done something unpleasant and unnecessary, isn't it? A sense of achievement, though? Nope.

And maybe this is a lack on my part, from a strictly outdoorsman point of view. I actually get very little out of having done something just for the sake of doing it. If it doesn't result in anything whatsoever for anybody. There has to be something else. Not that my activity necessarily has to make humanity happier and the world more beautiful, although that would undoubtedly be fantastic. But there should at least be a great view at the other end. Or a kiosk. Apparently there's a kiosk on top of Galdhøpiggen. I like that. But reaching the top just to reach the top, that actually leaves me pretty cold, no matter how much I've used my body to conquer nature.

But okay, let's not exaggerate my absence of ambition either. I do, after all, want to achieve things I think I ought to achieve. I do feel

I want to be good at things I think I ought to be good at, because it suits my image or simply because it's how I earn my living.

But I don't want it *that much* either.

Let me try to give you an image: A person who has trained to be the best at one thing for their entire life and has sacrificed everything else, forsaken friends and family and life partners, dropped parties and after-parties and spontaneous weekend breaks and picnics in the park, and probably had a difficult and boring and damp and dull and frustrating time of it along the way, who then, one day, crosses a finish line three-hundredths of a second before the runner-up. And there he stands at the finish line tensing absolutely every muscle to be found in a human body and bellows "YEEEEEEEEEEEEEEES!"

I've never been there. And I believe I'll never get there. And maybe I'm a bit envious. It does seem like an absolutely fantastic feeling.

On the other hand, I can't think of a single thing for which it would be worth forsaking friends and family and life partners and parties and after-parties and spontaneous weekend breaks and picnics in the park. I can't think of a single thing I want to be *that* good at.

Plus: most of the people who train to become the best at one thing their entire life and sacrifice everything else and have a difficult and boring and damp and dull and frustrating time of it along the way never cross the finish line three-hundredths of a second before the runner-up. Maybe they'll come in an excellent seventh now and then, in the best of cases.

What's more, there are grounds for being deeply skeptical about seeking achievement for achievement's sake. If you aren't skeptical about this stuff too, I advise you to go at once to YouTube and search for "cycle Swede" or "mtb rage" or "angry Swedish cyclist" or some other combination of "cycle," "mountain," "forest," "Swede," and "rage." What you'll find is a short film about achievement. There are many versions of this film out there, with and without subtitles. The film is as hysterically funny as it is depressing. Two Swedish buddies, two men in their middle years, are out cycling in the forest. There's nothing to indicate that it's a pleasure trip. Their equipment looks expensive. Their shorts are tight. And here, there will be achievements. Now they're supposed to be getting up a hill. One of them has already got up, apparently, and now stands at the top filming his buddy. The buddy makes first one attempt. Then several. And he can't get up the hill.

And that's when he loses it. He throws his bike into the forest. He throws his helmet onto the ground time and time again until he's quite certain that it's totally destroyed. He shouts and curses loudly, again and again, enraged at his own uselessness.

He picks up the bike and tries to get up the hill one more time. And one more time again. It goes worse and worse. He gets angrier and angrier, and curses louder and louder. Eventually he becomes enraged about his life itself. The tirades become darker and darker and the prefix "cock-" is used more and more frequently.

That's how things can go if you're hung up on achieving things you don't strictly need to achieve.

Here's something it may be worth thinking about now and then: for every image of a tanned athletic man raising his arms to heaven on a mountaintop there's a grubby enraged Swede destroying his cycling gear and comparing his life to a sex organ.

And this Swede reminds me of something else that could also be a reason why I don't possess a drive for achievement or want to beat my breast and talk about *bagging* peaks: I find almost everything that's manly fundamentally comic or uninteresting. The Swede on the bike is funny. Among other things. And I'm not interested in doing what he does. Nor am I interested in engines. I'm glad engines exist, of course, although it isn't something I spend a lot of time thinking about, but no more than that. I'm not particularly keen on fixing things. Know zero about cars. Couldn't care less about extreme sports. Or weapons. Or whittling. I like soccer, as has maybe become apparent, but that's also because I like big events and lots of people. And I get the giggles about the manliest aspects of being a soccer fan. Put it like this, you'll never catch me saying: "You can switch women but you can never switch your favorite soccer team, har har…"

This is the kind of thing you sit and think about as you sip at your liquor by the fireside during an afternoon in the mountains. Dinnertime is approaching and the break is over for the people who work there. Before they go back on duty, one of them points at our hip flask and says: "You're not allowed to drink your own alcohol here."

For a second there I'd forgotten we were at summer camp.

WE'VE MADE A conscious decision that over dinner we'll tell it like it is. We won't be like the oil-rig guys and most of the others. We won't boast and say "easy-peasy." We'll betray the club and tell the truth.

But first, we have to do the things you do when you're preparing for supper in the mountains: take an excessively short shower and dress up in undershirt and sweatpants.

This is actually the first shower of the trip and I try to think the way you're supposed to think: that this shower will be so much more than just a shower now that it's been several days since my last one and I've used my body and bagged the peak.

This isn't that kind of book, so I won't say too much about what the shower experience was like, but let me tell you this at any rate: It involved expectations. It involved nudity. And it was over very quickly.

Because you need cash to get the shower going at this cabin. Cash, which is used solely by criminals and people who think it's 1982.

Naturally, we don't have a lot of cash with us but we find just enough coins for each of us to have a shower that is just a little too brief.

FOR DINNER, WE'RE SERVED a lot of meat. Of course.

We find ourselves sitting beside the friends who aren't especially eager for company and who took pictures of each other. They aren't terribly chatty now either. But they are well brought up and capable of grasping that the idea at these cabins is for people to talk to their neighbors, no matter how little they may feel like it.

We manage to drag out of them that they are, respectively, from England and France, and studied together. They say they did the hike over Besseggen in six hours. And already here I feel myself struggling with our plans to tell the whole truth this evening. Because I notice that neither the Head of Documentation nor I are remotely convinced by this. *Yeah, right—like these two really only took six hours.*

And if *they're* going to sit here boasting...

We sidestep the problem and try to shift the conversation onto another track.

There are limits to how long you can talk about how nice but expensive it is in Norway, how Brexit came as a shock, and how the British and the French have a slightly strained relationship. And it's quite impossible to fathom what these two friends are writing their doctorates about. And they're not especially eager for company either.

The woman sitting beside them, however, is. And she also makes it a bit difficult to keep up conversations in low voices. She is a Canadian woman slightly past middle age with a haircut that screams "schoolteacher." I'd bet it's school vacation in Canada now. She feels responsible for including everybody at our long table in everything— the kind of responsibility only people with decades in the school system behind them can feel so strongly. She talks loudly, looks at everybody and rounds off every sentence with apologetic laughter in case she's inadvertently said something to offend anybody. It's hard not to like her a bit. And it's hard not to be a bit terrified.

"I really am a vegetarian! Ha ha!" she shouts, smiling at every single person at the table. Then she says it isn't a big deal. Which maybe makes it a bit odd to shout about it, of course, but let's not get hung up on details.

"I'll just eat the vegetables! Ha ha!"

To show that she doesn't have anything against people who aren't vegetarians, she looks at the vast chunks of meat on her neighbor's plate with a mixture of disgust and feigned yearning and shouts: "Mm! That looks good! Ha ha!"

Then she tries to engage everybody at the table in a conversation about how to pronounce the name of the place where the Besseggen hike starts.

"Is it MemooroBOO? MemooROOboo? MeMOOrooboo? MemoorooBUH? Ha ha!"

The two friends who aren't especially eager for company are regretting their choice of vacation destination.

IN THE FIRESIDE LOUNGE, things have happened since yesterday. It seems a film festival will take place here in a couple of days. Because they have film festivals in the mountains to show us doubters that life in the mountains is just as exciting as life in the city, only in a much more impractical location. I do think that showing films outdoors in the mountains is borderline funny. Horror films in the darkness and fog, for example, would certainly be a bit cool. But is it horror films they're showing at this festival? No. They're showing mountain films. People sit surrounded by mountains and watch films about mountains. That's what I call being keen on mountains.

It's a peculiar business, this desire we have to read about, watch, and hear about precisely the thing we're doing as we read or watch or listen. The bookcases in the mountain cabins are, as I mentioned, entirely dominated by books about mountains and cabins. And many of us are also like this with music. We like to listen to music that is about precisely what we're doing as we listen to the music. If we're at a party in a great mood, we like to listen to music about being at a party in a great mood. If it's Christmas and we're putting up our decorations, we like to listen to music about Christmas and people putting up their decorations. If it's summer and we're lying on the beach, we like to listen to music about summer and people lying on the beach.

And here, then, it's a matter of films about mountains in the mountains. And it's clear in the fireside lounge that the people who will be working with or attending the festival have started to arrive. Everybody in the fireside lounge looks as if they work for a film production company. They all speak a bit too loudly and a bit too hoarsely.

THE HEAD OF DOCUMENTATION conducts an evaluation.

"I have to say, I'm a bit shocked by how much lying and boasting goes on," she says.

"Nobody tells the truth here, do they?"

"Yeah right—like those two friends really took six hours."

"They spent six hours just on their selfies beside the boat."

The Head of Documentation looks out at the darkness and the fog.

"What do you think?" she asks.

"What about?"

"About the rest."

"The rest?"

"Now you've had a go at forest in bad weather and mountains in bad weather. According to our schedule we're supposed to be hiking—maybe in weather just as bad as this—for eight hours in pretty steep terrain. And then we're supposed to be hiking eight hours the day after, up and down Norway's highest mountain, maybe without seeing a thing."

"What exactly are you getting at?"

"I do have a responsibility here. You're supposed to find salvation in nature."

"Mm. And?"

"Well ... It's important to adapt to the weather conditions in the mountains."

"I've heard that too."

"It's possible you may have overestimated your own abilities."

"I don't think so. But it's possible I may have overestimated what I *want* to do."

"Precisely. And you are supposed to like this, aren't you?"

"There is that."

"And besides, there's your knee."

The Head of Documentation has a way of talking about my knee injury that makes it sound mostly like an excuse. It's a proper injury; it really is. In fact, my doctor was a bit unsure whether it was a good idea for me to go hiking in the mountains at all with this knee of mine. And I hike with a brace on my leg. I have proof. I've actually hiked over Besseggen for five-and-a-half hours today in bad weather *with* a knee injury.

Not that this is anything to boast about. I'm just mentioning it.

And I do see her point. I'm really not tempted to hike down a steep hill for four hours with this knee. Especially after taking a pointless hike straight uphill for four hours in order to see precisely nothing.

We check the weather forecast. It'll be awful weather with close to zero visibility in the vicinity of Galdhøpiggen tomorrow and the day after and the day after that and every day up until New Year's Eve 2043.

There is another route to the top of Galdhøpiggen from another cabin. That trip is shorter and starts with a hike across a glacier on a rope with a glacier guide. The Head of Documentation is the one who knows this. And indeed she actually argues in favor of this alternative.

Maybe, I think. At least that'll involve something happening. A glacier! That's something else. And if there's a glacier guide, then at any rate we'll meet people. Or at least one person. Who knows the way. I think it sounds like a better option.

The problem is, of course, that this cabin is much farther away. We can't walk there.

So what should we do?

We can drive a car of course. Both of us know people who live not so far away and can probably sort out a car for us to borrow or hire. This is one of the advantages of not actively avoiding other people: you accumulate friends and acquaintances who can help you when you need it. This is a fine thing.

It's decided. We sort out a car.

We have a toast and congratulate each other. Two times eight hours in the hills have been transformed into a road trip, a glacier hike, and a shorter mountain hike.

I wonder a bit about what just happened. Was the Head of Documentation being cautious about conditions? Is she protecting me from myself? Or is it actually that she herself is a bit bored of hiking in rain and fog? I decide that it doesn't matter. Because tomorrow we'll be taking a road trip. And then we'll head up Norway's highest peak with a cool glacier guide. Wicked.

⸺

"OH, LOOK! THEY HAVE a piano! Ha ha!"

The inclusive teacher has entered the fireside lounge accompanied by a German couple who possibly share her profession. She looks at the film people, the Head of Documentation, and me to ensure that we have all grasped there's a piano. Then she adds: "Memoorooboo, ha ha!"

Five minutes later, she and the Germans are singing "My Bonnie Lies Over the Ocean" in harmony. As if to sweep aside any possible doubt about whether or not they are teachers.

"Sorry about that. Ha ha!" she shouts afterward, when everybody is clapping. "Well! Off to bed! Ha ha!"

People go to bed early here. And they pretty much have to. There's absolutely nothing else to do in these rooms but go to bed. In fact, there isn't room for anything else. Unless they sit out in the corridor repacking, of course. So they're prepared to get up early in the morning to repack one more time.

We empty our wine glasses and say good night to the film people.

MY OUTLOOK HAS brightened again. And I realize that tomorrow is actually the first day on this trip when we aren't supposed to be catching something. No trains, no boats, no danger that we'll end up standing in a forest in the pitch darkness. We can even sleep through breakfast and it won't matter, because we'll have a car tomorrow, and can drive wherever we want and buy stuff.

As early as 4:00 AM, I sleep. Like a log. Like a log on a rock. On a slippery wet rock covered in snus.

LISTEN TO INEXPERIENCED MOUNTAIN FOLK, PART 1

YOU'D NEED TO have spent a pretty long time totally unconscious to have grown up in Norway and failed to grasp that there's a thing known as the mountain code. The mountain code consists of nine rules for safe travel in the mountains. It was developed by the Red Cross and the Norwegian Trekking Association in the 1950s and was regularly broadcast to the entire population on both radio and TV at slightly too short intervals throughout my childhood. During the winter, everybody would hum the tune that accompanied the radio and TV campaigns: "Daydream," by the French easy-listening pioneer, Franck Pourcel. And everybody knew the mountain code. In 2016 the mountain code was revised. One of the classics in the old mountain code was "Listen to experienced mountain folk." This isn't included in the new version. And I can absolutely see why. You'd be much better off listening to inexperienced mountain folk like me. Here are some of my tips:

1. Don't listen to experienced mountain folk. Experienced mountain folk mostly tut and say, "it isn't far," "it's easy," "it isn't dangerous," "no problem," "you'll hike in line there," and "if you're in reasonable shape."

2. Experienced mountain folk also often say jaunty things like "All you have to do is get out of the house." That isn't true either. Maybe it's a bit true if you actually live right beside or on a mountain and own all the equipment you need to be able to hike in the mountains in all kinds of weather; but then you also have to consider the weather and hiking conditions first, then dress accordingly and pack things to take with you on your hike. If you don't live on a mountain and don't own what you need, you'll first have to spend $4,700 on equipment, then plan your trip, check the weather forecast, pack eighteen times, check train and bus schedules because you want to be environmentally friendly when you're using nature, remember that bus schedules vary by season and that if you're a quarter of an hour outside the high season, there are pretty much no buses running and no cabins open.

3. What's more, if you're a quarter of an hour outside the high season, especially if it isn't the weekend and especially if it isn't top-notch weather, you're in grave danger of finding yourself utterly alone in the mountains. There'll be nobody you can ask for directions. Or for anything else. Think about that.

4. There's nothing wrong with having a mild hangover and a golden oldie on your brain.

5. If you're going to hike over Besseggen, be aware that only around half of the hike is interesting. The rest of the hike is an endless wander down a gentle slope on pebbles that are slightly too big.

6. There's no such thing as cheating. Now and then it's unnecessary and pointless to do unnecessary and pointless things.

7. Don't say you're going to *bag* a peak. It just sounds silly.

SIGNS YOU OUGHT TO FIND IN THE MOUNTAINS

- You can turn back here; the rest of the hike is nothing special
- Flat and boring
- Fog
- Long
- No matter what anybody else says, you'll have to climb here

EVALUATION OF FOOD AND DRINK FOR USE ON HIKES

1: Low-calorie beer

What do you have to do to make this taste pretty okay?

Go on a hike that lasts at least five hours and involves scrambling that is borderline climbing in the rain and the fog with a knee injury.

What do you have to do to make this taste good?

Hike and climb for ten hours up a sometimes-steep slope in sleet. Suffer an ankle injury halfway through the hike so that you have to spend the last six hours limping.

What do you have to do to yearn for this?

Spend twenty-four uninterrupted hours looking death in the eye.

2: Vacuum-packed camping stew

What do you have to do to make this taste pretty okay?

Spend seventy-two hours hiking in freezing weather without any food.

What do you have to do to make this taste good?

In addition to spending seventy-two hours hiking in freezing weather without food: be regularly subjected to torture for half a year.

What do you have to do to yearn for this?

In addition to spending seventy-two hours hiking in freezing weather without food and being regularly subjected to torture for half a year: spend fourteen years locked in a dark room for no reason, being served nothing but cold gruel and catty comments.

THE RETURN OF "THE HAPPY WANDERER"

Fourth leg: Gjendesheim–Juvasshytta.
With a car. And a knee injury.

I DON'T REMEMBER what we ate for breakfast on this day. Meat, probably. I don't remember what we said to the poor wretches who left the cabin before we did to hike over Besseggen in the fog. Something catty that went over their heads, probably. I don't remember what else we did before we drove away from the cabin in a borrowed car at brunch time. Packing, probably.

What I do remember from this particular day is that it is the day I understand what poor visibility truly is.

I've experienced poor visibility before, of course. Most recently, yesterday.

But still...

And I did check the weather forecast yesterday. It did say there'd be poor visibility today.

But still...

And I have, of course, heard the expression: "You can't see your hand in front of your face."

But I've never had the experience of this actually being true: that you really can't see your own hand in front of your face.

After driving for a couple of hours, we start on the ascent toward Juvasshytta, the cabin that is the starting point for the hike up to the top of Galdhøpiggen. Before we start the ascent, we see just enough in brief glimpses to register that the road we'll be taking up the mountainside is all hairpin bends and has no crash barrier. And the road is narrow. We think. And then there's absolutely no more visibility.

When it's like that, you drive slowly.

When it's like that, you drive very slowly.

This is, of course, the day when—for the first time—we don't have to be in time for anything. I think the glacier guide starts the hike to Galdhøpiggen at around nine tomorrow morning. I'm starting to feel uneasy about our chances of being in time for that.

We laugh of course. What else can we do? We're on a trip that's supposed to convert me to mountains and nature and cabin life. And views. And here we sit on day four in a car on our way from one cabin with poor visibility to another cabin with even worse visibility.

And there *is* the cabin. Suddenly. We nearly collide with it before we see it.

⏶

IT'S DIFFICULT TO SAY anything for sure, of course, but it looks as if it's a pretty big cabin. Dark brown, of course. Some time or another central decision-makers decreed that cabins may now have Jacuzzis and carports and helipads but they must still be dark brown.

There are no cars outside. No people. The little we can see of the landscape around us looks like the lunar landscape we hiked through in the last half of our hike over Besseggen. There's rock and mist and it's deserted. We've read that there's a summer ski center right beside this cabin. We can't see it.

"You chose the wrong week to be converted to nature," says the Head of Documentation.

"You can't choose that kind of stuff. People have time off when they have time off and that's when they have to take trips. And besides, the weather in this country isn't always brilliant—to put it mildly."

"That's why proper people of nature are always ready to head out at the drop of a hat."

"Yes, they wander around the store in hiking pants and windproof jackets, don't they?"

"Exactly. In case it breaks up."

"Then they immediately drop everything and storm to the nearest mountaintop."

"It'll never break up."

"It'll never break up."

We start to wonder whether the cabin is even open. There really isn't any sign of life here. Maybe the people who run the cabin looked out the window one morning, realized they were staring straight into a gray wall for the fifth consecutive day, and said to each other: "We really can't be bothered with this anymore." Then they cremated their hiking pants in the courtyard in a simple ceremony, locked the doors, and moved to the coast. And there they now sit, gazing out across the sea and wondering why they didn't do this ages ago.

"Do you think anybody will notice we've sneaked off?" one of them says maybe, to the sound of crashing waves.

"I can't imagine they would. Nobody would dream of heading to a cabin 6,500 feet up in the mountains in thick fog."

"They probably wouldn't even get there. That road's lethal enough even in blazing sunshine, isn't it?"

"And there isn't a crash barrier, either."

"No sane human being would dream of driving that road now. It's madness."

"Like climbing up Besseggen in zero visibility and rain with a knee injury."

"Scrambling."

"No. Climbing."

▲

A DOOR OPENS. A man in a chef's uniform comes out. He leans against the wall, lights a cigarette, gazes out into the fog, and wonders what went wrong with his life.

"Maybe that means lunch is over."

"We must have lunch. It's been hours since we ate a huge chunk of meat."

▲

I SHOUT "HELLO" as we open the door. And I half expect an echo. A person appears behind a counter. A woman in mountain gear. She nods. We say we reserved a room. She smiles a tiny smile that tells us we could safely have spared ourselves the effort. We ask if it's still possible to get lunch. She looks at the clock and vanishes through a door. After a while she comes back. She nods again. In a way that says we should count ourselves lucky to get any food even though it's getting toward 2:30 PM. Apparently she had to interrupt the chef as he stood outside, busy dreaming of life in another country.

This cabin is different from the previous one. From being alone in the forest with a knife under the pillow in a cabin with nothing but inedible stew and undrinkable water, we went to the low-standard high-budget summer camp beside Besseggen. Now we've taken yet another upward step. This actually is beginning to look like a hotel. We get a room with a shower. A shower that can be used at any time and only by the people occupying the room. And the beds have duvets. The duvet is most definitely an underrated invention. But to make sure you won't forget you're in nature, an animal skull looms over the bed and a picture of a polar bear adorns the wall. And to make sure you won't forget you're at summer camp, posters about the common areas being internet-free zones hang on the walls. As we wait for our food, we look around for other posters. "We take our hats off indoors here." "We leave nasty magazines at home." "Your mother doesn't work here."

The dining room is also different from the one at the previous cabin. Here, you aren't placed at a long table looking straight into the face of an underwear-clad person who tells you that Norway is beautiful and that they took six-and-a-half hours to get over Besseggen. No, here it's all about views. There are huge floor-to-ceiling windows, and everybody is placed so that they face these windows. Which becomes a bit comical when all you can see outside the window is a few feet of rock before everything fades to gray.

A gang of jolly pensioners is busy breaking up as we sit down. We talk a bit with some of them who tell us they're on a weeklong bus trip to all the finest viewpoints in southern Norway. So far, they haven't seen a thing, they say. And then they laugh heartily. I kind of want to join them for the rest of their journey.

Two women also empty their coffee cups and walk out behind us. So now we're the only ones there.

Our food comes. It's meat with extra meat, and meat pudding with meat sauce for dessert.

So we sit there all alone in a huge room, eating meat and looking straight ahead; and straight ahead, we see nothing.

We start to laugh again. Of course we start to laugh. But we pull ourselves together. I'm a bit scared somebody wearing hiking pants and a name badge will come along and put us in our place. I look around for posters: "We don't laugh at the view here." "There's no such thing as bad weather."

The hostess comes in. We make an effort to get a grip, try to behave like adults, and ask what you'd normally see out of these windows.

And here you normally see pretty much everything. Among other things, you see Norway's two highest peaks. There's something fascinating about the fact that Norway's two highest peaks lie right in front of us and yet we can't see them. We're not talking about a coin you lost on the floor here. We're talking about mountains.

"Would you like some coffee?"

"Yes, please. Very much."

"Would you like anything with your coffee?"

"Would it be possible to have a little meat?"

I DIDN'T SAY THAT. I can behave myself when I have to. Mostly.

Outside the dining room, we meet the two women who lunched just before us. Only now do I notice that one of them has a Band-Aid on her face. And everything about them indicates that they've been out hiking today. Their clothes are a bit damp. Their cheeks a bit red.

We don't go out on mountain hikes without doing our prep, so we know, of course, that everybody hikes from here to Galdhøpiggen in groups, and that these groups don't come back so early in the day.

The women tell us that yes, indeed, they did join the hike to Galdhøpiggen but they lost their way.

Wait a minute. *They lost their way?* Where on earth?

On their way to the glacier.

Wait a minute. On their way *to* the glacier?! So before the hike even started. So more or less right outside the cabin?

Yes, right over there someplace.

Wait a third minute. Isn't there a professional glacier guide along on these hikes?

Oh yes.

THE TWO WOMEN tell us they're here with two other friends. The four of them and a few others set off on a hike with the glacier guide early today. They'd gone some distance when our two new friends sat down on the ground for a little breather. When they were about to carry on, they couldn't see the rest of the group anywhere. After a while they decided it was best to turn back. Then they probably went the wrong way. Which isn't remotely difficult to understand. As I've said, there's zero visibility here. It's impossible to differentiate between rocks on the ground if rocks on the ground are all you can see.

"Where are your friends now?"

"Up Galdhøpiggen probably."

They stress that they aren't angry with their friends but are a bit disappointed in the glacier guide.

But their mood is excellent. And the lunch was good.

We should have taken these two along with us and joined the pensioners on the bus. That's what we should have done.

WE ASK THE HOSTESS what she thinks about tomorrow's outlook weather-wise. It looks as if it will, if possible, even be slightly worse tomorrow. Not so much rain maybe. But more fog.

More fog? *Is* there any more fog?

And then she says this: "So there's no guarantee you'll see all that much."

Huh?

And then: "But it's a nice hike regardless."

WELL. I AM, as I said, well brought up. But now I'm on the point of speaking out. What is it with these mountain folk? They're totally incapable of admitting anything whatsoever. Here she stands, two yards away from me, looking me straight in the eye and saying things she knows aren't true. And she knows I know they aren't true. She's Donald Trump in hiking pants.

Of course it isn't "a nice hike *regardless.*" It's a hike regardless. I can stretch that far. But there *is* such a thing as bad weather. It *is* a nicer hike if the sun's shining and you get a view halfway across Europe from the top than if there's such thick fog that it's perfectly possible to get lost on your way out of the cabin even when you have a mountain guide with you. Can't we just agree on that?

And "There's *no guarantee* you'll see *all that much.*"

I am here right now. I've looked out. There is an absolute guarantee that you won't see a thing.

I'd actually been thinking of asking her whether you get anything out of going on this hike if it's wet with zero visibility. Is it dangerous? Is it unpleasant? Would we be better off waiting a day and going on a nice hike down in the valley instead?

But there's clearly no point.

THE HEAD OF DOCUMENTATION has been thinking exactly the same thing as me, as it turns out.

"They all just say things," she whispers in the internet-free fireside lounge afterward. I don't even react to the fact that she's whispering. Of course you whisper when you're in places with reproving posters on the walls. "They don't think about what they're saying or what it means. They just say the same things over and over again. 'It's nice to go for a hike regardless.' "

"Good to get out!"

"You just need to wear the right clothes."

"No, it isn't dangerous."

"It's so good to get there."

"The food tastes so much better."

"It's good to use your body."

"Nobody's actually said that today."

"Just wait. You can bet your bottom dollar somebody'll say it before the day is out."

"Guaranteed."

HERE, TOO, BORN-AGAIN nature lovers are like religious people. The most literal-minded religious people. Who don't ask questions. Who don't allow themselves to be affected by changes around them. Who just repeat what's been said before. Because it's true and right for time eternal.

And they probably think they're right. Because nobody's ever told them any different. Because nobody's opposed to the idea of you wandering about in nature. Nobody is critical of this activity. It's healthy and it's good for you and it's natural and it's authentic and it's Norwegian. You're told that at school. And in public health campaigns. And on social media. The government is for it. Your parents are for it. Your environment is for it. If you wander about in nature, you're doing something everybody knows they really ought to be doing. To be interested in the experience of nature is to be interested in something you will never have to explain or defend. It isn't like saying you like the Eurovision Song Contest, or you don't drink alcohol, or you're into role-playing games, or you listened to a lot of Chris de Burgh in your youth. It's never embarrassing to say you wander about in nature.

I'm convinced that it does everybody good to wholeheartedly commit, at least once in life, to an activity they know it'll be embarrassing to tell people about later on.

Mountain folk quite simply don't face enough resistance. On the contrary, they constantly receive affirmation when they say the same things over and over again.

THAT IT'S GOOD to use your body.

That it's a nice hike regardless.

That there's no such thing as bad weather.

That it feels good to experience a sense of achievement.

All you have to do is get out of the house.

▲

DEAR READER, HAVE you seen the film *The Truman Show*? Where Jim Carrey plays a man who doesn't know that his life is a TV reality show and that all the people he meets in the slightly too successful town where he lives are actors playing people who are a bit too positive and say the same things over and over again?

Dear reader, have you seen the film *Groundhog Day*? Where Bill Murray plays a man who wakes up to the same day every day? Each morning, he wakes up to "I Got You Babe" on the radio and to people who say the same things over and over again?

Picture yourself in a mash-up of *The Truman Show* and *Groundhog Day* in very bad weather and you'll understand how we're feeling.

▲

IF WE ARE TO FORM a qualified opinion about what we'll get in return for hiking up—sorry: *bagging*—Galdhøpiggen in thick fog, we must clearly do our own research. And so we must have internet. And that's forbidden in the common areas. But we're allowed to use the internet in the reception area. There's a table there that is visible to all, allowing the hosts to glare at you disapprovingly, and allowing everybody who comes into the cabin after using their body in the Great Outdoors to see, the instant they come in, that you're sitting there, a worthless slave to the internet who's incapable of logging off, even here in the mountains where other people come for peace, contemplation; but not you: you have to have *likes*—gotta have them, just gotta have them—you're a junkie, nature isn't enough for you, you have to have the whole world in your hand, here, now. And as if it wasn't bad enough that this table might as well have a big shiny idiot-arrow pointing at it as you sit there shamefacedly Googling away, you're surrounded by walls covered in newspaper clippings and photos of the people who once built this cabin, and the road that leads to it, and the kiosk on top of Galdhøpiggen, and who carried tons of material up here several times a day in all weathers, in all seasons without getting a single *like*.

And there you sit. Googling. To find out if the weather will be nice enough for you tomorrow.

We don't find out anything different from what the hostess just told us. Everybody agrees that the weather won't be great tomorrow either. And that it's a nice hike. But when it comes to sober information about mountain hikes there's nothing, of course, because everything written about mountains on the internet is also written by mountain folk, and mountain folk lie.

There are eight of us at dinner. The four friends—the last two now apparently back from the top—a couple who have just arrived and are also wondering whether or not to do the hike tomorrow, and us. We eat meat, talk quietly, and enjoy our twilit view of nothingness.

Afterward we all go to the fireside lounge, because there's no place else to go unless you want to sit out in reception, an object of derision, and check Facebook.

The group of friends sits in the fireside lounge talking about theater. Of course. After all, every conceivable statistic indicates that we are dealing here with highly educated, well-heeled cultural consumers. I throw myself into the conversation because that's the kind of thing I do. Theater, I mean, not throwing myself into conversations— I do that more rarely. Soon we find ourselves talking about everything else too. Jokes are cracked. There is laughter. The mood is excellent and these people seem, in every possible way, like people we'd gladly spend six or seven hours with in a hotel bar.

But I know, of course, that sometime sooner or later, we'll be obliged to talk about it—the hike.

And then, anything could happen.

"You've been up to the top today?" I start.

"Yes."

"Did you see anything?"

They laugh and show us pictures from the top. They've taken goofy photos of themselves standing gazing out over the landscape—except that there is no landscape to gaze out over. It's all swaddled in gray. I ask them if it was unpleasant hiking since they didn't see anything.

"It was fine."

"It was a bit unpleasant when we had to climb maybe."

"Well, there's climbing and climbing. Was it really climbing?"

"It wasn't far off."

"It was pretty slippery, wasn't it?"

"And slick."

"Difficult to get a grip."

"Yes."

"And we couldn't see where we were putting our feet either."

"We couldn't see a thing."

"Not up on top, either. Absolutely nothing."

Brief pause.

"But it was a really nice hike."

"Yes. A really good feeling to get to the top."

"And it isn't any problem at all hiking up there in weather like this as long as you dress right and are prepared for it. And are in reasonable shape."

"Not at all, and then you get your reward afterward!"

"A really nice hike."

"Yes. Good to use your body."

AT THAT POINT, the hostess comes into the fireside lounge. Clearly there are no Googlers in the reception for her to scowl at. I ask her about the history of the place. Because that's the kind of thing I do. Then I ask her how many times she's been up Galdhøpiggen.

"Around five hundred."

Five hundred?!

THAT'S WHEN I UNDERSTAND why there's no point asking her if you'll see anything from the top in this kind of weather. It's been *such* a long time since stuff like that has played any role whatsoever for her. For her, it's just a hike. If you go up to the top of Galdhøpiggen two or three times a week for several years, of course you forget how nice it is there. You forget the view. You forget how it was the first time. If you hike up there more or less every day, it's even possible that now and again you'll forget you've taken along two women who paid you to get them safely to the top of Norway's highest peak.

"I hike up in all weather," she says. "It's a nice hike regardless."

"And it's so good to get there."

"Right?" agrees one of the friends on the sofa. "Good to use your body."

The friends get up off the sofa and walk over to the hostess.

"There's no such thing as bad weather," one of them says. And then they all laugh a bit.

And then the hostess starts to sing.

Leaning forward slightly, she launches into "The Happy Wanderer."

The friends chime in too.

As they reach the end of the first verse, the chef and two newly arrived guests pop their heads through the door and all give a very cheery rendition of the chorus.

Now they all start to dance. They're holding backpacks, which they swing playfully to and fro as they intone the second verse, looking straight at me and singing louder than ever.

And now Jim Carrey comes in, dressed as Truman from *The Truman Show*, and joins in with the chorus.

WE CHAT WITH the other couple instead. After all, we're in the same boat. All four of us are wondering whether we should go for a hike tomorrow.

The Head of Documentation tells them she's hiked up Galdhøpiggen before but that time she went from Spiterstulen, which is a longer and tougher hike. What's more, she tells them we hiked over Besseggen in similar weather to this yesterday. And that we did the hike pretty quickly.

When we leave, the Head of Documentation has a shocked expression on her face.

"Did you hear what I just said?" she whispers. "I've started boasting."

"What do you mean 'started'?"

"Very funny. But did you hear me? I said I did a longer and tougher hike to the top."

"Yes, I heard that."

"And that we did the Besseggen hike quickly."

"I heard that too."

"It had nothing to do with the issue."

"No."

"Zero. Zero relevance."

"No. Zero."

"Do you realize what this means?"

"No…"

"We're becoming like them!"

Good heavens! You probably don't notice it all that easily your-self. You start boasting a bit, quite innocently. You start fibbing a bit. The next day, you've probably forgotten what it was like to hike over Besseggen, so you tell people it's zero problem to take your three-year-old and your cat and your invalid grandmother up there in a blizzard—as long as you dress for it. It's a nice hike regardless! Easy-peasy! Love the outdoors!

"We can't stay here," the Head of Documentation says.

"But aren't we supposed to . . ."

"We can't stay here, I tell you."

"Aren't you supposed to be irritatingly positive?"

"Screw that. Everybody else here is irritatingly positive. I just can't become like them. And nor can you."

"But isn't the whole point that . . ."

"We must *never* become like them. We have to get away. Now."

This is absolutely not going according to plan. And I'm very much enjoying it.

"No," I say. "We really can't stay here."

"No."

"We can't go up to the top of Norway's highest peak and not see anything! Just for the sake of doing it."

"That is precisely what we can't do. That would make us like them. That's one step away from starting to talk about how good it is to get there."

"And use your body."

"If we're going to hike anywhere tomorrow, we're going to a place where we'll see something absolutely fantastic!"

"Yes! We've been on this trip since Sunday and the only view we've seen so far is from the bar in the Oslo Plaza."

"Which is a very nice view."

"Very. But the point of this trip is to be converted to nature."

"And that won't happen to you here."

"Exactly."

"We have a car. We can go wherever we want. We can go to a place where there's nice weather."

"And a view! And people! Preferably masses of people. People who don't just repeat the same ten sentences over and over again."

"Yes!!"

⸺

WE NEED TO FIND OUT where there's sun and a view and people. In other words, we need to have internet. And we pull out our phones. And go online. Even though we're sitting in the fireside lounge. An internet-free zone.

We. Are. Living. On. The. Edge.

And it's not as if we're bothering anybody either. There's nobody else here. The others have gone to bed. After all, it's past 9:00 PM.

The Head of Documentation quickly finds a photo a girlfriend has posted today. From Preikestolen, that insane mountain plateau in Rogaland, which—as its Norwegian name, "Pulpit Rock," suggests— looks just like a pulpit, assuming you're inclined to think along religious lines. Which hangs there almost in thin air 1,800 feet above the fjord. With views in all directions. Which has been photographed from every angle gazillions of times, with good cause. Which has appeared on several lists of the most fantastic places in the world. This is one of Norway's biggest tourist attractions. A quarter of a million visitors go there every year. Many of them foreign tourists who've never so much as seen a hiking shoe.

The weather looks fantastic. The hike takes two hours each way according to UT.no. Probably half that time for us, as the Head of Documentation points out. What's not to like?

"It's a very long way there."

"But it's a nice trip."

"And we have a car. With a roof. And music."

EVERYTHING'S LOOKING BRIGHTER NOW. We go to bed. We sleep eight hours in *bed linen*. We get up. We look out and see nothing. We laugh. We pack. We eat breakfast. We tell the couple from yesterday that we've decided to head off. They look at us with genuine envy. Then they look outside. And wait for it to break up.

It'll never break up.

We get into the car. We turn the music up to top volume and drive into the light.

So long, suckers.

LISTEN TO INEXPERIENCED MOUNTAIN FOLK, PART 2

1. Don't hike up a mountain if the weather is crappy and you won't see a thing. You'll understand this yourself. Find something enjoyable to do instead.

2. If the point is to use your body, there's no need to use it in a place where it's thoroughly unpleasant. Your body can also be used in the lowlands, in parks, in city streets, and indoors.

3. There is such a thing as bad weather. But it is possible to run away from it.

4. If you're supposed to cross a glacier and climb a country's highest peak, check in advance that your glacier guide is the type who won't leave you in the lurch three yards from the cabin.

5. Bed linen is underrated.

INTO
THE LIGHT!

Last leg: Juvasshytta–Preikestolhytta by car.
Preikestolen, on foot.
Estimated time: Who cares?

YES. WE'RE HEADING FOR the light. And a view. And people.

But first we have to drive a pretty long way downhill at two miles an hour with an inch of visibility along a road that suddenly takes a 180-degree turn and has no crash barrier and is pretty narrow and runs along a mountainside where there's a real danger of meeting a bus. The dashboard display reads: temporarily out of operation due to blocked vision.

But this is temporary. We drive down slowly. The fog loosens its grip. We drive west. And that's when we start on what is decidedly the best part of our trip to date. It even beats the elevator ride up to the bar at the Oslo Plaza.

I have been known to say—because I'm an immature jerk who can't resist needling nature lovers—that I think mountains are best seen from below.

But I really do. I grow happier with every passing yard as we drive along the floor of the valley, and see mountains on all sides—mighty, imposing. Not to mention when the landscape opens up and we see that someplace far up ahead there's a small town center where we'll certainly be able to eat lunch. At a place with tables and chairs and cutlery. And people in regular clothes.

It's important to do your prep, so along the way in the car, we also read about Preikestolen on assorted websites; and already at this point, I get a good feeling about this hike. Because here, in fact, there's an almost complete absence of boasting; indeed, here it's close to the opposite. There's a lot about how you mustn't underestimate the hike, how it may be harder than you think, and how you have to set aside plenty of time and dress sensibly. All this is probably owing to the fact that Preikestolen is visited by so many tourists who aren't used to mountains and think the plateau is right in the middle of downtown Stavanger—a city that is actually one-and-a-half hour's drive west—with an elevator to the top. On UT.no hikes are graded according to difficulty. In a Norwegian post about Preikestolen, it says the hike is of "average" difficulty. In the English version, however, the hike is described as "demanding."

Maybe we have a bit too much belief in ourselves when it comes to the mountains in Norway. On the other hand, we don't have a great deal of belief in others.

I call the tourist cabin beside Preikestolen. It's full. That also makes me strangely happy. This must mean there are a lot of people there. It's the weekend. The weather's nice. It'll be a veritable mass migration to Preikestolen.

We manage to get a bed in a nearby hostel. It'll be tough to return to bunks and shared toilets after the luxury holiday camp in the foggy heights. But we'll cope. We can cope with anything now. There's one day left. A day of sun and views and people. After lying down in wooden things that night, I feel for the first time this week that I'm looking forward to a hike.

It doesn't even annoy me all that much that the whole hostel is woken up at five o'clock by a bunch of people who get up then, probably to hike up Preikestolen while it's still cold, dark, unpleasant, and empty up there.

⟁

AT LAST, I DISCOVER something that hikers have told me that is in fact true: people really do hike in line here.

And I love it. I hear seven languages in the first ten yards. People are wearing regular clothes. In fact, we're the ones who stand out. Of course, I always stand out in this jacket, but needless to say nobody has noticed it in the other places where we've hiked because there haven't been any people there. After around twenty yards, we meet a Chinese man who's given up. He's sitting on a rock gasping for breath. We meet a young couple on their way back down again. They walk arm in arm. He has a little speaker on his shoulder. It's loudly playing bhangra music.

And why not?

There are people of all ages here. I listen, the way I like and tend to do, and pick up snippets of the conversations. And—as you've realized long ago, of course—people here don't talk about how far they've hiked and how long they've taken and where they've been before and where they'll go next. Here they talk about politics and the news, about marriage, about children, about restructurings at work, about music and books, about how studies are going. One girl says to her mother: "I think it's more fun going to the gym." Another girl says to another mother: "You're getting too far ahead of us, Mom. No need to show off."

No there isn't; that's exactly it.

Once we get to the plateau itself (in roughly half the estimated time, though we needn't make a big deal of it), the view is insane. It's something that actually has to be experienced. Enough said. And there are a lot of people there. Who are doing the stuff people do when they're at places with insane views. They take pictures of each other, arms raised to heaven. They sit dangerously close to the edge, eat their picnics, and chat, and laugh. A group of mature men tell us they're on a class reunion and ask if we can get a video of them lying down on the plateau making snow angels. That's what this group of one-time classmates do: they meet up now and then, head off to extraordinary places, lie down, and make snow angels, regardless of whether or not there's any snow. It's silly; it's embarrassing. And you'd be a real sourpuss if watching this didn't put you in a good mood.

Just before the plateau itself, a man with a camera stands shouting to his buddy who's standing right out on the edge.

"Tom Cruise! *Mission: Impossible!*" he shouts, probably because it's recently been in the news that scenes for the new *Mission: Impossible* movie are going to be filmed here. He lifts his camera. His buddy does his best to look like Tom Cruise. He is very averagely successful. And the photo is taken. Other people who notice what's going on laugh and clap.

I think: *Which of the experiences we've had this week could beat this?*
Tree root? Tree root? Tree root?
A snus trail in the fog?
Conversations about achievements in stocking feet?
Memoorooboo?
All the experiences we've had up until now on this trip sound like bad poetry collections.

▲

HOW MANY REALLY GOOD STORIES have you heard that involve being totally alone?

Let me tell you a simple story about being with people. A person I know was traveling with some buddies. The last night. They were supposed to be flying home the next morning. They got back to the hotel that night—not especially late—and agreed to have a last thanks-for-the-trip drink in my buddy's room. And there they sat, having a lovely time and chatting and laughing. A great night. And then the gathering broke up, everyone went back to their rooms and agreed they'd simply meet at the airport. My friend set his alarm and went to bed. In the morning, his alarm went off and my friend got up, had a swift shower, got dressed, packed, put on his jacket and shoes, and left the room.

And had the distinct feeling that something didn't add up. He didn't know what it was. But something was wrong.

He ate breakfast, still dogged by the same feeling. He left for the airport. Still with this feeling that something right now was different from usual. Eventually he managed to identify the feeling. The feeling was located in his feet, or more precisely: in his shoes.

His shoes were warm. And they had been warm when he put them on in his hotel room.

He believed he'd gone to bed at a reasonable time and slept for hours. But his head probably barely hit the pillow before the alarm went off. He hadn't noticed how many hours had passed as he sat there with his good buddies, chatting and laughing. That's why his shoes were warm when he put them on. Because he'd only just taken them off.

I think this is something to aim for. It should be a goal in life to make sure not to let too much time pass between the times when you get up and put on warm shoes. That's when you know the night turned out better than anybody expected. Those are the best nights— the ones that are unplanned. When you're on a trip with buddies and you're really only supposed to be popping into one of their rooms briefly. When you have a chance meeting with somebody you haven't seen for ages. Or when a quite ordinary evening with the people you live with never ends. And you don't notice that an awful lot of time has passed until it gets light, or you hear birdsong, or the morning rush hour, or church bells. Or you wake up and put on warm shoes.

If you're absolutely alone and put on warm shoes the next day, you're just an insomniac.

△

AND WHO'D HAVE THOUGHT IT? Who do we meet halfway up Preikestolen? We actually meet our Canadian friends from Besseggen. The man who ran off in the fog to search for Ts and the woman who hiked after him wetly.

It is a joyous reunion. It turns out that since we last saw them, they've been in Flåm. I don't know how familiar you are with Norway, but Besseggen, Flåm, and Preikestolen are absolutely nowhere near each other. These people mean business. They dash back and forth across Norway to hike on rock.

He says: "It's really beautiful here." Of course.

She says: "Too many people." Of course.

△

I MEAN, HELLO?! Have you taken a look around you? Have you seen the view? Have you seen the plateau and how it plummets hundreds of feet straight down into the fjord?

It's dramatic, it gives you butterflies in your stomach, it's beautiful, it's overwhelming; it's pretty much unlike anything else, it's fairly easy to hike here, you don't need fiendishly expensive equipment, and it isn't all that far from a couple of fairly large towns. Why in the world *shouldn't* there be a lot of people here?

And it really isn't all *that* jam-packed here either. It isn't as if you risk being shoved off the edge. It's a day off, it's noon, there's blazing sunshine, but there's still plenty of room to stroll around, look at the view from different angles, sit down and have a picnic, or lie down and make snow angels.

And surely you must want others to be able to experience this. If not, why take all those pictures and write #getoutdoors?

And only now do I notice there's a line in the middle of the plateau. One by one you walk toward the edge, as far forward as you want and dare. And then your friends can take a picture of you where it looks as if you're standing quite alone on Preikestolen. Hikers don't like lines, but they are clearly willing to make an exception for a line that allows you to be alone.

Mr. Canada surprises us greatly by seeming to enjoy all this pandemonium much more than his wife does. He's a keen and—I believe—pretty good photographer and, unlike his wife, he's very eager for us to stand in line to take a picture. I like that. He simply lets himself get swept up in the moment. He laughs and claps as the others have their pictures taken in weird poses. When it's our turn, he sets us up. He calls out instructions and directs us. He's on board.

Then they have to go. Of course they must dash back down to the cabin. Tonight they'll stay in Stavanger, they've told us. I profoundly hope they'll find themselves a nice restaurant, meet some fun people— maybe the angel gang—and end up standing on a table at three in the morning singing, "The Winner Takes It All." Then wake up early tomorrow morning and put on warm shoes.

Mr. Canada sends us the picture he took. The Head of Documentation is raising her arms to heaven. I am not.

But I'm really not all that far off.

SO HOW DID *YOU* FEEL ABOUT IT?

WE'RE BACK DOWN AGAIN. We sit outside the relatively modern Preikestolen cabin, with its view of a parking lot, a bunch of people, and a bit of nature. Soon we'll fly home and dress in regular clothes. We're drinking beer out in the sunshine. At the neighboring table sit the angel gang. They're also drinking beer, and squinting, and laughing.

"Okay," the Head of Documentation says. "Time to sum up. What's your impression of hikers?"

"Hikers are people who move around the place according to a rough plan. They don't wash all that often. They don't change their clothes all that often. They never dress up. Carry around backpacks that are way too big. And mostly talk to other people with backpacks that are way too big about where they've been and where they're heading and how long it took."

"So what you're saying, then, is that hiking from cabin to cabin is like Interrail for people who like going to bed early."

▲

OF COURSE WE didn't say that. Nobody talks like that. It's just something I made up later to show off. See: I have learned a bit from spending a week in the company of mountain folk.

This is what we actually said:

HER: Have you been converted to hiking?

ME: Not quite.

HER: I thought maybe not.

ME: What about you? How do you feel your job of being irritatingly positive went?

HER: So-so.

ME: But there has been an improvement, hasn't there?

HER: Yes. Because today was the best day?

ME: Easily.

IT GOES QUIET for a while.

ME: Just think—it's only a week since we stayed at the Plaza.

HER: Yes. That was nice.

ME: Mm. Very nice. We should do it again.

HER: Definitely.

1ST ATTEMPT: TO JOTUNHEIMEN IN SEARCH OF SALVATION.

EVALUATION.

Itinerary:

Day 1: Preparation (Completed.)

Day 2: Downtown Oslo–Nordmarka
(Completed, with poor navigation. Rain and fog.)

Day 3: Nordmarka–Jotunheimen
(Completed according to plan. Rain and fog.)

Day 4: Besseggen (Completed according to plan.)

Day 5: Gjendesheim–Spiterstulen (Replaced with a car journey,
Gjendesheim–Juvasshytta. Rain and fog.)

Day 6: Galdhøpiggen (Replaced with a car journey, Juvasshytta–
Preikestolen. Nice. A bit of rain. A bit of sun.)

Day 7: Relaxed day trip and evaluation (Replaced with a hike to
Preikestolen and a beer outdoors in the sunshine.)

Purpose of the trip:

- Find inner peace (not achieved, but borderline there in the sunshine on day six)
- Realize how small I am (not achieved)
- Experience something that's difficult to explain (I still think it's difficult to explain why people do this but nothing beyond that)
- Feel a desire to raise my arms to heaven (I was nearly there at Preikestolen, but there was also a whiff of irony in the air)
- Find out whether food and drink taste better, and whether views look better, if you've walked a long way (yeah, but you need to have walked a *really* long way)
- Talk to, understand, maybe even like people I meet at cabins with peculiar names (I've done my best and I've met some pleasant people—but on the whole, I met very few people)

Conclusion: First attempt = Failed

Five
Months
Later

I EXPLORE MYSELF AND MY CITY

FEAR OF DYING has an undeservedly bad reputation. Yet the blend of machismo and wimpishness makes it very easy to see the funny side of the fear of dying. It's easy to imagine a photo of a fifty-year-old on a mountaintop: he's trying to smile, but you can tell he probably has bad knees, and you can tell that behind those white teeth and that tanned skin is a tiny little human being saying: "I've lost my hair and my humor and I'm really scared of dying. Please like me."

But fear of dying is, after all, an expression of a desire to live a little bit longer and that can't be all bad. In fact it means you believe a future will come that will be nice enough for you to want to experience as much of it as you possibly can.

And if we're going to try and say something positive about the era and the kind of society in which I (and probably you, dear reader) live—the olden days get more than enough praise as it is—then here's one thing at any rate: quite a lot of the things people like us are doing in our lives today are based precisely on our belief that a future will come and it will be nice.

This must be why we go around fixing up our homes all the time, for example. It isn't because we plan to die young in fancy apartments.

It's because we think that one day in the future we'll finally have acquired the most perfect home and by then we'll be pensioners, maybe, so we'll have masses of time to just sit there thinking how perfect everything is.

This must be why we save for retirement too, and buy ourselves vacation homes—in the mountains, by the sea, in warmer countries. It can hardly be because we've set ourselves a goal of leaving as many unused buildings behind us as possible when we kick the bucket at around sixty-five. It's because we believe a day will come when we'll have time to use these vacation homes, when time is the only thing we have enough of, in fact, and then we shall also be economically comfortable and simply enjoy life.

And to keep ourselves healthy and sprightly long enough to experience these days to the fullest, we exercise. We cycle on bikes that don't go anywhere, we jog on floors that move and hold us in place, we go climbing and clambering in forests and mountains, and take an interest in healthy homemade fare. All in the hope that when we become old enough to have fully renovated homes and plenty of vacation homes and ample time and finances, we'll be in excellent shape and look damned good. And have masses of times to just wander around looking good. Along a seafront, maybe, in a pale, light summer shirt and shorts in colors that are startlingly bright for one so old.

And we truly believe this time will come. Most of us who live in societies like the one you and I live in, reader, we may think there's a lot that's peculiar about politics and there may be many tendencies we're not keen on, we may even think things have taken a turn for the worse, but despite it all we do not believe society will fall apart in the near future or that the system will collapse. We think things will turn out fine.

Yes, there's a lot of aggression in our society, there are a lot of people who think society is heading for a precipice, and who shout and scream about this loudly and angrily. But most of us are not there, despite it all. Not really. And all the people who shout and scream and are aggressive agree to an astonishing extent on the fundamental analysis, whether they're on the far right or the far left or from some extreme version of one or other of the world religions: that Western society today is going to hell because everything is changing and nobody is defending the good old-fashioned values. But most of us who don't belong to extreme versions of anything at all, we think: It'll probably be fine. We'll work it out. We always do. There'll be a future. It'll be nice. And I want to be part of it. Now I'm going for a hike. Bye.

"Okay," says the Head of Documentation, who's been listening to me talk about this for a pretty long time. A couple of hours, actually. We're at our local back in Oslo. It's freezing cold outside. There's a fire in the hearth and the pub is full of people and you can get good beer here without having to take a five-hour hike first. Our regular waiter, who speaks with an impressively thick French accent for a man who's lived in Norway for thirty years, walks past our table and asks: "Another?" It isn't really a question. We're here to plan the next attempt to convert me to nature. We actually decided immediately after Preikestolen that we couldn't give up just when we'd had a tiny glimpse of hope. We have to try one more time. One more trip. And learn from the mistakes we made on our first trip.

But time passed. You know how it is. There's so much else on. There are people to be met, pubs to be visited, jokes to be cracked. There's reminiscing to be done. You have to listen to music. There's reading to be done. There are series you have to watch. You have to talk about these series, and about series you haven't watched. There's silliness to be had. There's dancing to be done. There's silly danc-ing to be done. There's coffee to be drunk. Suddenly one day, the weather's unexpectedly good enough for an outdoor beer late into the autumn. Then it's Christmas and New Year's. And people come to visit. All in all, there's a lot going on. So nothing's come of it. But now we've decided again. Now we shall make a plan. That's why we're sitting here. And that's why I've spent a couple of hours talking about fear of dying and belief in the future and upper bodies.

"Okay," the Head of Documentation says, then. "So the only positive thing you have to say about people who hike in the mountains is that they're scared of dying."

Of course, it's a bit irritating to find that my blinding analysis can be summed up so accurately in seven seconds but...

"Yes, that probably is what I think."

The Head of Documentation nods.

"What about you?" she asks. "Are you scared of dying?"

"I don't know if I'm especially scared of it. I don't really give it all that much thought. But of course I don't want to die."

"See!" says the Head of Documentation, who hasn't forgotten that it's her job to be irritatingly positive. "There's something you have in common with nature lovers, at any rate."

OR IS THE POINT that I would like it better if a few more nature lovers actually did say: "I've lost my hair and my humor and I'm really scared of dying"?

But that isn't what they say. They make hiking in the mountains and forests a philosophical choice, something semi-religious, worthy, almost like a service to society. They want to stop time and switch off, find breathing space and silence and time, time to experience something that's difficult to explain, something that's bigger than yourself, something that gives people the peace and energy they need to carry on existing and contributing in a stressful world.

And this is something I am forced to acknowledge if I'm going to make another attempt to be converted to nature: All this semi-religious stuff, it's not my bag. I probably don't have it in me. I probably don't have a need for it, now that I think about it.

Something that's bigger than myself? Something that's difficult to explain?

Stopping time, slowing the tempo, shutting out the world? Peace? No. No. No. No. And no.

▲

PEACE?

I have enough peace in my life. I spend a lot of time working on my own. If I want silence, I can just turn off the music or shut the window. And generally I don't want to. I like sound.

▲

STOPPING TIME, slowing the tempo?

No. I don't want to stop time. I think time is moving along at just the right tempo. It's easy to believe things are going too fast. And it's common to think that, and it's almost natural to think things develop in a given direction, that everything's going faster and faster and becoming more and more advanced all the time.

But it just isn't so.

Some thirty to forty years ago, you could fly from Europe to America in just over three hours. You can't do that anymore. The plane that could cross the Atlantic in three hours is no longer in use. Because it made an enormous racket that shattered windows and terrified people and animals; because the tickets—and the plane itself—cost a tremendous amount of money; and because one of these planes crashed. People are certainly keen to get places quickly but not if it ruins things for other people, costs ludicrous amounts of money, and is potentially dangerous. Now it takes at least seven hours to fly from Europe to America—or fifty-six. It depends a bit on what airline you choose.

Besides, a fair number of people nowadays think we ought to fly less for the sake of the environment. That doesn't necessarily mean we actually fly less, but we *think* we ought to. And that may be the start of something else. I know several people who, several years back, thought that they ought to stop smoking and who have done it now. On the whole, planes aren't entirely unlike cigarettes: planes, too, were cool and stylish and modern once. Now a lot more people are critical.

Maybe we'll take sailboats to America in a few years. Or stop traveling there altogether.

It could happen!

Telephone calls: We also thought they'd develop in one direction and one direction *only*. Before, we used to have landline telephones that occupied a place of honor in our homes, wired into the wall on their very own table, which was more like an altar. Then came the first mobile phones, where you had to carry a cable and a huge battery, so strictly speaking they weren't so much mobile phones as pieces of luggage. And then the phones just got smaller and smaller and lighter and lighter and more and more mobile, and that's the way we thought it would continue, because that's what you think. But then came the smartphone. And then phones started to get bigger again. And heavier. And they needed more power, so their battery life was shorter, so we started having to carry cables around again, just like with the first mobile phones. And some smartphones have to be charged so often that they have, in practice, taken a huge step backward in the direction of landline phones again. Maybe in a few years, we'll keep our massive smartphones standing permanently in a place of honor in our homes, wired into the wall on their very own table, which is more like an altar.

It could happen!

Do you remember when microwave ovens arrived? Do you remember how we thought that now everything would change? Do you remember how we thought: now that somebody's invented a way of making food that takes one minute and fits into a small box, everybody will throw out their regular ovens and never look back?

That's not how things went. Mainly because microwaved food tastes like cardboard. Or hiking stew. On the contrary, in the past few years, we've started to gain status from taking as long as possible to prepare food. If you want to impress your friends with a meal now, you'll need to have planted it yourself; cultivated it yourself; watered it yourself; fertilized it yourself, naturally (don't ask); harvested it and prepared it yourself; and served it on a plate you designed yourself, and which then, itself, can be eaten for dessert.

Once upon a time, fast-food was the future. Now skepticism sets in if a restaurant serves you too quickly.

And suddenly, people are starting to buy vinyl records again. Even though this is totally unnecessary.

For that matter: we've finally become modern and advanced enough to escape the whims of nature, and that's when people start wandering about in nature, *by choice.*

These things happen! All the time!

People are odd and things rarely turn out the way you expect. All this is what you're missing if you stop time and shut out the world.

AND I THINK, quite honestly, that I experience things that are bigger than me all the time. On a daily basis. Things that are difficult to explain. Miracles, even.

For example: Imagine you're out and about in your neighborhood. And you see a hole in the road. If, like me, you're a conscientious citizen, you think: *Somebody ought to do something about that,* and then you continue on your way.

And—*ta-da!*—something very often is done about it. Not always. And not always terribly quickly. But as a rule, sooner or later, the hole in the road is fixed. By somebody or another. I don't know who.

And I don't know how that person found out about it because nobody reports it, of course; everybody just thinks, *Somebody ought to do something about that*, then continues on their way.

And yet it gets fixed.

That is hard to understand. That is bigger than yourself. That is a miracle!

Okay, maybe it isn't a miracle. But think about this: All societies that more or less hang together—a village, a town, a country—are a daily orgy of achievement. And most of what we master are things nobody mastered a hundred years ago, even though they were probably better at chopping wood in those days. We've made rules, some of them written and implemented in advanced systems, a lot of them just things we know because we realize it's best for everybody if we do things this way or that. If everybody suddenly stopped giving a damn about laws and rules and consideration and just thought about themselves, society would collapse almost immediately. Even the most advanced societies are based to a large extent on people generally behaving well. And people do. Not everybody. Not all the time. But enough of them behave well often enough for things to function. We work things out and get things done. *That* is bigger than yourself, for sure.

A mountain just stands there.

"YOU DO KNOW that you sound a bit born-again when you talk about that stuff, right?" the Head of Documentation says.

"Yes, sorry. I'll dial it down a bit."

"Everyday miracles in society. It's a bit much."

"Yes. Maybe. But it is what I think."

"No doubt about that."

"Traffic lights! Have you thought how fantastic traffic lights actually are?"

"Traffic lights?"

"Not in themselves, maybe. But the fact that there's a loudspeaker beeping beside every pedestrian crossing? So that people who can't see know when they can cross the street? Have you ever thought what a beautiful idea that actually is?"

"No."

We drink. We think. The Head of Documentation returns to business in hand.

"Okay," she says. "So this time we won't go looking for something that's bigger than ourselves in nature."

"Nope."

"And maybe we won't go in for macho peak-bagging, either?"

NO. MAYBE NOT THAT EITHER. I know peak-bagging is the trend nowadays. It's what people do. But, as you know, I have a low competitive instinct and find it hard to avoid giggling at manly achievements. And I tried going straight up a mountain once and didn't get much out of it. And the fact that I did that hike on slippery rock without seeing a thing probably should have just made my sense of achievement even stronger. But no. Nothing.

For a while we considered going to my old stomping ground in Stranda and *bagging* a peak there. I've spoken to several people I grew up with there who are now nature lovers and started to notice a tendency for nostalgia when, for example, I was reminded that our extremely nature-loving homeroom teacher waxed the skis of every single pupil before we headed out on a field trip. That was what my school days were like. And the people who work at Gjendesheim and some of my old friends have told me they were forced to go on hikes as children, hated it for a while, but then started to love it as adults. So perhaps that would happen to me too if I returned to my childhood realm, spent a bit of time sitting on the storehouse steps, and

gazing out across those enormous plains, and bagged, say, Slogen—
one of the most legendary peaks in the district.

But then I read up a bit on Slogen. And the internet discussions
about Slogen were ominously reminiscent of the internet discussions about Besseggen, except that in this case, there were even a fair
number of people who admitted to having thought it was "a bit airy"
on the way up to the top. As I understand it, "a bit airy" is outdoors-
speak for "scary as hell." There was even the hint of a debate not so
long ago when a very experienced mountain hiker said it made no
sense for the Norwegian Trekking Association to write on its website that this hike was suitable for children. He thought it should be
labeled as "risk-exposed" and unsuitable for small children. We who
have learned the talk of mountain folk will grasp that this probably
means there's around a sixty percent chance of dying on this hike.

So no.

And quite honestly, why should I start to love something I was
forced to do in childhood? What kind of thinking is that, really? It
hasn't happened with much else that I was forced to do in childhood.
I'll soon be fifty and I haven't yet started to love playing the recorder,
calculating the circumference of a circle, or jumping over a pommel
horse.

"Okay. Nothing macho. Nothing evangelical." The Head of
Documentation is working systematically now. "So what does that
leave us with?"

"Fear of dying."

We don't say anything for a while.

"You don't *have* to like nature," she says. "We can just drop it."

OR CAN WE? The other day I pictured a future in which this is the
only thing people do. Both at work and in their leisure time. People
wander around in nature. And do only that.

Okay, hear me out. It isn't as far-fetched as you might think.

Everybody knows the robots are coming. I recently read that a third of today's jobs will have been taken over by machines in twenty years. Robots are, for now, not as good as people at original and creative thinking, so in the first instance, they'll take over the routine tasks. But that's not all. I've read about this too: There are robots working as teachers and cooks. They probably aren't the most creative cooks, though they're probably much nicer to work with than, say, Gordon Ramsay. There are robot journalists. They probably aren't especially advanced robots. You just feed them a few sentences: "Party leaders have a lot to answer for." "This is thoroughly deplorable." "When push comes to shove." Then these sentences are simply repeated and repeated, year after year. There are already a few robots working as political commentators in major media corporations today, in fact.

So the question is of course: What will we do in the future when more and more jobs are taken over by robots and apps and software?

To deal with the obvious point first, a fair number of us will, of course, earn a living by making and developing and maintaining and updating and administering all these machines.

But what about the rest of us?

Well. Here we must learn from history. And all experience indicates that in the future we will earn a living from things we don't currently see as jobs. And things we laugh at today.

Twenty to thirty years ago, people snickered and said it was impossible for everybody to make a living cutting each other's hair. But it turned out that it actually is possible for a pretty large number of people to do so. I've traveled a fair amount around Norway. And there are local communities here with more hairdressers than inhabitants. There are pretty large numbers of people who now earn a living from cutting each other's hair, filing each other's nails, fixing each other's skin, lengthening each other's lashes, trimming the beards of baristas. And incidentally, that wasn't a profession forty years ago either. "I can make my own coffee," people said in those days.

And there are some professions that are experiencing growth at the same time as so much work is being automated. Veterinary nurses, for example, are experiencing strong growth. Forty years ago, people would have said: "I can stroke my own cat."

Another professional group enjoying strong growth is people working in fitness and exercise. In other words, people who make a living from standing beside people who are doing push-ups and saying, "Do push-ups." This is also a job that would have made people laugh forty years ago.

And last but not least, all these are jobs that are about people's leisure, about self-care, coffee drinking, exercise, fitness, cat-stroking.

And more and more things that were once about work are now about leisure. People's private cabins, for example. Many of them were once workplaces. They were once farmers' summer dairy farms; they were once fishermen's boathouses. And many people make a living out of providing services for the cabin folk. They clear their snow and light their fires so that it'll be cozy when they arrive. And people run tourist cabins in the mountains or make a living guiding people on hikes.

Do you see? What used to be work is now leisure. And more and more people make a living out of other people's leisure. Leisure becomes work, work becomes leisure. It isn't entirely unlikely that in the future we'll all spend our entire time wandering about in nature: half of us will have sold an app that has made us stinking rich and no longer need to work, while the other half will be professional hikers, or people who have local knowledge, carry our food up to the top, or give us a massage afterward. I believe PPW, professional peak walker, will be a perfectly ordinary job in a matter of years.

And there's no longer anybody left in the cities. The robots work and work, the pubs are empty, and our French waiter stands alone in the doorway, gazing at the deserted streets and wondering what happened. And what happened was that people wanted to live more simply, because they learn that this is responsible and necessary and the right thing to do politically, and because people think they need and have earned this. And because masses of books tell us so. (If you were to buy and own all the books ever published about buying and owning less, you'd have to build an extension on your house to make space for them.) And because the people we follow on Instagram show us that it's possible to live more simply. It is possible to make other choices. If you grow up, live, and forge a career lasting several years in a country with one of the highest average incomes in the world, you'll be able to afford to fly to one of the islands in the southern hemisphere with the lowest cost of living in the world and live there for a long time without working or shaving, and present it as a protest against excessive consumption and the quest for a career in the wealthy world.

Things never turn out the way you expect. Perhaps we'll all soon head off to the forest or the mountains or the beach.

It could happen.

▲

THE HEAD OF DOCUMENTATION doesn't take this analysis terribly seriously, I see, but she probably interprets it as an expression of my desire to make one more attempt to love nature. But if that's the case, we'll need a bit more to build on than fear of dying.

"We mustn't forget," she says, "that, in spite of it all, you are very fond of walking."

▲

THIS IS TRUE. As recently as today I went for a walk in my city. The walk took about an hour. Here are some of the things I saw and experienced:

A restaurant had a sign outside that said "Happy summer" with a drawing of a sun. It's January, it's winter, and it's snowy.

I met an old acquaintance I hadn't spoken with for a long time for divorce-related reasons. It was extremely pleasant. He'd grown a beard since last time I saw him, but we'll let that pass.

I saw a man with two full shopping bags who decided to take a chance on walking down a steep hill, probably a shortcut home. As I've said, it's January, it's winter, and it's snowy. And icy. He'd taken no more than two steps when he slipped and fell flat on his back, then sailed down the rest of the hill surrounded by milk cartons, fruit, bread, and cat food. He laughed the whole way down.

I saw a kindergarten class out taking a walk. The kids waddled along the river in a neat line, dressed for winter. Right behind them came a flock of ducks, walking in exactly the same way.

I saw an extremely jolly bunch dressed in shoes that were slightly too light and clothes that were slightly too nice open the door to a bakery at quarter to twelve in the morning and shout in: "Do you have any beer?"

I asked a small family of tourists with a map if they needed a hand. I feel a certain need to help people who've chosen to take a short break in Norway in January. Especially when it's a mother and a father and a teenager who's just a bit too old to be on vacation with Mom and Dad. They asked me the way to a vegan restaurant they'd heard about. I recommended a different lunch spot that is much nicer instead. The teenager smiled a bit.

I saw a young couple sitting on a park bench arguing, though it's strictly speaking too cold to sit on park benches.

When I was almost home again, I met an elderly man I know a bit because we worked at the same place many years ago. Entirely unprompted he told me a jaw-droppingly filthy story about a vacation to Iceland.

"SO WHAT YOU MEAN is that you like these kinds of walks better than mountain hikes?" says the Head of Documentation.

"Yes, maybe I do."

"And that's where we should start," says the Head of Documentation. "Those city hikes of yours, you take them every day, all year round, regardless of the weather."

"There's no such thing as bad weather."

"Yes there is. In fact, the weather's wretched today. It's cold and wet and nasty. And lethally icy. And you still went for a walk. On a day when other people dread going to the store or to work or just out to the car. The question we need to ask ourselves is: What is it that makes these walks different from the hikes we took in Jotunheimen? And to the cabin in the forest?"

"Asphalt?"

"Apart from the most obvious things."

"They're shorter?"

"But they aren't. You don't have any problem walking long distances."

"Or quickly."

"We walked at over Besseggen at a breakneck pace."

"Half an hour below the lowest estimate on UT.no, actually."

"With a knee injury."

"But of course a mountain hike isn't primarily meant to be a competition, is it?"

We snicker.

"We both know what the big difference is, don't we?" she says. "We hardly met any people in Jotunheimen. And the few we did meet were pretty irritating. And they lied. And repeated the same phrases over and over again."

"You were just as irritated by those people as I was, weren't you?"

"I let you down a bit in my role as the irritatingly positive one there."

"You made a pretty good recovery."

"Thanks."

"But it isn't just the business of meeting people," I say. "It's something to do with unpredictability. Can I share a little anecdote?"

"If it's the one about warm shoes, I've heard it before."

"It isn't that one."

"If it's the one about Iceland and the European Championship, I've heard that one too. In fact I was there."

"It isn't that one."

"Is it the one about the orange glove?"

▲

YES. OKAY. IT'S THAT ONE. But you, dear reader, probably haven't heard it. So, here goes:

The anecdote of the orange glove!

It's a soccer anecdote. But I promise it's the last one. And this one isn't really about soccer either.

It happened on a Saturday afternoon. The next day, a big, important soccer match was due to be played in the city where I live. The Norwegian Football Cup final, in fact. One of the teams was Ålesund. The team, as of course you remember, that Stranda knocked out of the cup in the historic year of 1983. Later, Ålesund got much better at soccer. So good that they even reached the cup final a couple of times in the 2000s.

So that's why Oslo was full of people from Ålesund that weekend. Dressed in orange. Because orange is the color of the Ålesund soccer team. Because Ålesund Football Club was one of the last teams that got to choose its colors.

Anyway. The city was full of people from Ålesund and thereabouts, full of people who come from the same part of the country as me. And on the whole they were in an extremely good mood.

This weekend, on the Saturday afternoon, I was out and about—I think I was just going to the store, or maybe I was taking my daily walk—when I felt somebody place a hand on my shoulder. Or rather, I didn't just feel it. I saw it. Because the person who placed a hand on my shoulder was wearing a gigantic orange foam finger.

I turned and saw a man I'd never met before. Around fifty years old. Almost six-and-a-half feet tall. A bit overweight. A bit drunk.

So he was wearing a gigantic orange foam glove on one hand. He was wearing a two-foot-high orange hat on his head. And he was otherwise dressed in a slightly undersized, slightly worn orange onesie.

This man examined me carefully from head to toe, then looked me straight in the eye and said:

"What are you doing going around dressed like that, you dick?"

Apologies for the language, but that's what he said.

I was wearing pretty ordinary jeans and a pretty ordinary gray sweater. *He*, on the other hand, was wearing a giant orange glove, a two-foot-high orange hat on his head, and a slightly undersized, slightly worn orange onesie.

And *he* was criticizing *my* outfit. And calling *me* a sex organ.

Folks. It's times like these—when a six-and-a-half-foot, slightly drunk fifty-year-old man with a foam hand and a onesie criticizes your outfit and calls you a sex organ—it's times like these when you really show what kind of a human being you are.

I mean, what are you supposed to say to that kind of thing?

You can of course say: "Actually I'm not a dick. I'm a human being."

You can say that.

You can get grumpy. That's an option too.

Or you can join the party. That's what I did. And it was extremely pleasant. And that, of course, is exactly what the man actually wanted. He actually wanted to invite me to join the party. He did it in a slightly peculiar way. We can all agree on that. But I also think that most of us can agree on this: if a perfectly normally dressed, fifty-year-old, slightly overweight, six-and-a-half-foot man you'd never seen before approached you on a Saturday afternoon, placed his hands on your shoulders, looked you straight in the eye and asked if you wanted to join the party, you wouldn't take him up on the offer.

And that's precisely what's so nice about these occasions when masses of people get together and the mood is excellent. Things happen then that don't happen otherwise. People do things they wouldn't do otherwise. You can say what you want about it, but it certainly isn't boring.

"THAT KIND OF STUFF never happens on a trip to the mountains," I say, to hammer the point home.

"No," the Head of Documentation agrees. "And if it did I'd be scared to death."

The Head of Documentation has a think. "We traveled at the wrong time of year. And in the wrong weather. If we're supposed to meet different kinds of people and maybe experience unexpected happenings. We have to take a trip at the same time as everybody else. And we have to go where everybody else is going."

I catch myself smiling.

"So what you're saying is we have to do the exact opposite of what all the hikers advise us to do," I say.

"That's precisely what I'm saying. That's why Preikestolen worked."

I like this. I sense that now I'm already looking forward to going up to the woman at the trekking association store, smiling my legendary smile, and saying: "Hi! I was wondering if you have any tips about where to go if you want to meet as many people as possible in the mountains? Lines! We want to walk in lines!"

She'll pass out. Or shut the store.

Of course this is the way to do it.

"We must go to the mountains to find people," the Head of Documentation says.

"And silliness. People and silliness."

"People and silliness. A bit like on New Year's Eve."

⚠

RIGHT. HERE'S SOMETHING I haven't told you, dear reader. I have, in fact, had one nature experience since the last time. Maybe I could even call it an extreme nature experience. Short but extreme. My birthday is on New Year's Eve. I'm just mentioning it so maybe you'll remember next time. This year, we celebrated by going for a swim. In the sea, I mean. It was below freezing. There were a few of us friends who were warming up for the New Year's Eve festivities by taking a trip to an enormous sauna in our city. They serve food there and there are masses of people and an excellent atmosphere. If you want, you can go outside and take a dip in a hot tub. If you're even tougher, you can walk a few yards farther and jump into the sea. That's what we did. In the Nordic region. In December. Below freezing point. So it isn't that I'm scared of a challenge or afraid of feeling the cold against my flesh. I can be a tough guy. Put it this way: there were tourists who took photos of us.

⚠

"MM. A BIT LIKE New Year's Eve. If we can get a trip to the mountains to be a bit like New Year's Eve, we're onto something."

Our French waiter passes by.

"Any more trips to the mountains planned?" he asks, laughing. He's asked about this before. And laughed. Because he heard about our previous trip.

"Yes, actually," I say. "We probably won't be here so often from now on. We have a skiing trip to plan."

"Okay," he nods. "See you tomorrow."

To the Hardanger Plateau in Search of People

Itinerary:

Day 1: Oslo–Finse
Day 2: Finse–Krækkja
Day 3: Krækkja–Heinseter
Day 5: Heinseter–Geilo
Day 6: Evaluation

Purpose of the trip:

- Meet people
- Be silly
- Get trips to the mountains to feel
  a bit more like New Year's Eve
- Again: Talk to, understand, maybe even like
  people I meet at cabins with peculiar names

JAM-PACKED AND DEADLY DANGEROUS

First leg: Oslo–Finse.
By train.

THE OLD ME would have been sad. And embarrassed.

We're walking through the city to the station to catch the train that will take us to the mountains. We're dressed in skiwear, we're carrying skis and ski poles, we have big backpacks. It's late March and the last workday before the Easter break. A lot of people have already started their vacations. Because they've been waiting for this. It's been an irritating winter. More snow than usual, colder than usual, icier than usual. And it's felt as if winter would never end. Until now. Winter ended yesterday, in fact. And today it's as if the whole city is grinning. The sun is shining. The snow is melting. Windows are opened. People throw off their jackets and wander around aimlessly in the streets. Outside our local pub they're setting out the patio tables for the season. Our waiter takes a break from his work, lights a cigarette, and stands with his face toward the sun.

The old me would have been sad. The old me would have composed a graveside eulogy in his head:

Dearly beloved City. You were abruptly and pointlessly snatched from us on the last working day before Easter, just when you were at your most beautiful. Just when you were about to start blossoming and growing warmer, when you were about to open yourself up to everything, just when life itself was about to begin, with all it has to offer: friendship, love, laughter, endless new opportunities. At just that moment, you were snatched from us because we had decided to take a train to a place far, far away where there's an awful lot of snow.

OUR WAITER COCKS HIS HEAD and watches us walk by in our skiwear. The old me would have been embarrassed.

But here I am smiling.

Here I am thinking that we've come up with a fantastic plan for this vacation. If this trip doesn't make a nature fan of me, it simply isn't going to happen.

Already now, before the trip has started, I'm pretty certain we'll achieve three of the four goals we've set ourselves for this trip:

1. Meet people.
2. Be silly.
3. Get trips to the mountains to feel a bit more like New Year's Eve.
4. Talk to, understand, maybe even like people I meet at cabins with peculiar names.

That last one is and will remain the most uncertain point but we'll manage the other three. Easily. We always manage to be silly. It's what we do best. And meeting people—we're guaranteed to do that. We'll meet enormous numbers of people in fact. I've investigated. I've Googled. I've read statistics and I've spoken to people who are in the know. And listen to this:

The Hardanger Plateau is the mountain region of Norway where most people go cabin-to-cabin cross-country skiing.

We're going to the Hardanger Plateau.

And that's not all.

The Easter break is high season for cabin-to-cabin cross-country skiing.

We're going to the Hardanger Plateau during *Easter break*.

And that's not all either.

We'll start our trip at Finsehytta, which was Norway's most visited tourist cabin in Norway's most popular mountain region, in the high season.

And that's *still* not all.

Easter this year will be *insane*. Everything points in that direction. There isn't a weather app in the world showing anything but huge, yellow, beaming suns in the Hardanger Plateau over the coming days. Easter is early this year (which is a sentence I've never said before but is the kind of thing mountain folk often say) and there have been abnormally large amounts of snow this year (see previous parentheses), so the weather and skiing conditions are fantastic. This is the kind of Easter people talk about, the kind of Easter that looks the way Easter looks in ads for things that are extremely healthy.

In other words, there will be *so* many people on the plateau this Easter.

A buddy I lost to nature long ago who's spent a lot of time hiking on the Hardanger Plateau actually pulled a face when I told him about our plans for the trip.

"Are you *absolutely certain* you don't want to start maybe a couple of days before the Easter break begins?" he said. "To avoid the very worst of the rush?"

And yes, I am absolutely certain. If there's one thing we don't want to avoid on this trip it's the very worst of the rush. We avoided the very worst of the rush by an extremely large margin on our previous trip. We're not planning on making that mistake again.

And we know what awaits us. My buddy isn't the only person who's emphasized just how full it gets in the most popular region and at the most popular cabins during the Easter break, especially when the weather and skiing conditions are good. Veritable hordes ski from cabin to cabin across the Hardanger Plateau, people tell us. The cabins are full to bursting. The walls bulge. People sleep in the corridors and on chairs in the fireside lounge. We've also had this confirmed by the hosts themselves. When I tried to make reservations at a couple of the cabins in advance I was told I could just forget about it. You simply have to turn up and hope for the best. Everybody who arrives at the cabin will get a place to sleep—they don't throw people out in the middle of nowhere when it's multiple degrees below freezing, after all—but nobody can count on luxuries like rooms or beds. You just have to pack your bag and assume you'll end up in a dorm or on a mattress on the floor. Or worse. The experienced cabin-to-cabin people start out at the crack of dawn and dash across the plateau to make sure they'll be the first to get to the next cabin, in time to secure the few available rooms. Then the amateur tourists come straggling along many hours later, cold and exhausted, with their lousy equipment and sunglass tans, and have to spend the night in the stove or the outhouse.

I'm kind of looking forward to this. It surprises me, but I actually am.

And listen to this: What have we done to ensure that our mountain trip will be a bit more like a New Year's Eve celebration? We've invited along the people we usually celebrate the New Year with.

Genius, right?

Most of them couldn't come, of course. They had other plans. Some of them were heading on vacation to places like, for example, abroad. A peculiar idea.

But two of our friends did want to come along. They're people we usually meet at pubs, in backyards, at festivals, at bars, or on balconies and terraces on nights that never end. They're a hair's breadth more mountain-savvy than me. Meaning that they have skis they rarely use. He's partial to good food and wine and doesn't strike me as the type to enjoy exposing himself to danger. She's positive and jolly and sociable but somewhat accident-prone. In other words, there's a small gang of us. A slightly less than averagely mountain-savvy gang in a slightly more than averagely party mood who will make sure the plateau is fuller than ever this Easter. This pleases me for several reasons.

One of those reasons is that I'm a bit worried about the Head of Documentation.

The thing is, I saw a new side of her that made me uneasy when, not so long ago, we were out on a trial cross-country ski. We thought it would be good to do this because we haven't actually been skiing together before. And besides I had to break in my new ski boots. Good footwear is, as you probably know, this and that. The end-all among other things. Besides, it would be good to find out if I still *could* ski. You see, with the exception of a roughly one-hundred-yard trip from a parking lot to a cabin, this is the first time I've skied in over thirty years. The last time I went skiing, Ronald Reagan was president, the Soviet Union existed, and Rick Astley was popular. Today, neither Ronald Reagan nor the Soviet Union exist. Rick Astley does exist, although not everybody is aware of it, and he's doing very nicely. In fact, he made it to the very top of the album charts in his homeland, the United Kingdom, as recently as 2016. The question is, of course, whether my ski technique is like the Soviet Union or Rick Astley. That's what I'm supposed to find out on our trial run in the countryside that lies just a short tram ride from downtown Oslo—a fact Oslo folk often like to boast about to people from abroad, who don't really see that there's much reason to boast about how quickly you can get out of your city, and to people from the rest of Norway, who don't see the point either, because their route to nature is generally even shorter.

Everything I'm standing and walking in, and standing and walking on is new. One aspect that is most definitely new since I last did cross-country is the ski poles. For one thing, the ski poles now weigh roughly 0.007 ounces. For another, the ski poles are now attached to your hands in a totally different way than before. In the days when I was an active skier, a pole was a pole. Now there's a complicated Velcro system that distinguishes between right and left, and has different holes for your thumbs and the rest of your fingers. And the most hellish part of it is that once you've found the right pole and the right hole and managed to attach one of the poles, you have to sort out the other pole with the sole aid of one hand that already has a ski pole firmly attached to it.

Being a positive type, I choose to see the half hour I spend on the poles as a warm-up. Then I'm ready. For my first ski in thirty years, with new narrow skis and new light poles it'll be close to impossible ever to remove.

So now the question is: The Soviet Union or Rick Astley?

Rick Astley, I find, after the first few dozen yards. I'm slightly off-balance, not quite in rhythm, a bit uncoordinated. Not unlike Rick Astley's dancing style, if you remember.

But then I feel it all coming back to me. The technique is there, the technique that, in those days more than thirty years ago, secured me several honorable second places and a teensy-weensy trophy. I find my rhythm. I let my skis do the job, as some coach once said to me long ago. I probably look like a blast from the past beside all those people skate skiing up the hills, but we're not going to the Hardanger Plateau to exercise and show off; we're going on a cross-country skiing trip. And on a cross-country skiing trip you use proper cross-country technique. Diagonal. There's a reason why it's also called "classic" style. And it's in my bones. And that feels nice. For roughly fifteen minutes. Then it starts to get monotonous and I look around for the Head of Documentation to ask how long a trip she thinks we should take.

And that's when I see it. She's standing slightly ahead of me, just outside the tracks. She's looking up at the treetops and smiling. She smiles a lot, it isn't that, just not in this particular way. It's a gentle smile, a peaceful smile. She poles a few yards farther. Then stops again, takes a picture of the treetops and smiles once more.

"Isn't this nice?" she shouts before poling onward. Middling technique, but happy. Very clearly happy.

What is it about that smile?

Is it a bit... enlightened?

A bit... born-again?

YES, I'M AFRAID OF losing her to nature. It does happen to people. And I've never seen her like this before. And, as I said, this is the first time I've ever been out skiing with her. For all I know, this may just be how she is out in nature in wintertime. If she has a blissful gaze and pious smile after a mere fifteen minutes of snow-covered treetops right outside downtown Oslo, what might happen to her after several days of dream weather and dream skiing conditions out on the plateau itself?

I take no pleasure in the fact that my technique is way better than hers. I just feel uneasy.

That's why I'm glad there will be a few of us along on this planned trip; a few of us who can bring her down to earth if she turns glassy-eyed and starts talking like Instagram. The last thing you want when you're out in the middle of the plateau dozens of miles from the nearest cabin is for your traveling companion to look you straight in the eye and declare earnestly: "Love the outdoors!"

Luckily, there will now be three familiar faces to remind her who she is and where she belongs: in bars, at festivals, on asphalt.

I know the idea is for me to let myself get swept up. I haven't forgotten that. But if the Head of Documentation becomes religious and irritating, and if her competitive instinct also runs amok in the battle to arrive first at the cabins and get the best sleeping spots, I'll have no chance of keeping up. And I'll have no desire to keep up either. If I'm going to enjoy life out in nature, then nature and I need to meet somewhere halfway. We need to find a compromise, a place where we're a bit alike, where we have fun together.

And this is what I hope our friends will help with.

I haven't told them this, but the fact is I'm hoping they'll be a bit shittier than I am at skiing. So that I'll be this mid-point between them and the Head of Documentation. That's where I want to be. My idea is that I'll be what binds them together. I'll be the group's glue. The person who tells the fastest ones to wait and keeps the slow ones' spirits up. The one with the jokes. That's how I can learn to love nature.

Incidentally, I have no reason to believe our friends are any worse than me. They've done more cross-country skiing than I have in the past few decades. But then, who hasn't? And my technique is in my bones. And I'm in decent shape. And I won a trophy. And I'm renowned for my good humor and winning smile. And I'm better prepared than they are. Didn't I plan and set up this entire trip?

Last but not least, I have all the very latest equipment. They don't. For example, I have skin skis, which are skis you don't have to wax, and that already places me one potential catastrophe ahead of the others. And I have everything else you're supposed to have too. Because, of course, after buying everything you already own prefixed by the word "hiking" in order to wander about in the mountains in the summer season, you have to buy everything you already own once again in order to wander about in the mountains on skis in the winter season, only this time prefixed by the word "ski." Ski gloves and ski shoes and ski pants and ski hats and ski sunglasses. And skis. And it isn't true that skis are just skis. There's different equipment depending on whether you want to skate ski, do classic cross-country, exercise, go ski touring, ski in loose snow, go uphill, ski at temperatures of ten degrees below freezing, ski in the sun, or ski when it's snowing.

It's hard to choose.

Not to mention that it's extremely hard to find ski equipment you'll be proud to be seen in. For it appears to have been decreed that exercise gear in general, and winter gear in particular, must be gaudy and ugly. It's yellow and bright green and pink, often all three combined. Looking at the selection in a sports store is a bit like looking at a party in the nineties, except that it isn't any fun. It's a bit the way it used to be with computer equipment only in reverse. The computer age was already well underway before it occurred to anybody that maybe it was possible to make computer equipment that wasn't clunky and beige. Apparently, nobody has yet walked into the open-plan office of a sports-equipment producer and said: "Hey folks, how about we make something nice?" Sports stores are one of the few places where I can catch myself thinking, with conviction: *What's so wrong with beige anyway?*

And I can't ask the guy in the store about this kind of thing because what on earth does he know about style? He's standing there wearing a ski hat and wraparound sunglasses indoors.

I am already the proud owner of the greenest windbreaker in Europe and I'll be taking it along on this trip too. If, on top of that, I have yellow skis, pink boots, a purple bathing cap–shaped hat, gloves in four different colors, and orange sunglasses that look as if somebody spray-painted them onto my face, I'll get bullied. Or taken away.

In the end, I manage to find a pair of skis that are black and red. Dammit—that's not bad. And a pair of ski boots that are pretty neutral. And only one color: Gray.

And this is good gear I've bought myself. In fact, it's the best equipment available for precisely the kind of trip we're taking. I know that because a guy who wears sunglasses indoors told me so. And right there, I'm way ahead of our two friends. They've simply grabbed the equipment they already own, which they probably haven't used for ages. They aren't prepared for this. Not really.

I hope they'll cause minor problems and mess-ups so that it simply isn't an option to go crazy and win competitions. We'll have to get our act together, laugh at ourselves, and stagger along at a middling pace cracking terrible jokes.

SO, OF COURSE, I'm happy when we meet the two of them at the station and I see he's dressed in tight black jeans, a city sweater, a city jacket, and Ray-Ban sunglasses that are designed to avoid a sunglasses tan when you're having a beer outdoors. She also has city sunglasses that don't look as if they were spray-painted onto her face. Otherwise, though, she looks like regular mountain folk. From 1983. She has a classic red parka that has seen a few skiing trips in its time. And she tells us how long she's had both skis and poles. Her ski equipment is, in fact, a family heirloom. The poles came from her mother. Already at this point, I've mentally christened her the "Head of Lousy Equipment." Let's shorten that to HLE for simplicity's sake.

"Ready for the trip?" I say, a bit too enthusiastically.

She nods, just as enthusiastically.

"I dreamt about avalanches the whole night," he says.

And with that, our trip has acquired its Worrier-in-Chief.

AND MAYBE HE'S RIGHT to be worried. Here are a few selected head-lines from the internet news sites the last couple of days before our departure.

"Easter Accident Fears."

"Record High Avalanche Risk in the Easter Mountains."

"Champagne Powder Snow Makes for a Dangerous Easter."

"This Year, the Easter Sunshine Is Extra Dangerous."

It is, of course, possible these are perfectly ordinary headlines that you'd find any year around Easter time and that I've simply failed to pick up on it because I don't normally spend my Easter break out in nature. I'm pretty certain the one about the dangerous Easter sunshine haunts the headlines every year. The Easter sunshine is sneaky. I heard this from the guy who was wearing sunglasses indoors too. The Easter sunshine can creep under your sun-glasses or over them or in from the side. That's why you need sunglasses that look like they've been spray-painted onto your face. You can even walk with your back to the sun and your entire face covered amid thick flurries of snow: the sun will still find its way to your face. The sun is fatal in the Easter mountains and it's out to get you. If it doesn't manage to burn up your face, it will, at any rate, steal your sight.

And that's how dangerous the Easter sunshine is *normally*. This year, as the internet said, the Easter sun is "extra dangerous."

Of course, if you're the worrying kind, this isn't the sort of thing you most need to read before your vacation.

The online newspapers also talked about a "record high" ava-lanche risk. That can't possibly be in there every year. And then, as we mountain folk like to say, there's been a lot of snow this year. And Easter is early.

I don't know what "champagne powder snow" is but if the mete-orologists have even the ghost of a sense of symbolism, it's probably something that seems tempting but if you have too much of it you'll end up staggering around then fall over and hurt yourself.

And on top of all this, in the last few days before we left, the news was almost entirely dominated by rolling updates about a viral outbreak on the Hardanger Plateau. This probably tells you quite a lot about how little happens in Norway at Easter, but still: people at the tourist cabins on the Hardanger Plateau have become infected. People have caught a stomach bug and had to be shipped out. There have been evacuations. There has been talk about the possibility of closing the cabins because of the risk of contagion.

And this is precisely where we're heading. In the sunshine. And we're going to ski from cabin to cabin.

Maybe there is cause for concern. On the other hand, I have the impression that mountain folk like it this way. Whenever I've spoken to people before this trip, it's struck me that the ones who boast the most about how fantastic the Easter mountains are also say, often in the same breath, that they are deadly dangerous. This is nature. You don't mess with nature. You have to respect nature. They like to say this sort of stuff. It makes them feel weather-beaten and wise and rugged even though they have office jobs and underfloor heating at home. You have to be prepared for all eventualities, they say. You never know what might happen out in nature. You may think it's safe but suddenly you'll be caught out by a hurricane or mauled by an elk. Our trip starts at Finse. The scenes on the ice planet Hoth in *The Empire Strikes Back* were filmed there. Maybe we'll meet beings from other galaxies. With wraparound sunglasses. Anything can happen out in nature.

It's almost as if people like us, who live in extremely modern and technological societies where we have rules for everything and most things sorted out, have a special need to convince ourselves and others that there are still things that we can't entirely control but that we nonetheless manage to tackle single-handedly without any help from society.

Nature.

The weather.

This must be why people feel proud when the town they live in sets a new record for cold or when it rains for more weeks in a row than at any previous time in recorded history. It doesn't matter, say the people who live there. We know what this is. We are prepared. We know nature. We'll get through this with rugged humor that nobody else can make head or tail of.

In a legendary Norwegian radio interview, a man was once phoned up live on air because he lived in a place where, according to the news, a record low temperature had been reached that day.

"Can you tell us what the temperature is over your way right now?" the anchorman asked.

"Well," said the man in a slow, country drawl. "It's probably around three or four degrees."

The studio went quiet.

"What—only three or four degrees below freezing?"

"Above."

"But . . . we've heard about temperatures of forty below."

The man at the other end of the line drew a breath before replying.

"Ah, yes. Well, that'll be outside, won't it?"

⛰

IT DOESN'T LOOK AS IF all the news about viruses and stomach bugs and the deadly dangerous sun and avalanche risks has made people revise their vacation plans because the train is jam-packed. The entire train, I mean, not just the seats.

It must be a totally bizarre experience for foreign tourists to arrive unprepared in Norway on any weekday during the Easter break, get on a perfectly ordinary train between Oslo and Bergen, Norway's two largest cities, and find everybody on board dressed in exercise gear. Put it like this: I'm not the one who stands out on board here in my brand new skiwear. On the other hand, the Worrier-in-Chief gets a few odd looks as he stands there in his black jeans and Ray-Bans trying to secure a pair of skis in a ski rack.

We rapidly conclude that if we're to have any hope of getting a table in the restaurant car, we need to go there right away and stay there for the entire trip. Naturally, the restaurant car is right at the other end of the train, which is extra long because it's Easter, and at Easter, everything is extra long. We battle our way through the cars, step over backpacks in the aisle, narrowly escape being skewered by ski poles and ski tips that are poking out all over the place, and arrive in one piece in the middle of the train and the war zone that is the family car.

The train has barely been going for a quarter of an hour but the family car is already well on its way to a collective breakdown. Parents with glazed expressions have already given up. I do what I always do: prick up my ears and pick up snippets of what people are saying.

"...we'll be sitting on this train for four-and-a-half hours, so..."

"I said no."

"...back here right this minute..."

"No!"

"Yes, but it isn't yours..."

"Yes, there's still a long way to go."

"NO!"

ONCE WE GET TO the restaurant car, I think we've probably put the most arduous part of our journey behind us now. Getting to the restaurant car feels like coming home. There are a few men sitting there with a lot of pockets, checking the weather forecast on their phones. Two friends in regular clothes have occupied the window spots at the best table and sit there drinking red wine and chatting, and everything about them suggests that they plan to sit drinking red wine and chatting right up until the train stops for good and they're ordered off. The friends and the Worrier-in-Chief actually nod to each other. They probably feel a sense of fellowship because they're the only ones on board in regular clothes. We take the last available four-person table and sit down just before everybody else on the train decides to take a trip to the restaurant car. They're too late. It's full here. We plan to remain here until Finse. We all order beer and train food, except for the Worrier-in-Chief, who orders wine and train food.

THINGS START OFF WELL, the way they're supposed to. We talk nonsense, which is what we do when we're together, but we talk nonsense about mountain-related things. The two worlds are in the process of coming together.

"If I were a criminal," the Head of Documentation says, "I wouldn't break into people's homes while they're on Easter vacation. I'd go to the mountains. It's much easier to take things there. Expensive things. The tourist cabins aren't locked. There are probably wildly expensive skis and ski poles stacked up outside, and ski clothes that are just as wildly expensive hanging up to dry all over the place. All you have to do is borrow a snowmobile and whizz across the plateau swiping masses of valuables along the way."

We agree that if all else in life fails, we'll start a criminal snowmobile gang. Easy money and fresh air. What's not to like?

"We'll commit crimes in the mountains," says the HLE pensively as she takes a slurp of her beer.

"We'll be mountain crimers," I say.

This is the kind of humor you can safely indulge in when you're on vacation, you're winding down, and you're in the company of good friends.

I catch myself starting to wish this train journey could last all evening and all night, and that we'll wake up with warm shoes.

But of course, that's not how it is. Reality bites. In an hour and a half we'll arrive in Finse, which is where we're getting off, and after that it'll be just us and the mountains. Our conversation takes a new turn.

"If you're swept away by an avalanche," the Worrier-in-Chief says as he studies the wine list, "you're supposed to spit and see which way your spit runs, otherwise you risk digging in the wrong direction when you're trying to dig yourself out. Bear that in mind."

He's a funny man, capable of self-insight and self-mockery, and of course he's exaggerating his fear so shamelessly for comic effect. But he does mean it a bit too. Now, for example, he thinks he's noticed that his eyes are stinging a bit from the bright sun in the Easter mountains.

"You do realize we that we *aren't* in the Easter mountains?" I say.

"But still . . ."

"We're in a railroad car."

"Yeah, yeah."

"And you're wearing sunglasses."

"I think I'm a bit sunburned too."

The Head of Documentation laughs at him. In a good way. She proposes a toast.

"I'm looking forward to this myself. I think it's going to be great fun," the Head of Documentation says. There's a dangerously born-again glint in her eyes. The HLE smiles and joins in the toast.

"I think so too," I say. "Quite honestly, how wrong can it go?"

The Worrier-in-Chief gives this some thought.

"We could get blinded by the sun so we don't see the avalanche that's heading for us and then, as we're lying buried in the snow, we could find ourselves lying upside down and discover we've caught the stomach bug."

THE ART
OF LOSING
A JAPANESE
TOURIST

**Second leg: Finse Station–Finsehytta.
Two hundred yards. On skis.**

TOURISTS OFTEN FIND it hard to deal with the fact that there's more than one facet to their travel destination. It may be as simple as there being rain in a place that's famed for sun and sandy beaches. There they stand, the tourists, in swim shorts and flip-flops, with injured looks on their faces. Tourists who head for Kenya often plan to go on safari. But spending part of their stay in a cosmopolitan city with a population of millions is one thing they've never packed for. So they find themselves sitting indoors in an air-conditioned luxury restaurant in Nairobi dressed in khaki and safari hats, and prepared for imminent attack by wild beasts.

Tourists vacationing in Norway often travel there for the nature and are prepared for a lot of extreme weather and wind here in the North. What they are not prepared for, however, is that Norway isn't *just* nature. That's why you can see foreign tourists in Norway in hiking shoes, woolly socks, and windbreakers right in the heart of one of Norway's largest cities in the middle of summer when it's 80°F and there's not a breath of wind.

The most out-of-place and helpless tourist I've ever seen, though, was dressed for carefree summer sightseeing and fine restaurants in a city setting but abruptly found himself alone, four thousand feet above sea level, in the snow.

Finse is the highest point on the train route between Oslo and Bergen. The station is marked as being 1,222 meters—or just over four thousand feet—above sea level. I suspect they placed the station in precisely that spot so that the plaque showing the altitude would look cool. Here, midway between Norway's two largest cities, you're in the proper mountains and there can be snow here even at mid-summer. This is the kind of thing tourists like, somebody probably thought. That's why the train lingers a few extra minutes at Finse Station, to give people a chance to get out and take a picture of the wild mountains and the plaque that says "1,222." And maybe also have a smoke in one of the few places in Europe where it's always way too cold to stand outside and smoke.

I've traveled a lot on this train in the past. Because for some years, my circle of friends was split neatly in two. Half of them lived in Bergen and half in Oslo. And we regularly went to visit each other to be rowdy and over-confident in each other's hometowns.

On one of these trips I shared a car with a bunch of Japanese friends who were on a trip together. The mood in the group was good. At Finse, of course, they got off the train to take a picture, like good tourists. As the train started to pull out of the station, I looked out of the window and saw a man's back. The man turned slowly and found himself standing there alone at Finse Station, dressed for summer, camera in hand, in the snow, four thousand feet above sea level, watching the train roll onward to Bergen.

The rest of the group returned to their seats in the car just in time to catch a glimpse of their buddy at the station. They discussed among themselves whether it was really possible that they'd seen what they just saw. Or at least I think that's what they discussed. Because after a while, they all looked at each other, registered that one of them was missing, and then they started laughing. They laughed and laughed. Loudly and uncontrollably. After a while, they pulled themselves together, got ahold of a conductor, and explained what had happened. After much phoning and mulling, they all reached the collective conclusion that the best thing was for their buddy to simply wait at Finse Station for the next train, which would come through in three-and-a-half hours. There's a hotel at Finse, so it's possible to spend a few hours there without dying of starvation or freezing solid. It's probably a bit boring unless you decide to take a hike, but the man wasn't really dressed for that.

Of course, I got talking to the other Japanese tourists. They told me about their plans for the rest of the trip. They'd reserved a table at a fish restaurant in Bergen that same afternoon and then they'd be heading onward, by bus or boat—I forget which. In any case, they had a whole tour of western Norway planned and a pretty packed schedule, and they laughed and laughed when they pictured how they would now go through this entire trip with their buddy hurrying close on their heels, always arriving just a bit too late to be in time for the train or the bus or the boat or the restaurant. How they laughed.

And to all of you who are thinking right now how unkind it was of these friends to laugh at their buddy, they didn't mean it. I met the whole lot of them again in Bergen later that evening, happily reunited. And they'd postponed the next leg of their trip so their abandoned buddy could join them. And they were still laughing.

IT MAKES ME GENUINELY HAPPY that we'll be starting our great ski trip at precisely the same spot where this man stood all those years ago; on the spot that should really be called "Abandoned Japanese Tourist Place" but which is actually called Finse Station. I'm filled with anticipation at the thought that it's possible to start an experience of nature with a few hours of banter and mild anxiety in a noisy restaurant car before getting off a packed train in a desolate place where Japanese tourists get abandoned.

This is where our wilderness adventure starts.

And it starts with panic. Because when you've managed to put on your outer clothes and wrestle your enormous backpack down off the overhead hat rack without causing excessive personal injury, and all you have to do is pick up your skis and poles from the baggage car on your way off the train, that's when you realize it's much more complicated than simply picking up your skis and poles on your way off the train. Because, of course, the place is packed with skis and poles. And a lot of people have similar skis. And nothing is exactly where we put it four hours ago. Because people have moved things around to make space, and probably to make sure their own skis will be easy to find when they get off. Idiots.

Still, my skis are easy to spot in the chaos, because I'm one of the tiny minority of people on board whose skis aren't yellow and pink. What's more, my skis are so new they're shiny. But now, as the train stops at the station, I realize I have no recollection of what my ski poles look like. Are they yellow? Are they green? Are they polka-dotted? Are they patterned with small gnomes? After all, I've barely seen them before.

The other people in my group are having trouble finding both skis *and* poles, and even more trouble getting them out once they've found them because the skis are fastened with straps and are also mostly tangled up together.

I sweat. I know the train spends a bit of time at the station before traveling onward. But I don't know exactly how long, just that it's roughly long enough for a Japanese tourist to lose himself in a daydream.

"We have to get off now," somebody says. I grab a pair of poles that look new and tumble off the train right behind the others, just in time to avoid a reverse-Japanese tourist situation.

There goes the train and here we stand on the platform in a mess of ski equipment. And all of us are a bit unsure what we've actually taken off the train with us.

I'm repeating myself, I'm well aware of it, but it has to be said that for an activity designed to soothe the soul, there is a surprising amount of logistics, hassle, and panic involved in outdoor living.

We calm down, do a tally, see that everything and everyone is here, and conclude that this is a good sign and that we deserve a beer.

WE DON'T HAVE TO GO all that far. In this precise area, the Finse mountains are at their finest: when you're standing on the platform at Finse Station, you are, practically speaking, also in the hotel reception. The hotel, which is, of course, called Finse 1222, is not an entirely average hotel. For example, you can't drive here by car. You can get here by train. Otherwise you have to travel by ski or on foot, or bike. Consequently, nobody in the reception area at this hotel wears ordinary clothes either. Apart from the Worrier-in-Chief, who still looks as if he's been airlifted out of downtown Oslo by helicopter and dropped in the mountains. Otherwise, everybody's in skiwear. And they're all beetroot-faced and wild-haired. We have obviously walked into the hotel just as all the guests are returning from their day's ski.

To our enormous delight, we see there's an open-air bar here. The Worrier-in-Chief and the Head of Documentation aren't just good at worrying and documenting; both are also remarkably good at finding space in places that are otherwise full. So we send them out at once and of course they manage to find the nicest corner on the jam-packed terrace, with a view of a lake that probably lies beneath all the ice, a glacier that apparently lies beneath all the snow, and people gliding along slowly on skis, faces turned to the sun. And there we sit, drinking our open-air beer with a view of nothing less than the legendary Easter mountains.

And yes, they're beautiful.

We share a table with a jolly couple from Bergen. Anybody who's ever met anyone from Bergen knows it isn't entirely unusual for people from there to be jolly. What's more, these two are bursting with stories about Finse and the Hardanger Plateau, because they've spent their Easter vacations in this neck of the woods for generations. Their parents brought them here when they were kids and they themselves have brought the next generation here. He tells stories from his youth, about the time they went to a party and took the train back to Finse in the night and had to make their way to the cabin on the crusty, icy Easter snow in patent leather shoes. Good times!

We toast one another and agree that the view is beautiful, that this Easter looks set to be fantastic, that Easter is early this year, and that there's a lot of snow. The people from Bergen confirm that many years may pass between Easters that look like this.

"It's the way you dream Easter will be."

They tell us that they're planning to take a trip around the cuckoo this morning. We nod, as if what they just said was a sentence that made any sense whatsoever. After a while it turns out that cuckoo is their pet name for the Hardanger glacier, the glacier that apparently lies right before our eyes beneath all that snow, for the simple reason that the Norwegian word for the glacier—Hardangerjøkulen—happens to sound a bit like the word for cuckoo.

We laugh a bit at them for having a pet name for a glacier. But I must say I do understand the need for abbreviations out in

Norwegian nature. It isn't just the cabins that have peculiar names here. Norwegian mountains, valleys, peaks, tops, plateaus, and lakes are often called things like Stormeaglecongresshill or Breakdevil-stanzatrout. Or they're called something or other plus "troll." Or some other being that doesn't really exist. Often in combination with a body part or a place you can live. Troll's Realm, Giant's Realm, Devil's Gateway. Troll's Wall. Troll's Tongue. Troll's Dick. That last one actually exists and is a tourist attraction that was vandalized in 2017, thereby becoming a major scandal and a news item; as a result, for a few glorious days in Norway, we got to enjoy the sight of grave-faced newscasters looking directly to camera as they discussed the sex organ of a mythical being.

But enough of that.

Since we happen to have people at our table who are thoroughly familiar with the terrain and thoroughly pleasant, we tell them about our planned route. After this beer, we're heading to the Finse-hytta tourist cabin. The Bergen couple laugh out loud and point at Finsehytta—the buildings are right over there, a couple of hundred yards away. Tomorrow we'll go to Krækkja. A well-known, classic trip to a cabin with a silly name. They've done that ski many times. It's just about sixteen miles. The male half of the couple reminisces about how his father used to take the kids on day trips from Finse to Krækkja and back again. I'm a bit concerned that the conversation is heading into boasting territory, and that the wife will follow up by telling us that in the good old days her parents used to force their kids to walk across the Hardanger Plateau on their hands before breakfast. But the man just laughs and shakes his head at the memory of his father who didn't understand the value of enjoying oneself and taking it easy on vacation.

These are our people. I like the Bergen couple. We propose a toast. We've proposed quite a few toasts today for people who are on a wilderness vacation.

How long do they think we'll take to get to Krækkja? The man looks at the sky, then the snow, then us, and says six hours. That's a bit more than I'd expected, I must admit, but I think he's exaggerated a bit because he sees us as inexperienced, lazy city slobs. Not without good reason. We've opened up about ourselves in the conversation so far. I've held forth about how I haven't been skiing in thirty years and have such brand new equipment that I'll probably end up with blisters on body parts I didn't even know I possessed. The HLE has given a lively account of how old her old and inherited equipment is. The Worrier-in-Chief has comically exaggerated his urban idiocy and told them he's already managed to suffer sunburn and a spot of snow blindness on the train journey. The Head of Documentation says her fingers are already freezing, which gives the Bergen couple license to shower us with their knowledge and tell us our gloves are way too thin.

We're good at this. This is beautiful. What we're doing here is bridge-building. We let the mountain folk laugh at us a bit. The mountain folk thaw up and let us laugh at them a bit. There's no harm in it. We're all human. We're all alike inside. This is how people grow closer to each other. It's exactly the way this trip is supposed to be. A bit more partying. A bit less in the way of revelations and things that are bigger than yourself. Nobody will go crazy, nobody will become born-again, but all of us will grow a bit fonder not just of the mountains and nature, but also of the city and each other, without any of us losing our sense of humor as a result. In brief, we will find the Third Way! The best of both worlds! City and land, hand in hand! You're my brother, you're my sister. We'll stick together. Hand in hand we stand, all across the land. A more perfect union!

Damn, that beer works fast in the thin air.

It's cold, too. Especially since we have pretty thin gloves. So we decide it's time to be on our way. To the cabin where we'll spend the first night and where, by all accounts, it will now have become even fuller since we've wasted an hour on a beer outdoors in the sunshine. It's getting toward late afternoon. The experienced guests probably checked in long ago. A lot of them probably went directly to the cabin from the train. All the rooms are sure to be taken and all the dorms will be full. People will long ago have started to roll out their sleeping bags in the porch and the bread box.

The Head of Documentation goes into reception and buys herself some thicker gloves. She's actually paying attention to the advice of experienced mountain folk.

In the meantime, I fall into conversation with a couple from Rogaland. My first impression of this Norwegian mountain region is that there are an awful lot of jolly western Norwegians here. Being a jolly western Norwegian myself, I wonder if maybe these are my kind of mountains. The people from Rogaland and I agree that this is a fantastic Easter. A dream Easter, in fact. Let's just hope we avoid this stomach bug. Ho ho.

These two also turn out to be very familiar with the area. Before they have a chance to get to know us and our story, I ask how long they think we'll take to get to Krækkja. They look at us and say four hours. I'm a bit too pleased about this.

Then we hear what sounds like an army marching toward us. It turns out to be a group of similar-looking men with noisy shoes. Apparently they're snowkiters. The Head of Documentation is the one who realizes that's what they are. She understands stuff like that.

It's hard to understand what on earth a bunch of snowkiters have been up to today since there isn't a breath of wind. But they've been outdoors, there's no doubt about that. They're in their early sixties, with reverse-panda tans on their faces, are studiously unshaven, and are extremely scared of dying. They ooze financial comfort, look like Men's Wearhouse models on vacation, and appear destined to exercise their way to arrhythmia over the course of the current season.

The mood in the room changes. These are not our people. This is not where we belong. We shall join the hikers. The cabin-to-cabin folk. The people who ski in classic style.

"Mom, Mom, the snowkiters are here!" I say after the Head of Documentation has worked out who they are. Our whole group snickers.

So far, I must say I like this trip a lot better than the last one.

THE FIRST FALL of the trip is spectacular and happens right outside the hotel, on flat terrain, before we've even started moving. Almost before we've got our skis on, in fact. Out of respect for personal privacy, I will name no names.

Then we take our first step on our first leg across the plateau: the two hundred yards from Abandoned Japanese Tourist Place to Finsehytta, where it is probably so jam-packed by now that guests are poking up out of the chimney.

After roughly twelve yards, the HLE realizes that one of her poles is broken. Not the whole pole, but the fastening on the strap, which has snapped. So the strap can't be used. And the pole is slightly bent. It may have happened during the fall.

The eighties gave us many things that have proven to be of lasting value. Rick Astley I've already mentioned. The portable Mac is from the eighties. And the first solo album by Stan Ridgway of Wall of Voodoo from 1986 is holding up surprisingly well. But ski poles from this era clearly last only about thirty years.

WE'RE A BIT TIPSY. The Worrier-in-Chief is sunburned and partially snow blind. The HLE has started to live up to her name and has already broken a ski pole.

We've gone thirty yards. We're on our way to our first night's lodgings. There are fifty miles of the planned trip still to go.

WHERE OLD FOOD GOES TO DIE

"I'M AFRAID WE'RE absolutely full. No beds left."

"Yes. We pretty much assumed that."

"It's Easter, you see. A lot of people want to ski about in the mountains."

"Yes. I realize it's hectic here at Easter."

"Especially when it's as lovely as this year."

"Yes, it's fantastic in the mountains when it's like this."

"It's the way you dream Easter will be."

"Right?"

"Easter is early this year, you know."

"I know. And there's been a lot of snow too."

"It's nice out on the plateau now."

"Yes, it's very nice out on the plateau now."

"Let's just hope we avoid the stomach bug. Ho ho."

"Ho ho."

"But anyway. Of course we'll find a spot for you here. We don't turn people away. How many of you are there?"

"Four."

"Oh dear. Let's see . . . No, the corridor's full too."

"I see."

"And all the furniture and the floor in the fireside lounge."

"Goodness."

"And it's full in the storeroom."

"Storeroom?"

"And in the chimney."

"Heavens."

"How do you feel about sleeping on your feet?"

NOT REALLY. This is the conversation that actually took place at reception when we arrived at Finsehytta:

"HI. THERE ARE FOUR OF US."

"Right, you can have Room 18. It's a four-person room."

"Okay."

I CAN'T LIE: it's disappointing. Aren't these supposed to be the jam-packed Easter mountains? And isn't this supposed to be the most popular cabin in the country too? And yet we get a four-person room, just like that, without any effort, even though we came stumbling in tipsily with broken ski poles at 5:30 PM, which is getting on for bed-time at cabins like this based on my recollections of our previous trip.

Can't you rely on anything anybody says about cabins and moun-tains? Does this mean it's not true that there are masses of people in the mountains at Easter either? Not even here, in one of the world's most popular Norwegian tourist cabins, in the world's most popular Norwegian mountain region, during the world's most fantastic Eas-ter break? Of course I've already learned that a lot of cheating and exaggeration goes on out in nature but my most important source of information about the Easter mountains is a friend of mine. True enough, he's a friend I lost to nature, but even so, I honestly believed I could trust him. Or at least that he was smart enough to realize he'd be found out. This friend has also told me it takes four hours to ski from Finse to Krækkja. Can't I rely on that either? The jolly Bergen couple at the bar said six hours. I ask a guy who happens to be standing in reception studying a map.

"Seven hours. Maybe a bit longer. It depends."

Right.

⚠

THE RECEPTION DESK is occupied by a young woman whose main aim in life appears to be to express herself exclusively in single-word sentences. She looks down and the conversation between us feels slightly like an interrogation.

"Member?"

"Yes." (I assume she's asking whether I'm a member of this trekking association and not, for example, of the Ornithological Society.)

"Four?"

"Yes." (I think I'm telling her how many of us there are, but I'm far from certain.)

"Dinner?"

"Yes, please."

"Half past six."

... (This isn't a question, so I don't answer here.)

"Breakfast?"

"Yes, please."

"Sandwiches?"

"Huh?" (This is the wrong answer. I can see that myself.)

"Sandwiches?"

"Uh...no?"

"For tomorrow." (Here she makes an exception, using two words and rolling her eyes for clarity's sake. I appreciate that.)

"Uh...yes, please."

"How many slices?" (She's becoming positively chatty now.)

"Uh..." (This means: "Are we supposed to decide *now* how many sandwiches we'll want to make early tomorrow morning?")

"Hm?" (Yes, that's clearly what this means.)

"Uh...Four? Per person?"

"Thermos?"

"Uh..." (Thermos?! I see they're selling thermoses in reception, which also serves as a bar and a store. But what does she mean? Is she planning to go through all the objects here in the cabin and ask if I'm interested? Thermos? Woolen underwear? Souvenir undershirt? Sunglasses? Sunblock? Snowmobile? Dog?)

An older man in thermal underwear takes pity on me and tells me that what she's trying to ask is whether we want to fill our thermos flasks tomorrow morning before we leave on our trip. Ah! Of course that's what she means. What else could she possibly mean? If a person in reception anyplace else asked "Coffee?" I'd never assume it was a pleasant offer to which I could respond, "Yes, please" or "No, thank you," would I? Of course, I'd assume that what she's asking is whether I plan to help myself to coffee in thirteen hours' time.

"Yes, please. Two thermoses."

I THINK I'VE ANSWERED all the questions correctly and we go to Room 18. We don't get a key because they don't go in for that kind of thing at these cabins. If anybody wants to come into our room and bother us in the middle of the night we'll just have to put up with it. We're free people out in free nature.

Our room looks ever so slightly like a jail cell, except that everything is made of wood. There are bunk beds in there, and a discussion about upper or lower bunk beds starts up at once. We're back at summer camp again and everybody thinks it's pretty good fun. There's some snickering in the group. It helps to be a bit tipsy at summer camp. Bear that in mind, kids.

A lighthearted conversation about snoring ensues as we change for dinner. The Worrier-in-Chief is still wearing his tight jeans and now puts a crumpled shirt on over the top of his T-shirt. At a tourist cabin, this is roughly equivalent to wearing a tux. The rest of us change into sweatpants.

THERE'S A LINE outside the dining room. A Dutch family stands looking at the line. *We've traveled all the way here to vacation in one of the world's richest countries,* they're probably thinking, *and what do we see? People dressed in old underwear standing in line for food.*

Why are people actually standing in lines? Everybody's been assigned a seat at the table. Isn't there room for all of them? Isn't there enough food to go around? Is it first come, first served? Will some people have to eat on the floor? Or *off* the floor? I don't know.

And I still don't know because when we come in, all the long tables are marked with room numbers. Everybody is told where they're supposed to be sitting. There was no reason to stand in line. There is order in the ranks here. We sit at long wooden tables. Some soup already stands on our table when we sit down. I'm about to dig in, or whatever it is you do with soup.

But first there's a speech!

Our hosts introduce dinner. A delightful woman who looks as if she was born and bred outdoors tells us about the menu. We'll be eating lasagna. Then she tells us a little bit about the virus that is ravaging not this cabin—luckily, ho ho!—but other cabins on the Hardanger Plateau. She tells us how important it is for us all to wash our hands thoroughly and often. She talks about this for a long time as the soup grows cold, and she says it only in Norwegian. Down at the far end of the table, the Dutch family sits smiling uncertainly, probably wondering when people start eating in this country. And of course they haven't understood a word of what the hostess has said so they'll undoubtedly infect the entire plateau with viruses.

The woman to my left leans toward me and says: "This is exactly like being at summer camp."

Well whaddaya know! There's a like-minded soul at our table!

Soon we'll be able to start eating but first two girls are supposed to tell us about the program for children this evening and tomorrow. When they're finished, they direct a stern gaze straight at us and say, "No entry for adults." It's possible we may have been gigglier than we'd realized.

Then it's time for food!

But first they just have to explain the line system. For people who don't care much for walking in lines in the mountains, mountain folk are remarkably keen on standing in line when they're indoors. Table 1 will serve themselves first, we are told, and then it's Table 2's turn. Most of us can probably guess the rest but to be on the safe side, we are also informed that after that it will be Table 3's turn.

As we slurp down the remains of the ice-cold soup, we laugh a bit more about summer camp with our neighbor. She's Norwegian but lives in Australia. And she tells us she's here to celebrate her fortieth birthday.

And everything indicates that she is alone.

Of course, you want to ask: Have you traveled halfway around the world to celebrate your fortieth birthday alone among strangers in a cabin on the Hardanger Plateau?

Of course you want to ask.

Of course you're also a bit scared and a bit inclined to switch tables.

But that isn't allowed!

Of course you also want to excuse yourself, run away, and lock yourself into your room.

But that isn't possible!

Fortunately it turns out that she's waiting for some friends who are arriving tomorrow. So she's not totally insane. Just a bit.

She lives in Perth, in the far west of Australia. Not to boast or anything but I've actually been to Perth. And Perth is quite simply the opposite of Finse. Perth is a relatively modern city of two million inhabitants with an annual average temperature of 68°F. If you drive some way out of the city, you hit the desert. Maybe Perth is where you have to go in order to long for Finse?

The Worrier-in-Chief is naturally worried that we might not get anything to drink with our food. A smart-ass wearing underclothes tells us that if you want to drink anything other than water you have to bring it with you from the bar when you come in.

A half-hour information bulletin and nobody informed us about that.

We drink water and laugh even more about summer camps. The HLE shares the story of her ski pole that was destroyed twelve yards into the trip. We open up about ourselves. We're good at that.

When at last it's our turn to serve ourselves, we get a scolding. Well, maybe not a scolding. A mild reproof. We stand in line, as you do, and a mature woman in aged underwear says to us in a way that makes it crystal clear she doesn't mean it:

"By all means, do go ahead of me."

We don't understand why and protest. That's the kind of people we are. "No, no, no, of course we won't go ahead of you."

"But you must, it *is* your turn. We just didn't know when you were going to serve yourselves..."

So it turns out that we've taken too long. We at Table 2 have spent a bit too much time chatting away about Perth and wine, while Table 3 sat waiting their turn and getting grumpy. In the end, Table 3 gave up and went to serve themselves, like lawless rebels. And that's precisely when we from Table 2 got up to serve ourselves.

Chaos at summer camp!

We realize the woman will insist that we go first even though we don't deserve to. So we smile our famous smiles and apologize.

And then comes the evening's next great experience.

▲

EARLIER, I DISCUSSED the fact that traveling in Norwegian nature is like traveling to a Norway that no longer exists; a monocultural, harmonious society where you live at one with nature as if it were the most self-evident thing in the world. I've also mentioned that at these cabins out in nature, you are mostly served traditional Nordic meat. Seen from that perspective, it is shockingly exotic of them to serve lasagna here.

But!

As it turns out, they serve the lasagna with ... potatoes!

Talk about a trip back in time. This is something I've only ever heard about. In historical terms, it isn't especially long since Norway was the way people up in the mountains pretend it still is. You need go back no further than the sixties to find a Norway that was almost free of exotic food.

When pasta made its big breakthrough in Norway, people were still so unfamiliar with other food cultures that many believed dinner could not be considered dinner unless potatoes were involved. Which is why in those early days, to ensure a smooth and gentle transition to the new era, pasta was often served with boiled potatoes.

I've heard of this. I have never experienced it, until now.

And that's not all. There's a dessert table too. A dessert table! This dinner is just like being at a christening or an eightieth birthday party hosted by a tradition-steeped family from rural Norway. People eat dessert and engage in strained conversations at long tables as everybody wonders whether they can get their hands on any alcohol.

And on the dessert table—*ta-ta-ta-daaaa!*—there's aspic. For any readers below the age of 150, I should explain that aspic is a quivering, transparent lump of savory jello containing chunks of, say, vegetables and prawns. Aspic was party food and a cold buffet favorite for many a decade until the dish was invited to a confirmation in the eighties and never returned.

But here it stands, quivering.

We all find it extremely exciting.

"Heavens," the Head of Documentation says to the HLE. "This cabin is full of dishes from the days when your ski poles were made."

THE MOST BEAUTIFUL THING about this is that several of the guests here are too young to have any relationship to phenomena like pasta with potatoes or prawns in aspic. For them, this must be *actually* exotic.

But when you look across the dining hall, which *is* a hall even though it's called a room, the most striking thing is that nobody else appears to think that any of what people do here is either strange or exotic. Everything people do here is the most natural thing in the world.

Sitting at sparsely decked long tables eating food from another era? Perfectly natural.

Being forty-odd years old and getting scolded for chatting too long at the table? That's the way it's supposed to be.

Eating dinner in the company of strangers without getting properly dressed? What's so peculiar about that?

In fact at one of the tables, a young man now sits eating pasta with potatoes. His upper body is clad in a sheer mesh tank top and nothing else. This is an outfit you can only get away with in two kinds of establishment: tourist cabins and gay nightclubs.

OVER DINNER, BY THE WAY, the Worrier-in-Chief incurs an injury. During a moderately gallant attempt to pass something to our friend from Perth (water, probably), he manages to burn himself on the candle that is the sole decorative item on the table.

"The group has suffered its first injury," I say. But the Worrier-in-Chief reminds us that this isn't the first injury, since he is already snow blind and sunburned. Besides, he's still struggling a bit with a pub injury he suffered two days before our departure.

"And my ski pole is injured too," the HLE reminds us.

The group is doing well.

△

AFTER OUR INVOLUNTARILY alcohol-free dinner in the relatively warm dining hall, we feel like having a cold beer. So does everybody else at the cabin, which means there's nothing to do but stand in line again. I do believe people at tourist cabins try to stand in line as much as they possibly can for the shortest possible time while they're indoors to maximize the contrast with the sense of freedom they enjoy out in nature.

△

IF YOU'RE ONE OF THOSE PEOPLE who generally hangs out at cabins in the winter season, you probably won't realize this, but those of us who are just passing through notice very quickly that it can be difficult to keep up with the conversation. In this respect, unpretentious mountain life has a great deal in common with the most pretentious academic language there is. Academics may turn up to conferences entitled "Criminal Liminality and Pan-Cultural Autonomy in Regressive Dance—Facts or Plenary?" without understanding why people laugh at them.

But mountain talk can be just as exclusive. You have to concentrate to keep up with the one-word interrogation at check-in, for example, or you risk ending up with an empty thermos and a new dog.

If you've learned to read maps, you have to learn everything all over again before you can do a cabin-to-cabin trip. I received a quick introduction to symbol use from a man with a lot of pockets when I bought a map of the Hardanger Plateau before our trip.

"Staffed cabins are marked with a filled red square. And then there are the no-service cabins: a transparent square outlined in red. Self-service cabins: half-red square. No-service cabins that have to be reserved: red square with diagonal hatching. Then there are various private cabins. Marked with red or blue outlines and diagonal hatching or color fill. Any questions so far?"

"Will I be tested on this?"

"No. No-service cabins with food: pink triangle. No-service cabins without food: purple rhombus with an outline. Cabins where you can't use the master key: parallelogram with stars. Cabins you have to dig out and break into: crowbar."

THAT'S THE WAY IT IS out in nature. One of nature's foremost tasks is to ensure that you will at all times feel slightly stupid. To be a first-time traveler in the mountains is also to have a constant sense that there's something you ought to know that is already known to everybody else. Now, for example, it's finally my turn at the bar. I notice that the sole beer brand they're serving is called Finse. Being a pleasant, interested type, I ask if the beer is actually brewed here.

"Yes," says the woman behind the bar. "Edvard's the one who makes it."

Everybody else here knows who Edvard is.

I leave the bar, filled with shame.

THE TRIP FROM the bar to our table is thirteen yards. On my way back, the beer grows warm. Because it's 140°F in the fireside lounge.

IT'S FULL HERE but when I left the dining hall, it struck me how quiet it was. I didn't give it any more thought. But now I understand why it's so quiet here. People simply can't be bothered to talk. Nuclear families stare apathetically at board games. They can barely bring themselves to lift up their Ludo pieces. And there are a couple of things we need to remember here: These people may not be wearing all that many clothes, but what they are wearing is probably made of wool. And most of them have spent hours outside skiing in the sun. They were baked before they got there. And here in the lounge the fire has been stoked to hellish heat levels.

It's almost as if the hosts want to get the guests to go to bed as early as possible. First of all they're supposed to wear themselves out completely with seven or eight hours of skiing, then you stuff them with lasagna, potatoes, and aspic, and then you turn the heating up to the max.

People don't hold out for long then.

We're tired too. And we haven't even been out skiing today so we think it's a bit embarrassing that we aren't managing to contribute to life in the lounge. The HLE has something to do at least, so she's keeping active. She bought herself a new strap from reception, and we play handymen, provisionally fixing her pole. After that we have no strength left. We had been thinking of drinking red wine, because that's what you're supposed to do at cabins, but we can't face anything as heavy as that. Besides, it's such a long way to the bar. We decide to play Yahtzee but can only be bothered with forced Yahtzee. Free-scoring Yahtzee is too demanding. I don't know who wins. Or whether we finish the game.

The evening is becoming more and more like a competition to hold out as long as possible in a sauna. People scowl at each other beneath leaden eyelids. A bunch of young guys in a corner sneak over to open the door a crack. I think this is the first time a door has been opened here since the days when aspic was contemporary. We notice what's happening and switch to a table nearer the open door. It helps. A bit.

More and more people give in and admit defeat. Chins sink onto chests. People suddenly slap their thighs and say, "Right, then . . ." At one table after another, board games are packed away. By half past nine, the fireside lounge is a quarter full. The bunch of young guys who opened the door give up too. As does our Australian friend, who I suspect has long been sleeping behind that book of hers. By just after ten, we're sitting almost alone again. The one-word girls have started clearing up.

They are winning.

We can't let ourselves be defeated! This isn't who we are! We are people who stay up all night. And we're here to make mountain life seem more like a New Year's Eve celebration. We can't start our vacation by spending a few hours on a train and then going to bed at half past ten.

"We must have a cigarillo!" the Head of Documentation says.

The Worrier-in-Chief looks scared.

"I haven't brought any with me," he says shamefacedly.

This requires an explanation, I can see that. Of course we wouldn't normally indulge in an activity as imprudent as smoking, but on big, festive occasions we do sometimes have ourselves a cigarillo. And the Worrier-in-Chief is normally the one who has that kind of thing with him. Because as well as being worried, he's also very good at parties.

"We have some," I say. "After all, we are the tour guides."

It's as if his worries finally loosen their grip.

"Is that so?"

The Head of Documentation shows him the packet.

"Heavens," says the Worrier-in-Chief. "I didn't think this was . . . that kind of a trip."

IT IS THAT KIND of a trip.

There's an ashtray outside the cabin, so this has happened before, but it still feels delightfully criminal to stand smoking a cigarillo outside a cabin on the plateau in subzero temperatures way after normal bedtime.

In fact it feels very good to be outside. Maybe that's why they batten down the hatches and hurl a ton of wood on the fire in there? So we'll appreciate the cold more?

It's quiet. The Head of Documentation looks dreamily up at the sky and again I grow slightly uneasy about what might happen to her when we set off skiing tomorrow.

My unease is interrupted by a door opening. All four of us instinctively hide our smokes behind our backs. A man sticks his head out.

"Can you see the northern lights?" he asks.

Of course, that's the only possible reason why anybody would be standing outside in the middle of the night.

⚠

BACK INSIDE THE CABIN everything is empty and closed. The time is 10:59 PM. There's nothing for it but to find our room and hope that there isn't already somebody sleeping in there.

⚠

EVERYBODY AGREES IT'LL BE NICE to have a ski trip tomorrow. The air will be nice. The subzero temperatures will be nice. The HLE's ski pole is fixed. We'll get plenty of sleep and be bursting with energy.

We call it a day.

"Good night," I say.

"Good night," says the Head of Documentation.

"Good night," says the HLE.

"Remember that it's lethal to charge your cellphone at night," says the Worrier-in-Chief.

THE NEXT DAY, our first day of skiing, starts with lines. At breakfast there's one line for hot food, another for bread, and another for coffee. I think. I'm not sure, because I was constantly in the wrong line. In fact, I don't think I've made so many mistakes in such a short time since a math test in eighth grade.

And maybe I'd already made other mistakes before I even got to breakfast. This is possible.

The day got off to a lively start with the Head of Documentation playing "The Happy Wanderer" to the group on her phone to get us in the right mood.

The HLE is excited and ready to go. The Worrier-in-Chief had a bad sleep but is in good spirits. He reminds us that we must remember to put on sunblock. And then comes the part where it's possible to go wrong: What should you wear? Or rather, how much should you wear? Because it's cold. We're talking at least 5°F. The Head of Documentation presents the idea that we should wear two sets of underwear, a thought that hasn't even occurred to me. Is that necessary? In addition to ski pants and fleece jackets and windbreakers? And two hats, maybe? And this is a choice you can't afford to regret. You don't start changing your underwear on the middle of the Hardanger Plateau at 5°F.

We opt for two layers. And an extra layer of sunblock on our faces. The important thing when you're going out to enjoy nature is to do everything you can to keep nature at bay.

And then we wash our hands.

⬧

AT THE BREAKFAST TABLE sits a woman with a map who looks mountain-savvy. She's from Bergen and is waiting for some friends who'll be arriving on the train, and then they'll ski together to Krækkja. Even though it's tempting fate because the virus has apparently struck there. Ho ho! We agree that it's a fantastic Easter and that Easter is early this year and that there's a lot of snow. And she estimates that the trip to Krækkja takes five or six hours. She thinks she'll wax with blue, but maybe green. The wax discussion continues around the table. The two men on the other side of us are unsure whether to use blue or green. This is something I don't have to relate to. I think the others look down on me a bit because I don't have to wax my skis. Wax-free skin skis are the skiing equivalent of pop stars lip-synching to playback.

⛰

WHILE THE OTHERS are waxing their skis, I talk to the skiers in reception about how long the trip to Krækkja takes. Some say five hours, some seven. I check the internet. On one page about organized tours across the Hardanger Plateau, it says the trip from Finse to Krækkja takes between eight and nine hours.

There's only one thing to do.

Leave.

But first, I wash my hands.

LIQUOR AND CIGARILLOS

Third leg: Finse–Krækkja. Sixteen miles. On skis.
Estimated time: between four and nine hours;
it depends a lot on whom you ask.
Questions we expect to find answers to during the trip:

- Will the Head of Documentation
  become religious?

- Are we wearing enough clothes?

- Are we wearing too many clothes?

- Will the Worrier-in-Chief survive the trip?

- Will the HLE's provisionally repaired
  ski pole survive the trip?

- And last but not least: How long does
  it really take to get to Krækkja?

AFTER TEN MINUTES, the HLE's ski pole breaks. The other ski pole, I mean. And exactly the same thing happens this time too. The fastening on the strap, which has made itself useful for thirty-odd years, snaps. There's a lot to be said about ski-pole production in the eighties, but it looks at least as if the quality is pretty consistent from one pole to another.

△

AFTER FIFTEEN MINUTES, the pole is fixed. The Head of Documentation has taken on the role of the group's MacGyver. What's more, the HLE has shown a great deal of foresight, buying several straps at the cabin before our departure. The straps are tested. They actually seem solid.

Fifteen-and-a-half miles of today's leg remain.

△

AFTER TWENTY-FIVE MINUTES, the last ten of them in silence, the Head of Documentation has started to look a bit impatient and asks whether we're happy with the pace. Okay, a bit worried that her competitive instinct is now stirring. But she is, at any rate, showing no signs of her quasi-religiousness from the trial run. Maybe because it is in fact overcast, no matter what the weather forecasts claim.

△

AFTER THIRTY MINUTES, the Worrier-in-Chief announces he has a blister. Naturally enough this comes as no surprise to him.

△

AFTER THIRTY-FIVE MINUTES, the HLE is lagging slightly behind. I think the explanation for this is that her ski poles, though solidly repaired, are pretty short. She did inherit them from her mother after all. Maybe her mother is simply shorter than her. Or maybe ski poles, like so much else in life, have been getting bigger over the years. I seem to remember from my days as an active cross-country skier that ski poles were supposed to reach your armpits. But the poles I have now are much longer than that. And this is the way poles are supposed to be now. Or at least that's what the guy at the sports store told me, the one who wore sunglasses indoors. And I do feel as if these poles get you moving faster. If you have to bend down as you pole, everything takes more time.

AFTER THREE-QUARTERS OF AN HOUR, we take a coffee and chocolate break. We do an evaluation. The Worrier-in-Chief has spotted signs of a second blister, but that is as expected. The HLE is breathing a bit quicker than the rest of us, but smiles broadly and says she's in good spirits despite her poles. But obviously there's a fine line between good spirits and bravery, and between bravery and hysteria, especially when you're poling twice as often per minute as everybody else but still going slower. The Head of Documentation seems a bit impatient maybe, but otherwise neither she nor I have any shortcomings or defects, in body, mind, or equipment. But we are, after all, experienced mountain folk.

And this is what we're good at: Standing around drinking coffee and shooting the breeze. And again, we manage to shoot the breeze about mountains. We discuss what we would call the various mountain formations we see if we had a chance to christen them. And we abide strictly by the rule that if a mountain formation is to become famous and popular, its name must combine a creature that doesn't exist with a body part or a place where you can live.

"Troll's Spleen."

"Unicorn's Ankle."

"Santa's Thigh."

"Goblin's Diaphragm."

"Vampire's Vagina."

"Banshee's Buttocks."

"Wizard's Wiener."

"God's Gallbladder."

"Werewolf's Studio."

"Satan's Basement Apartment."

We don't get any further than that. Because it's cold. And over-cast. If you stand still much longer than five minutes, you really do start to freeze.

But I'm glad we managed to shoot the breeze a bit. Because if we're going to shoot the breeze, we'll have to do it while we're outdoors. At the cabins, there's so much else on the agenda in the evenings. There's talk to be had of hours and minutes and miles and conditions and routes. And after that you're supposed to talk about how early Easter is this year, and how fantastic it is when it's like this. And then you're supposed to ask if there's a single place in the world where you'd rather be right now. And then you're not supposed to answer: the Seychelles. I'm speaking from experience here. And then you're supposed to discuss waxing and skin skis. And then you're supposed to crack manly jokes about avalanche risks and viral out-breaks. And all this you have to get through before going to bed at half past ten at the latest. So it goes without saying that there isn't a lot of time left over for aimless banter.

What's more, if we're going to get any talking done while we're out skiing, it has to happen while we're taking a break and standing still. Because—and I can't remember anybody mentioning this in among all the praise of the great meditative silence and the won-derful conversations in the mountains—cross-country skiing is terribly noisy. Skis against snow make a noise. Poles in snow make a noise. Windproof clothing makes a quite insane amount of noise. What's more, there's often only one set of tracks, so we can't ski alongside each other but have to go one behind the other instead, and we have our hats pulled down well over our ears, some of us even have two hats pulled down well over our ears, and we have scarves covering our mouths against the cold. So, as you'll under-stand, we don't get to solve many of the world's problems while we're skiing.

And I haven't even mentioned the noisiest thing of all: hoods. If your hood is up, you can just forget about conversation. In fact you should be happy just to escape without hearing damage. A hood, which you often put up if it's cold or windy, has the property of gathering all the sound up behind your head and then sending it back past your ears again. It's like walking in a wind tunnel. It's like *being* a wind tunnel.

If we want to hear each other as we ski, we have to shout. And the Worrier-in-Chief has refused to let us to do that because loud noises can trigger avalanches.

AFTER AN HOUR, we start to wonder where all the people are. We've been skiing quite alone the whole way. We are diligently following the marked tracks. We respect nature. There are tracks here, after all. Not exactly groomed tracks like the ones you see at the Winter Olympics, but there are tracks here nonetheless. Somebody has skied here before us. But where are they? Maybe they've already reached Kraekkja? Maybe a hundred people set off in a mass start at seven o'clock in the morning? We didn't leave until half past ten. I'm guessing people view that as the afternoon here in the mountains. Maybe we're simply the very last skiers? But no. The woman we met at breakfast was also heading for Kraekkja today and she had to wait for her friends who were arriving by train. They must be behind us. But we can't see them anywhere. Nor can we see many people in front of us—and we can see a long way. There are a few scattered dots up ahead but there are long gaps between them. Hordes skiing from cabin to cabin, my ass.

AFTER ONE HOUR AND TEN MINUTES, I decide to focus on my technique. Let the skis do the job. I get into it, sense that I've found my rhythm, that I'm whizzing across the Hardanger Plateau. I feel my body working. After five minutes, I also feel that I'm no longer interested in this.

AFTER ONE-AND-A-QUARTER HOURS, I try to remember "Do-Re-Mi." With a bit of effort, I manage the entire chorus. So both brain and body are functioning.

△

AFTER ONE-AND-A-HALF HOURS it breaks up. We take a short breather, enjoy the sun, and do an evaluation. The Worrier-in-Chief has acquired another blister, on his Achilles tendon, as expected. The HLE is on good form. Very good form, in fact. She's still breathing more hectically than the rest of us, and her ski poles haven't grown since last time, but the straps that the Head of Documentation MacGyvered are working like a dream. And the HLE has that happy, enlightened smile on her face as she stands squinting at the sun. Maybe she's the one who'll turn religious? Then again, there's a fine line between religious and hysterical.

△

AFTER ONE HOUR AND THIRTY-FIVE MINUTES, we start to freeze and have to carry on.

△

AFTER ONE HOUR AND FORTY-FIVE MINUTES, we still haven't got going. The HLE can't get her skis back on. Because ski equipment is astonishingly ill-designed to function in the snow and cold. If a tiny bit of ice or snow gets into the binding or under your shoe, you're in trouble. And if your equipment is also older than Ed Sheeran you'll obviously end up standing around for a quarter of an hour before you can get your skis on and continue on your way.

And if you end up standing around for quarter of an hour, you really have time to feel it. And all of us do now. The HLE thinks, with good reason, that she's holding up the entire group, and her efforts to get her skis on are becoming less and less constructive by the second. Her smile is on the point of crossing the line. My hands are horribly cold but I know from experience that this will pass as soon as I get moving again. It's incredible how quickly you acquire experience in the mountains. Those two, whose equipment isn't as new, also notice that their fingers are freezing. What's more, their glasses are fogging up, and their hats are doing nothing whatsoever to keep out the cold.

The one doing the most thinking now is the Head of Documentation. This is the point when anything could happen. Those of us who know her well, and who aren't too busy putting on a pair of skis or unable to see anything because of fogged-up glasses, we (I mean me, in case you missed it) see that behind that forehead and beneath those two hats, a ferocious internal battle is raging between the impatient Head of Documentation with her competitive instinct, and the responsible and sociable Head of Documentation who takes care of her friends and keeps people together. The impatient one looks at the dots far ahead on the tracks, which are maybe a bit closer than a while back. She sneaks a discreet glance at her watch. She takes deep breaths. She probably feels a bit like saying the group should split up, so that those of us whose equipment and fitness levels permit it can dash on ahead and reach Krækkja in time to drink beer by the cabin wall and laugh at the ones who arrive late.

She looks at the group: a man with frost in his beard, a hat that's far too thin, and big-city glasses he can't see through; a woman with an ever-more hysterical smile who is kicking a couple of yuppie-era skis; and a guy in a green jacket who's just standing there like an idiot gawking at her forehead.

She sees what anybody else would see: these people need help.

Her competitive instinct has lost. We can kiss that quasi-religiousness goodbye.

The Head of Documentation takes charge. And she'll probably continue to do so as long as anybody in the group is in trouble. And I'm now starting to feel certain that, in this group, somebody will always be in trouble.

Since the Head of Documentation and I are extremely well prepared (or were totally screwed over by the man who wore sunglasses indoors, that's also a possibility), we have two of almost everything with us. The Head of Documentation issues commands, in a tentatively friendly fashion. Hats and gloves are redistributed. Everybody is a bit better equipped than they were before the break, and we're starting to get ready to carry on.

And by now, the HLE has also managed to get her skis on.

AFTER TWO MINUTES AND FIVE SECONDS I can feel my fingers again. And now the terrain has flattened out after sloping gently upward all the way from the cabin. And the sun is warming. And the plateau is endless. The Head of Documentation smiles. The HLE smiles. The Worrier-in-Chief smiles. And it's beautiful. Of course it's beautiful.

And...?

And here's the thing I have most trouble explaining to those friends I've lost to nature. When they start telling me about a trip they think will convince me, which is what they do—they're missionaries after all—they often say stuff like: "You'd manage that trip," or "You'd cope," or "It isn't all that difficult."

But that isn't the point. Of course I'll manage it if I must.

I just think it's a bit...boring.

I think it's pretty okay. And "okay" is a word that only exists in the vocabulary of proper mountain folk in its ironic variant. When proper mountain folk write on social media that it's "pretty okay" out on the Hardanger Plateau right now, they always do so with evident irony because anybody who has a heart and a brain and sees the picture you've posted of ski tracks in the sunshine will understand that right now it's *totally fucking fantastic* on the plateau, and of course everybody is envious of you because you're there and not stuck in an office or a bar that's full of human noise. When I say it's pretty okay on the Hardanger Plateau now, I actually mean just that: that it's pretty okay.

And I know that means I ought to feel less worthy or realize that I'm not trying hard enough, that I'm a slave to our hectic age. And that you just have to carry on for five more minutes, then another half hour, and then an hour on top of that, and that's when you start to feel that the monotony is the actual point of it; it's the fact of repeating the same movements through a landscape that is also repeating itself; the repetition itself is what fills you with peace. This is the meditative aspect of skiing everybody talks about.

Or is it just New Age bullshit?

Or maybe it's just the story of the world's best fish soup all over again.[2] If you've spent your vacation heading in a straight line at a moderate pace in a monotonous landscape for days on end, it goes against the grain to admit that it was quite simply boring. So you have to call it something else. Meditation, for example, which is at least both boring and comic.

Of course it generally goes against the grain to admit that our experiences are merely okay or perfectly ordinary. This must be why we're so hung up on finding the authentic when we travel as well, on finding places no other tourists have found. Or no—that isn't what we want. Because finding places without tourists is, after all, very simple, no matter where you are in the world. All you have to do is head for an industrial district. What we dream of is, of course, discovering the tourist cliché—but entirely free of tourists. We want to turn a corner in a French city and find a square nobody else has seen where all the women look like Amélie and all the men have baggy pants and baguettes, and nobody has any intention of speaking English as long as they live, and all the food is based on recipes involving

---

[2] If you've already forgotten this story, see "Indoor Mountains and Popcorn on the Campfire."

various combinations of full-fat butter, locally sourced foie gras, and malodorous artisan cheese, and there are no other tourists. That's the tourist dream. That's why the internet is crammed with tourists giving other tourists tips about places where they can avoid tourists.

▲

AFTER JUST OVER TWO HOURS, we take a break. It's important to take breaks. And there's nothing we have to be in time for anyway. Not even the Head of Documentation has to be in time for anything now.

I bring up what I've been thinking about. That it's just a bit boring to ski like this, hour after hour, no matter how beautiful it is. The HLE doesn't agree; she thinks it's fantastic. So she's back on track, then. Or else on the point of tipping over into hysteria. The Worrier-in-Chief doesn't have time to get bored because he has so much to think about.

"We must ask people about this," says the Head of Documentation. The responsible side has won out and now she's also taking responsibility for my research work.

"If we meet any people," I say.

"We will. If not before, then at the cabin this evening. There must be other people who think this is boring even though everybody just goes on about how fantastic it is."

Then she takes responsibility for the rest of the trip and draws up a plan so we'll all have something to aim for despite the boredom, despite the fact that we'll never get to overtake anybody, despite blisters and ancient ski poles, despite it all. We agree to eat lunch once we've been going for two-and-a-half hours. We'll lean against a rock and eat our pack lunches and feel the sun on our face and look like Instagram. And after three-and-a-half hours we shall have—ta-da!—liquor and cigarillos!

Of course the Head of Documentation has her hip flask with her. She's a hair's breadth away from having to change her name to Head of Everything.

I don't know whether it's the prospect of liquor and cigarillos or the sun that does it, but things go pretty well after this. I smile as I ski. Of course it helps a lot that we've started to meet a few people now. We still haven't seen any sign of the hordes we've heard of, but now and then a couple, or a small family, or a woman with wraparound sunglasses passes by and says "Hi!" Because that's what you're supposed to do in the mountains. This greeting helps define us as the kind of people we want to be. When Americans make small talk, or when the British say thank you and sorry about all sorts of things, it's easy for us to think of this as superficial; but when Norwegians out in nature stretch to uttering a two-letter word to strangers when we're so far from civilization that it'll probably be an hour before we next have to speak to anybody—that's authentic. This is why it's considered a betrayal of the flock not to say "Hi!" and not to stop and have a chat when somebody invites you to. I catch myself taking a certain pleasure in stopping people who obviously don't want to stop at all because it'll ruin their flow. And their meditation. Oh, come on—I have to find something to make the trip more fun, too.

And I honestly think this business of strangers stopping to talk to each other is one of the more likeable aspects of life out in nature. There should be a lot more of this in our everyday lives. So we speak to most of the people we meet. Everybody agrees that it's fantastic when Easter is like this and that this is what life's all about and that Easter is early and that there's lots of snow and we've waxed with green or blue or have skin skis and they work perfectly well even though you don't get all that much glide in these conditions. And we ask whether they know how far it is to Krækkja. Everybody replies in miles, which doesn't help us a hell of a lot since we don't have a speedometer so we can't work out how many miles an hour we're skiing. But generally speaking, it has to be said that it's farther to Krækkja than we think. Every time.

AFTER ALMOST TWO-AND-A-HALF HOURS, we've apparently reached the spot where people eat lunch. Or the time when people eat lunch. At any rate, we see groups of people taking a break around and about. Since these groups seem to have taken all the best spots, we carry on a bit farther until we find our own spot.

AFTER TWO HOURS AND THIRTY-FIVE MINUTES, we've taken off our backpacks and skis and poles and taken out our pack lunches and thermoses and realized we've probably found the coldest spot on the Hardanger Plateau to eat lunch. We have to wolf down our food and get moving again while we still have fingers to eat with.

But first the HLE just has to get her skis back on again.

After two hours and fifty minutes we're on our way again.

AFTER TWO HOURS AND FIFTY-FIVE MINUTES we meet a woman towing a heavy sled skiing along at a brisk pace. She tells us she's training to cross Greenland on skis. Okay. She skis several hours a day with the sled. That's how she's spending her Easter vacation. The Head of Documentation does as we agreed and asks her if she doesn't think it's a bit boring just skiing along like that with this sled. She doesn't. She thinks it's fantastic. And what a nice Easter. There's no better place to be when it's like this. Green. But blue might have been better. More than six miles to go. And then she continues on her way. Because her breaks can't be too long, you see.

She looks perfectly normal. She could be a teacher or an insurance underwriter. She could work in a daycare center or a communications agency, serve in a kiosk or play violin. She must have a home and a social life and go about in her hometown like a normal human being. You can't tell by looking at her. But she spends her spare time preparing to cross the world's largest island on skis.

I've sometimes thought that living in Norway is a bit like living in the old East Germany, only with nature playing the role of the Stasi, the state police force. You're watched the whole time; there's always somebody keeping an eye on you. The people of nature are everywhere. And you never know who they are, so you're never entirely safe. They may be friends. Neighbors. It is impossible to know.

A few years back, I met a musician with a gentle disposition and sensitive fingers. Interested in theater, music, art. In short, a man with all the distinguishing characteristics of people who have focused on anything but physical exercise in their youth; who have, from an early age, cultivated indoor interests that make you different, proficient, and pale, and ensure that you don't make very many friends until you meet like-minded souls on some course of higher education for nerds in your twenties. I'd known him for a pretty long time when he suddenly mentioned in passing one day as he sorted through some sheet music that he had just been on a guys' trip to the Alps, where he'd gone downhill skiing.

You never know who they are!

You may think it's safe to poke fun at outdoor folk, but no! Anybody at all could belong to Nature's Stasi.

If I've understood the essence of doctor-patient confidentiality correctly, I'm allowed to tell you about my physician. It's only when it's the other way around that it's not okay. At any rate: A while back somebody told me they thought this doctor, who's been my doctor for many years, had been a talented skater in his youth. "I just can't see that," I laughed, because I just couldn't see that. You see, my doctor doesn't look like a skater. Or any kind of athlete whatsoever. That goes a long way toward explaining why I like him. He's jolly and chatty and rather short and always has one button too many unbuttoned on his shirt. He looks like the kind of guy who belongs in a sidewalk bar in the Canary Islands, a satisfied smile on his face and a slightly unsophisticated drink in his hand. A man who's often had a very pink nose. But I became curious so I Googled him. And that's how I found out that my doctor had indeed been a skater in his earlier life. And he was pretty good too. What's more, he made it into the Guinness Book of Records for cycling 1,242 miles without sleeping. He has also cycled around the world in eighty days and skied across Greenland, and to the South Pole with hundred-year-old equipment. Naturally this affected my relationship with the man. I no longer go to him and complain that I'm feeling a bit under the weather.

You never know who they are. The people of nature are everywhere. It could be that tipsy lard-ass at the back of the bar. It could be that listless librarian who looks as if she hasn't seen a ray of sun since the nineties. It could be that fellow in white face makeup wearing a leather jacket with a skull and crossbones on the back.

It could be anybody at all. And they're watching you.

△

AFTER JUST OVER THREE HOURS, it starts to go downhill in earnest. The terrain, I mean. After a while, it starts to become downright steepish. We agree that once we get to the bottom of this steep hill, we'll have liquor and cigarillos. Then we set off. It goes pretty fast. Right at the bottom of the hill there's a big hole where people have fallen over earlier. The Worrier-in-Chief falls over there. The rest of us manage the hill, just. No people or ski poles come to harm.

This time we've found exactly the right place for a break. The sun is warm here. And we have a view of all the people falling over on the hill, as well as all the people who really messed up by starting out in the opposite direction, so now they have to go *up* this hill.

We smear ourselves with sunblock. We've done that during all our breaks.

And then we stand there, with a total SPF of 300 on our faces, sending around the hip flask and smoking cigarillos. It isn't so bad.

The Worrier-in-Chief grins and starts talking about all the things we'll do when we get there. Drink beer by the cabin wall, of course, then after dinner we'll read and drink red wine and play Yahtzee. We'll live cabin life to the full.

It's *fatal* to start talking about getting there.

A woman skis past, stares at us for slightly too long, and says "Hi" in an accusatory tone before starting on the uphill stretch. Stasi for sure.

To save time and prevent any freezing of fingers, I've stopped removing my skis when we take a break. A man in skis but without poles who goes just outside the tracks to take a leak in loose snow may not look elegant but he certainly improves the good humor of the group. That's my contribution.

AFTER ROUGHLY FOUR HOURS, we get it into our heads that we'll soon be there. It's a bit unclear why we believe that. It may be because somebody told us the trip takes four hours. But somebody else said nine. It may also be that the positive atmosphere created by the liquor-and-cigarillo break has made us immune to reality. But I think the real reason is that a woman we met a little while back told us there was a pretty steep hill, after which it was just over three more miles to Krækkja. And we did actually whizz down a pretty steep hill just before our break.

We ski across an ice-covered lake and are pretty sure that the cabin is at the other end of the lake.

AFTER FOUR-AND-A-QUARTER HOURS, we realize that the cabin can hardly be at the end of the lake. What *is* at the end of the lake, however, is a steep hill. We agree among ourselves that once we get to the top, we're sure to see the cabin. But first we have to get to the top. And the hill goes straight up. I notice that my dancing-injured knee isn't all that keen on herringboning up the hill. So I go up sideways.

Each of us chooses our technique, and each of us loses a little bit of our good humor with every step.

And this is where the Head of Documentation combines her sense of responsibility with her competitive instinct, deciding to become the best person in these mountains at keeping up the group's spirits. She leads us upward, ten steps at a time. "One! Two! Three!" she shouts. It would be totally infuriating if I weren't a bit too bored to be bothered by it.

Halfway up the hill, we meet some people with a sled heading down. The Worrier-in-Chief asks if there's a cabin up there. They say no.

AFTER FOUR-AND-A-HALF HOURS, we're at the top of the hill and it looks exactly the same as the rest of the plateau. And there's no cabin in sight.

After four-and-three-quarter hours, one of us hints that maybe the hill the woman mentioned was the one we just went *up*, not the hill we whizzed *down* before the cigarillo break. If so, there are still three miles left. We all agree that no, that can't be right. The group is in denial.

AFTER FIVE HOURS, the mood starts to turn sour. The blisters aren't diminishing and the Worrier-in-Chief is no longer the only one reporting this kind of problem. Both the Head of Documentation and the HLE are observing the same tendencies. And sunglasses are fogging up. The plateau still looks like a plateau. And it's clouded over again.

AFTER FIVE HOURS AND TWENTY MINUTES, cursing occurs. We think we've seen the cabin several times but each time it's turned out to be a rock or just more plateau. We haven't met or seen any people for ages. Heaven knows where the legendary hordes of the Hardanger Plateau are when you need them. Is there a quarter of an hour to go? Three hours? Nobody knows. We try to find the cabin on our cell-phone GPS. The phone tells us the cabin doesn't exist. The computer says no.

"Maybe the cabin really doesn't exist?" I say. Nobody finds it funny.

AFTER FIVE-AND-A-HALF HOURS we reach the critical point, the point where you're forced to make a tough decision. And that's what we do. We decide to embrace the gravity of the situation and take an extra liquor-and-cigarillo break.

Here, at least, it's possible to have an open-air cigarillo without people giving you dirty looks. But of course, as we're standing there in the middle of the tracks smoking and drinking, *that's* when somebody turns up, for the first time in an eternity. And of course he looks like a man who was born, bred, and confirmed in a film promoting the outdoor life. And of course we have to talk to him.

He mostly looks confused when he works out what we're doing. But he is at least able to tell us that we don't have far to go. Half an hour max, he says. From the top of the hill at the end of the lake, it's supposed to be just under four miles to the cabin. In other words, that *was* the hill the woman meant.

Then the man heads straight out of the marked track, right into the loose snow and vanishes. He's sure to be taking the shortest route to Stasi headquarters to report that the rumors are true: four middle-aged people, two with lousy glasses and one with extremely short poles, are going around smoking cigarillos on the Hardanger Plateau.

AFTER ALMOST SIX HOURS, we still haven't seen any sign of the cabin. Suddenly, we're overtaken by a man on skis being pulled along by three dogs, which must certainly count as cheating. He stops to talk a bit. It's fantastic when Easter is like this, in case you're wondering. The Seychelles? Pah! The Seychelles can go jump in a lake along with all the South Sea Islands. Let's just hope we don't catch the virus. Ho ho! Blue actually. Right around the bend.

"Have you skied far today?" we ask.

"Oh no," he says. "Only from Finse."

▲

BUT HE CLAIMED that the cabin was right around the bend.

So we round the bend.

And there, at the bottom of a little hill, is the cabin.

▲

AFTER SIX HOURS, an ice-cold lunch, two cigarillo breaks, an inner struggle by the Head of Documentation, four or five apparently huge blisters, two broken ski poles, and certain technical problems involving skis and sunglasses, we have got there. We took exactly as long as the jolly Bergen man at the bar told us we would. You should always listen to jolly Bergen men at bars.

Krækkja does exist.

IMAGINARY WILDERNESS

OF COURSE I'VE done my prep and have read up on Krækkja. I haven't found any explanation for its silly name but I have found out that Krækkja is a historic site in several respects. It was the first tourist cabin on the Hardanger Plateau. The oldest building dates back to 1878. Moreover, ruined settlements right next to the cabin show that people have lived here for several thousand years. And when you go inside and see the man standing in reception, it's easy to believe that he, himself, may have stood in this reception for several thousand years. The entire man exudes bizarre life wisdom and ancient anecdotes as he stands there with his unkempt hair, sly smile, stooped back, and impenetrable facial hair. He looks like a man who does things at his own pace and in his own way, and who could burst out into inscrutable words of wisdom about nature at any moment. Because, of course, we believe that people who spend a lot of time in nature possess a special wisdom. That's why we often share stories about harmonious and rather naked people of nature we've seen on TV, who have sixty-eight different words for running water but no word for war.

What will this man say when we ask to be checked in?

"The trees don't grow on rock when the melting snow drowns the owl"?

"One rodent in the marsh does not a springtime make"?

"The mountain holdeth not back if hope falleth in vain"?

"Ah, so you made it in the end?" is his opening gambit. And I love it. I have a soft spot for anybody who makes a bit more of an effort than "Hi," or "Welcome," even though—or perhaps especially if—they are catty. He likes us. And he probably doesn't like just anybody. I think it's because we're not in a hurry. We're so happy to have got here at last that we're not in a rush to do anything anymore. We laugh and make small talk with him. We express enthusiasm for the local beer brand he has in the refrigerator. All this probably helps, as the line behind us lengthens.

The man cracks a joke about the local beer and tells us a story from the sixties about somebody who was in a bit too much of a hurry. This fellow, he says, came panting into the cabin. He was barely able to speak. He'd taken two-and-a-half hours from Finse. "What's the record?" he spat out. "What's the record?!" Then he ordered a wort beer, which he guzzled down before throwing up, sleeping around the clock, and being sent home again.

I feel as if we did exactly the right thing by taking six hours. Maybe we should have taken longer.

There's a wooden sculpture standing on the floor that looks like the man in reception. I have so many questions, but the line is simply too long now, so it'll have to wait. Besides, it'll be dinnertime any moment now.

WE HAVE A FOUR-PERSON ROOM this time too, but at least we're directed to a cabin away from the main building, a cabin that must surely be older and more ramshackle. I bet it's the one from 1878. But it could also be the one that's several thousand years old. It's difficult to tell because you can barely see the cabin. It's completely buried in snow. A bunch of people sit and drink beer on what I had, until now, believed to be the ground. I now see that they're actually sitting on the cabin roof. I recognize a couple of them from the fireside sauna lounge at Finse yesterday. They look more awake now. They're toasting each other. Lucky devils. They've probably got a place at the second sitting for dinner. We won't have time to sit on the cabin roof drinking beer. We've been assigned the first sitting in a quarter of an hour. And if you get there too late, I reckon you have to go to bed without any dinner.

Somebody has simply dug a passage in the snow down to the cabin door. This really is tremendously exotic. We'll practically be living in an igloo. Which is run by a thousand-year-old man who tells good stories and keeps a wooden version of himself standing in reception. This is probably where our wilderness adventure will really begin.

There isn't a toilet in our cabin either. Living the dream.

We drink a toast with local beer we've brought with us from reception and do a swift evaluation as we fish out our sweatpants. We agree that sixteen miles is too far, that blisters hurt, that there actually is some point to these glasses that are spray-painted onto your face, that it's perfectly possible to get bored on a ski trip, and that the Worrier-in-Chief will have red wine with dinner.

A LOT OF THINGS are the same at these cabins. There are questions about thermoses at check-in. People stand quite unnecessarily in line to be let into the dining hall. We sit at long wooden tables with beetroot-faced strangers. A lot is similar. And that's when you also learn to be more appreciative of the few differences that do exist. For example the acoustics in the dining hall at Krækkja, which are quite unique. When it's full in the dining hall, it's extremely difficult to catch what's being said at the other end of the table. What's more, they've employed a cheerful, obliging waitress who not only stands at the end of the table, which makes it difficult for her to hear what's being said, but also proves to be the only Swedish waitress in the world who doesn't understand a single word of Norwegian. People try and try. People shout. And to speak English to a person from the neighboring country would, of course, be a failure of Nordic cooperation. A twelve-year-old comes close to admitting defeat and saying yes please to a bottle of wine after trying to ask for soda in five different ways.

We're sharing a table with a tiny little mountain-savvy family. The man beside me has spent generations going from cabin to cabin on the Hardanger Plateau. And now he's brought his teenage daughter with him. If he's been dragged from cabin to cabin on the Hardanger Plateau in his youth, he's damned if the next generation is going to get off any easier.

The Head of Documentation is quick on the uptake. After a few introductory pleasantries about the day's trip, she asks straight out whether they don't find it boring to ski for hours on end.

They don't. Or at any rate, he doesn't. His daughter simply shrugs, but of course if your dad's in the Stasi, you can't really speak freely.

The issue of blisters comes up, as it often does at the dinner table. Yes, indeed, apparently he does get blisters, but it's nothing to complain about. It's part of the trip.

Some way into the conversation, he tells a beautiful little tale of bonding in the mountains. He tells us that he and his daughter take turns motivating each other while they're out in the mountains.

"But if you have to motivate each other," says the Head of Documentation, who's in top form, "you must actually think it can get a bit boring now and then? Or difficult? If it was totally fantastic, you wouldn't need any motivating, would you?"

This is so obviously true that silence falls around the table. Or at our end at least. At the other end of the table they may be bellowing but it's impossible for us to know with these acoustics.

Our neighbor admits that he hasn't given this enough thought.

Seriously? You've spent generations going from cabin to cabin in the mountains and not once have you thought the thought: *Right now it's a bit boring?* Or, *That blister is actually a bit irritating?* Or, *I could really do without all this snow up in my face?*

Another couple at the table pick up on the mildly confrontational tone of our conversation. Let's call them Per and Kari, because those are the kind of classic Norwegian names people seem to have here.

"And yet here we sit, the whole lot of us!" Per laughs at us, making a toast. I'm a bit unsure if he's being catty or is trying to smooth things over. Or if he just wants to toast the people sitting at his table. For what it's worth, I'm a fan of all three options.

The Worrier-in-Chief tries to distract attention by ordering more wine for the table. The Swedish waitress nods and smiles and returns with a cucumber.

Of course the atmosphere picks up again quickly. You don't linger long on unpleasant questions in the mountains. And in fact I think our neighbor found it slightly interesting to have to think about why he actually goes wandering about here on the plateau, and why he's never thought about it before. I think he's approaching an existential crisis.

Next Easter they'll probably go to the Seychelles.

AFTER A WHILE, the Worrier-in-Chief grows uneasy. He thinks we—or at least some of us—need to leave now if we're going to get ourselves a good table in the fireside lounge afterward. The people of nature may have six thousand words for sleet and may be able to tell what the weather will be like in two weeks' time by looking at a tree trunk, but we have with us a man whose instinct for precisely when you need to leave to secure a good table is sound as a bell.

That's what's so good about knowing people who do more than wander around in nature. They often have several qualities. The Worrier-in-Chief, for example, is both scared of avalanches and fond of red wine. In addition to having this intuition, which assures us the best table in the fireside lounge. In the middle of the room. Like a kind of power hub. The Head of Documentation is (as you well know, reader, for you are familiar with her now) both fond of winning and good at taking responsibility, both irritatingly positive and extremely impatient. And she's also confrontational enough to ask questions the somewhat conflict-averse author would rather not ask himself at the dinner table at Krækkja.

And the HLE! Not only has she proven particularly good at maintaining her humor for six hours despite short and broken ski poles, but she's also good at drawing and capable of coming up with an idea like this:

We will map our injuries.

The HLE sits down at the power-hub table and sketches all four members of the group. Simple but recognizable. Then she draws in the injuries we have sustained on the trip so far, color-coded to indicate when in the trip the injuries occurred. And all of the injuries will be included. Sun-related injuries. Damage to our equipment. Blisters.

I get off lightest. She draws a mark on my right knee to indicate that I set off my old dancing injury again when I herringboned up the hill today. And then she points out that my nose is sunburned. Which is pretty impressive considering I used SPF 1000.

The Head of Documentation has a couple of blisters on one of her feet but is otherwise fit as a fiddle. The HLE is coping well physically despite the inevitable blisters. On the other hand, there are several places marked on her sunglasses and ski poles.

The sketch of the Worrier-in-Chief looks absolutely dreadful.

OTHER PEOPLE AT OUR TABLE are watching. Our dinnertime neighbor has come and sat at our table. So he probably does like us really. And if that isn't Per and Kari sitting over by the window. And behind us sits the woman we met over breakfast at Finse, now reunited with her friends. This is like a family.

But then I have to go and ruin the atmosphere a bit by reminding the others that according to our planned route, we're supposed to ski just as far tomorrow as we did today. The Worrier-in-Chief rubs his blisters and reminds us how we agreed just now that maybe twelve miles was a kind of limit for us. There's another cabin that's closer by but is still on the way to where we're going. I've always kept this cabin in reserve as a Plan B although I haven't made too big a deal out of it. The cabin is called Tuva, which is cute, it being a girl's name. We agree we're in no condition to work out how far away it is from the map. And that we'll have to ask the receptionist. After all, he has been running lodgings here since the 1800s, so he should know.

As if on cue, he appears in the fireside lounge. He scans the room and comes over to our table. He knows who his people are. Before we're able to ask him anything he tells us, entirely unprompted, a fair number of stories about the Norwegian philosopher and environmentalist Arne Næss, who had a private cabin on Hallingskarvet, which is the mountain we can see from the window. Apart from that, he tells us it's twelve miles to Tuva and that the trip is easier and less hilly than the trip from Finse to Krækkja. Our neighbor doesn't think it's as far as twelve miles. More like ten miles. Maybe eleven.

Here we go again. Can they never make their minds up?

And there's probably somebody out there now who's dying to point out that you can't really say exactly how far it is from one point in wintertime nature to another because the tracks aren't always in exactly the same places. It depends on conditions and how deep the snow is and avalanche risks and the time of year and probably a whole lot else. In short, it depends on nature. And by the way, the Inuit have six thousand words for snow and not a single one for irritating smart-ass.

▲

IT'S EASY FOR US to decide to go to Tuva tomorrow. Our mood picks up even more after that. We drink wine and exchange toasts with our new friends at the neighboring table. We arrange a quiz for everybody at our table and it goes surprisingly well. And just when the evening is becoming the evening that proves outdoor life can be like New Year's Eve, at the precise moment when I'm starting to look forward to waking up tomorrow morning and putting on warm shoes—that's when two things happen.

The first thing to happen is that a new person arrives at the cabin. Where in the world she has come from is of course the question on everybody's lips. It's late and it's dark and has been that way for a long time. Naturally she sits at our table—who wouldn't? And she tells us she arrived in Finse on the afternoon train and then she skied from Finse to Krækkja. Alone. In the dark. It took her three-and-a-half hours.

She looks perfectly normal.

You never know who they are.

▲

THE OTHER THING to happen, of course, is that the place shuts down. And at Krækkja, they really shut down. At 11:00 PM on the dot, they switch off the power.

▲

AND THEN THERE'S nothing to do but go to bed. And then you can't get to sleep because you hadn't been planning to go to bed. And it's ice cold because it's -4°F outside and we're staying in a cabin that's more snow than cabin, and the heating is switched off.

And then you end up lying there thinking. And then you think that you shouldn't be bothered by things like this. It's *supposed* to be cold. It's part of the trip. It's cold, you get blisters, it hurts, there's an abrupt change in the weather. You never know what awaits you. You have to be prepared for every eventuality. Nature is capricious.

And maybe you have to go for a leak in the middle of the night. That means you have to go outside. It's -4°F. And dark. And maybe there's a guy standing out there in the darkness with peculiar facial hair carving a wooden figure of himself with an ax. So what? We can cope. We're prepared for the fact that in nature anything at all can happen at any moment.

AT THE SAME TIME, though, life at these cabins is very routine. You're swaddled in safety. Here, there are absolutely no surprises. You know what you'll be asked about in reception when you arrive. Everybody dresses the same. You get your food at a fixed time. And you know roughly what food you'll get. And you go to bed at the same time every night. The only variation in the interior is the age of the wood. Everybody talks about the same things. It takes nothing at all to knock the people of nature entirely off balance. Mandatory neckties at dinner would, for example, be enough. Or mandatory clothing of any kind, for that matter. In fact, all it takes to spread terror through the cabin is one innocent question about whether it might be boring to go hiking. Yes, of course, it livens things up to have a dyed-in-the-wool eccentric in reception, but other than that, there's minimal sign of any variation. In here, a secure framework shelters like-minded people who all talk about the same things.

But out there! On the other side of the wall! That's where Nature is. And she can be lethal. And out there we can get by on our own, thank you very much.

Here's another similarity between religion and the outdoor life. If you really want to get a telling-off on the internet, all you have to do, as we know, is say something about religion. Saying something about outdoor life achieves roughly the same outcome, at least in Norway, and at least if you cautiously suggest making nature safer and more accessible and less dangerous to be out in.

Just don't.

▲

TRY GOOGLING "safeguards + some well-known mountain desti-nation or another" and just wait for the outpouring of bile. In the mountains, you're supposed to get by on your own. Anything else contradicts the very principle of the thing. When I was preparing for this trip, I strayed into an internet discussion where somebody cautiously asked: "Am I the only one who thinks it's peculiar that there aren't any safeguards at [insert well-known Norwegian moun-tain destination]?"

Here are some of the answers this person received:

"You can't make the whole of nature safe."

"If you can't cope with nature stick to the park."

"If people don't understand it's dangerous and that they have to take care, then I don't know…"

"You spend time in nature at your own risk."

"It would be unnecessary interference with nature."

"If you don't like heights don't go there."

"If people are so stupid they don't realize they have to be careful up there, then tough luck."

But that's precisely what everybody obviously doesn't realize. You don't need to have spent much of your life on social media to grasp that there are people who will happily have themselves filmed dan-gling off a precipice by one hand. But they're probably the ones who fall into the category of "stupid people—tough luck." Or let's tell it like it is: foreign tourists. Who don't have it in their bones the way we do. We have an innate respect for unspoiled nature, a respect you lack if you grow up in silly places like abroad.

Here are a couple more quotations from the same conversation.

"It's the hallmark of Norway that we have so much wild, unspoiled nature, which you have to treat with respect."

"We'd be better off handing out the mountain code in all the different languages at border crossings and airports."

Right. We have to teach other people how things are. Because we're the ones who know how to get by in wild, unspoiled nature. We, who have lived our entire lives in the world's most socially democratic, most thoroughly organized, and safest society but who like to spend our weekends taking pictures of ourselves in places without guardrails.

One of the few times Queen Sonja of Norway has had a telling-off from the people of nature was when she had the misfortune to suggest that it would be nice if nature could be more accessible for disabled people too. The queen doesn't come in for a lot of telling-off in general—she is the queen after all—but it is especially rare for her to get a telling-off from the people of nature. Because she's one of them. She's often out in nature, often on foot, and is, of course, an honorary member of the Norwegian Trekking Association. For her eightieth birthday, she received a statue from the association that depicts the queen in hiking shoes, sitting slightly awkwardly on a rock with an old backpack beside her; a statue that would be seen as lèse-majesté in most monarchies, but has been given pride of place right beside the castle in Norway, because this statue shows that the queen is one of us even if she is interested in modern art.

BUT IN MAY 2017, the queen went too far. At the opening of a new cable car, she was quoted as saying that we should have "a lot more" cable cars in the country so that people who have difficulty walking can also have a chance to experience our beautiful nature. You may well think that was an uncontroversial, well-meaning, and politically correct statement.

Far from it.

A spokesperson for Friends of the Earth Norway thought this sounded "terrifying" and went on to say: "The joy of Norway's simple outdoor culture comes from traveling on foot." That's a wee bit disrespectful to all those people who *can't* travel on foot—the very people the queen was talking about in the first place—but that can't be helped. The trekking association said something along the same lines when they commented on the queen's bombshell: "Norway has a very strong tradition of outdoor life of which we should be proud. It's about experiencing nature under your own steam."

Okay. We get it now. If you can't walk there yourself, you can just forget it. No arms, no cake. And if you don't understand without being told that nature can be dangerous even when it's a tourist attraction, then it's just your tough luck if you plunge two thousand feet to your death.

Because we are people of nature here in the North.

Not all the time, of course. Not in our everyday life. Not at work, or school, or daycare, or on the street. There, we want—nay, expect—society to look after us and make sure everything is safe. And not just when we're at home either. We may be far from home, on the other side of the planet, where we've traveled to find ourselves and liberate ourselves from society's demands. And if we happen to screw up while we're there, we count on society coming and getting us out.

But specifically in nature, that's where we want to cling to the illusion of total freedom. That's where we want society and civilization to keep away. Not too far away, though. We want them to be there as well, in case anything goes wrong, but preferably not in such a way that we can see them. And certainly not in such a way that they show up in our photos.

And if civilization offers us help, we want to have the option of wiping the sweat from our brow, stroking our beard, and saying: "No thanks, I'll get by on my own."

And that brings us back to this idea that only in nature are we free and ourselves. That nature is where we are the way we really are, at our best.

This is why you can get away with saying things in discussions about nature that you can't get away with in any other circumstances. Or at least not without seeming like an irresponsible person or an asshole or indeed an irresponsible asshole.

During the winter of 2017, there was discussion in Norway about introducing mandatory helmets at ski resorts. In a radio item about the issue, people at a ski slope were interviewed. One of the many who considered mandatory helmets a good idea thought it probably wouldn't work. "Some people don't want to ski in a helmet. That's just the way it is."

You couldn't use an argument like that in any other discussions about safety.

"Some people like to drive past daycare centers at 120 miles an hour. That's just the way it is."

"Some people like to knock back a bottle of liquor before sitting behind the controls of a passenger plane. That's just the way it is."

And while we're on the subject of drunkenness: In Norway, people are strictly prohibited from driving drunk in civilized areas. But it's sort of allowed out in nature. If you're in a boat, you have the right to be a little bit drunk. Because you're free then, out in the archipelago. So society can just shut its trap. In Norway, the blood alcohol limit for drivers is 0.02. At sea, the limit is 0.08, which means you can drink just the amount it takes to reach the level where it gets tricky to judge the amount it takes to reach precisely that level. Most Norwegians think the blood alcohol limits should be just as low on sea as on land. But then again most Norwegians don't own boats, so they don't know what they're talking about. And any attempts to introduce a ban on driving over the limit at sea are ritually and predictably seen as an attack on—that's right—the freedom of the boat folk.

Because when rock or water comes into the picture, or hills and snow, different rules apply. We want to be free then. And we can get by on our own thank you very much. Back off, nanny state!

In one of the many books marking jubilees of the Norwegian Trekking Association, there's an interview with a man who lives at and runs one of these cabins in the mountains. He shall remain anonymous. In the interview he says: "Why dream when I'm living the life everybody else dreams of?"

There's a picture of him in the book. He isn't an old man. And yet he's already stopped dreaming. It's actually sad. But if I can manage to set aside all sympathy for the man—and I most certainly can manage to do that—the question remains: What sort of a statement is that?! And who else could get away with saying that sort of stuff?

A pop idol or a reality TV star? They'd be seen as assholes.

Who else? An auditor? A surgeon? A teacher? A minister? A prime minister? A president?

No. No. No. No. No. No.

All for different reasons, but no.

It's nice that you're happy up there in your little cabin. But presuming that other people dream of being happy in the same way as you? That just goes to show that fresh air can inflate your ego.

Stop dreaming? That's what we call stagnation. Not out in nature, though. Because that's where we are the way everybody really wants to be.

This is probably also why the idea of luxury hotels in the mountains never took off as much as the planners believed it would in the last millennium. Free people don't stay at hotels. Free people must have their own individual cabin. *With* hotel standards.

And if anybody ever suggests from time to time that it may not be feasible for everybody to have their own private cabin, which stands empty most of the year, or that the way we currently use nature is contributing to the destruction of that very same nature, it's the national equivalent of sitting at the long table at Krækkja on Easter break and asking if it isn't actually pretty boring to go cross-country skiing.

THIS IS THE KIND OF STUFF you may think about in sub-freezing temperatures at Krækkja cabin. And this is the way you may poke fun at people who are so busy feeling free in nature that they won't even admit they need help when they actually do.

It's easy.

But then one day, suddenly, you're there yourself, in a situation where you have to choose.

And this is exactly what happens to us the following day. Somewhere between Krækkja and Tuva. Out in the middle of nowhere.

The accident has happened and now we must show who we are, what we're made of, which side we're on, whether we're for us or against us, what all this mockery of the people of nature is actually worth when push comes to shove, when there's something at stake.

Because now we're there ourselves. We can choose the way of the wilderness folk, or we can give in. We can get by on our own or ask for help from civilization. Now is when we'll show what we are.

Man or mouse?

MAN OR MOUSE?

Fourth leg: Krækkja–Tuva.
On skis. Sixteen miles, maybe.

UNTIL THE CRISIS HITS, this day is a ball.

True, we wake up in a room that's freezing cold and many of us have slept poorly, but the previous day and the red wine and the decision to revise our route have left us lighthearted and in excellent form. There is optimism in the group. There is much humming of "The Happy Wanderer." I'm so extremely cold that in a moment of confusion I become convinced it must be warmer outside. Let's get out of here! Quickly! The Worrier-in-Chief cautiously reminds us that we have to ski almost as far today as yesterday, and these blisters are only going to get bigger and more painful. But that doesn't make an impact. We tape and plaster ourselves and put our clothes on and go to the breakfast room and for once we don't stand in the wrong line—we're on a roll—and we thank everybody for the previous evening and we're all friends and we know what to do with the thermoses and we pack our pack lunches and the man in reception thanks us for our visit and tells us that the wooden sculpture of him was made by a local chainsaw sculptor and will soon be placed in a more central spot. And we leave and find the right track almost at once and today the weather is just the way it's meant to be and Easter looks like Easter in the ads and the sun is baking and we're in the flow and it's flat and we take pictures and we look great and the HLE's ski poles are holding up and it's almost as if they've grown longer overnight and after a while we cross a highway and we take fun pictures of ourselves with asphalt beneath our feet and we know that no matter who we choose to listen to, we have now, by crossing the road, already put roughly a third of the day's trip behind us, and didn't that go quickly? And on the other side of the road, there are groomed tracks, like at the Winter Olympics! And we speed onward and we see private cabins everywhere on this side and there are a lot more people on the tracks on this side and they ski faster and they have more expensive clothes and more expensive equipment and they're in too much of a hurry to say "Hi!" because they have to put a certain number of miles behind them before getting back to their cabin and making interesting, locally sourced, hand-pressed food for the occupants of their cabin before going to bed early enough to be rested enough to go and put more miles behind them tomorrow too and one way or another there's an awful lot they have to get done before they die—*and that could happen at any moment*—and we stop briefly and talk to each other about the enormous difference between the two sides of the road and we agree that the exceedingly few people we met on the supposedly jam-packed Easter ski tracks on the other side were nicer than the slightly larger numbers we've met here—at least they say "Hi!," we like people who say "Hi!," we agree, but the tracks are fantastic and it's still flat and lovely and look at that sun! This is the way it should be, this is Easter, this is what they talk about, all those people, and could it really get any better than this? And what could possibly go wrong now, And the Seychelles?! Don't get me started on the Seychelles! And we've eaten lunch without freezing to death and we've had a liquor-and-cigarillo break without anyone being bothered by it, and the only thing we're wondering about now is whether we'll soon be getting close to the cabin.

And then.

▲

THE HEAD OF DOCUMENTATION and I have slightly better glide than the others and sail on ahead after a small downhill. We stop and wait, because that's the kind of people we are. And then we think we've been waiting a bit too long. When we turn around, we see the HLE and the Worrier-in-Chief standing halfway down the hill.

And there they remain. In the end, we turn and head back toward them, because that's the kind of people we are.

The HLE gazes at us in genuine desperation.

"I've cracked my boot," she says.

"You've done what, now?"

"Cracked my boot."

"Sorry—one more time. What have you cracked?"

"My boot."

"Your boot?"

"My boot."

"Is it possible to crack a boot?"

▲

IT IS POSSIBLE. Part of her boot is stuck fast in the ski binding. The rest of the boot is on her foot.

One has planned and read up on things; one has sought tips from people with experience; one is convinced one has prepared for everything that could possibly go wrong in nature and packed accordingly.

Spade? Check.

Extra ski tip? Check.

Plenty of water? Check.

Headlamp? Check.

Bandage? Check.

Shoemaker? Oh, dammit.

AND THIS IS THE POINT where you show which side you're on. Because we are, actually, all perfectly aware that we aren't all that many miles away from a tourist cabin run by people who are used to pretty much anything happening in the mountains, and we even have the phone number of this cabin, and we have functioning cellphones, and this cabin probably has a snowmobile, so they can come and pick up the HLE. We know all that, of course. Actually. Even though it looks as if we're infinitely remote from civilization from where we're standing right now, in the middle of nowhere with half a boot.

And that's when the savage beast awakens in the HLE. There will absolutely be no ringing for snowmobiles. Snowmobiles are embarrassing. We'll get by.

MACGYVER GETS TO WORK. What we need, she says, is gaffer tape. We have none. What we do have, however, is some pretty useless medical adhesive tape that we brought with us in case any of us happen to crack a body part rather than an item of footwear.

An attempt is made to repair the boot with straps and tape. It holds for precisely twenty-two yards.

The snowmobile option is raised again but there's no question of it. The HLE discovers that if she can just avoid lifting her right foot, she can move forward. As long as it's flat, at any rate.

I see the Head of Documentation's face twitch slightly. And we probably feel the same about the HLE's new technique: "Okay, so you are sort of making progress. But if we forget the snowmobile, that means we'll *all* have to ski to the cabin at your pace, and that means we're not going to get there in time to enjoy a beer by the cabin wall before dinner today either—if we get there in time for dinner at all."

But this isn't our battle. This is a battle between the HLE and nature. And she has made her choice: to press on with one-and-a-half boots and a loose ski.

I won't deny it: There's some murmuring in the ranks now. Some-one asks, in a low voice, whether snowmobiles aren't there to be used too, and whether it's even defensible to set out on a long ski trip with equipment from the previous century.

There are fewer people out on the tracks now than earlier today but now we see a woman coming toward us. We tell her about our mishap and ask if she happens to have gaffer tape or a shoemaker in her backpack. She doesn't even have a backpack. But she consoles us and says it's no problem. The cabin is right around the corner. She's just come from there herself. Maybe the best thing is for one of us to just pop to the cabin and pick up some reserve skis and boots, which they'll almost certainly have there.

At this news, relief spreads through the group. Or at least three-quarters of the group. Because I have a sneaking feeling that this isn't entirely true. The thing is, I remember that some miles back we met a young couple by a signpost. This signpost said it was 5.2 miles to Tuva. The couple, who had skied from Tuva themselves, said there were only two signposts between Krækkja and Tuva. One of them showed 5.2 miles. And the other said 2.5 miles. I remember this because we joked a bit that the people who make the signposts on the Hardanger Plateau can apparently only write fives and twos.

And I can't remember having passed a sign that reads "Tuva 2.5 miles." And I would have remembered that. There isn't a hell of a lot of variation out on the plateau. It's mostly snow and ski tracks. You notice eye-catching stuff like signposts. Another thing is that I can't see any signposts up ahead either. And this is a plateau. You can see a long way on a plateau. In other words, most of the evidence suggests it's at least three miles to the cabin. Probably farther. Maybe a good deal farther. If one of us were to "pop" to the cabin that is "right around the corner" and back, it would take at least an hour. And that's if we send the fastest and most impatient member of the team (the Head of Documentation). It'll take one-and-a-half to two hours if we send the member who's keenest on liquor-and-cigarillo breaks and goofing around.

The others have started skiing, or limping, or whatever you call limping on skis, and looking out for the cabin. I don't think they picked up on the conversation by the 5.2-mile signpost. I decide I must have heard wrong or achieved the extraordinary feat of passing a signpost without noticing it.

That must be the explanation.

It is the only possible explanation.

So we ski and ski. The savage beast HLE in the lead, stubbornly limping, the rest of us right behind her. We'll get by. We are people of nature.

Progress isn't especially speedy, but I'll give the HLE this: She's pretty quick to discover a technique that works impressively well on flat terrain; she finds a rhythm and eventually achieves almost normal marching speed. If there were such a thing as a world championship in skiing on the flat with a loose ski, she'd make a fantastic showing.

And the group's spirits are rising.

And then we see something, a fair distance ahead of us.

IT ISN'T A CABIN, in case that's what you were thinking. No such luck.

No, it's a cluster of people. After a while, we see that this cluster of people is looking at something.

They're looking at a signpost. There's a pole planted in the snow and attached to the pole are signs pointing in all directions.

We've reached a crossroads on the plateau. And we have, I see, probably reached the point on our trip when at least one of our party is going to lose their shit.

The Worrier-in-Chief hurries over to the signpost. He reads it. He reads it again. Then he skis the few yards back to the rest of us and says, genuinely aggrieved:

"There are still 2.5 *miles* left to go. NOW!!!"

"Don't shout," I say. "You might trigger an avalanche."

But he has no sense of humor right now.

A

WE TELL THE PEOPLE by the signpost about our mishap. They are sympathetic but also laugh.

"It's a gentle downhill all the way from here to Tuva, though," one of them says.

And this is what the mountains do to you: I've become so distrustful now that I ask control questions.

"You've come from Tuva?"

"Yes."

"So you just skied the stretch from Tuva to here, is that what you're saying?"

"Yes."

"Right now?"

"Yes."

And then one of the others asks: "And from here it's all downhill?"

"Yes, from here it's a gentle downhill all the way."

A

AFTER SKIING FOR twenty minutes on terrain that is unquestionably uphill there's nothing for it but to accept that we know nothing. For all we know, it could be seven more miles to the cabin and the last four hundred yards could go straight up. Anything is possible. Because you simply can't trust any information provided by anybody here. We have just gathered information from three different sources. None of them said a single thing that was true.

The Worrier-in-Chief is starting to get enraged. The HLE is mainly focused on keeping up her technique and her spirits, someplace in that no-man's-land between bravery and hysteria. In the midst of all this, the Head of Documentation and I are both a little bit pleased that the other two have had this experience. Since our Jotunheimen trip, we've spent a lot of time talking about how people lie and boast all the time in the mountains. And I think our friends all thought we were exaggerating a fair amount ourselves when we talked about it.

But now we've just met people, several people, who lied right to our faces. And for no reason whatsoever! Because what we've heard today isn't even boasting. It's just lying. And they've lied to somebody who's had a mishap and has to ski at half the normal rate with broken equipment. Telling lies about distances and terrain to a person in a situation like that is nothing short of evil.

What's wrong with these people?

Hey you! The woman we met supposedly around two miles from the cabin (although who knows?): Do you always behave like this? Or are you only crazy out on the plateau? If you're in the downtown area of some city and you meet a person in a wheelchair, a *manual* wheelchair, and that person tells you his wheelchair is broken, that one of the wheels won't turn so he needs to get to a place that can fix the wheel, and he's found out that there's a place like that at such-and-such an address, and you know that this address is in a neighborhood that's three miles away from downtown and he asks you if it's a long way—what do you say then? Do you say that it's right around the corner and only show-offs take taxis?

Probably not. Because nobody would behave like that. Not in civilization. But out in nature, everything is different apparently.

Is it the mountain air that does it? Or maybe that virus has other, far worse complications than diarrhea?

Maybe there's something in the food? In all those dishes that haven't been served anywhere but the mountains since the eighties? Maybe there's something in the vintage food from the eighties that brings out the dishonesty in people? Maybe if you eat enough roast pork and aspic you lose your ability to distinguish between truth and falsehood?

I don't know whether you, dear reader, are old enough to remember the eighties, but I remember them. And people exaggerated quite a lot in the eighties, too. There really isn't any need for shoulder pads that big. The eighties was the decade of boasting. It was an attitude that was celebrated in those days. You were supposed to show off, and pretend you could cope with anything, and were world champion of pretty much everything.

In the rest of society, this behavior died out with the eighties.

But not in the mountains. It must be something in the food.

It's the aspic talking.

IT ALWAYS HELPS to overtake somebody. And if you can only lift one foot, it's also a pretty impressive achievement.

The person we now overtake turns out to be the woman we breakfasted with at Finse the day before yesterday, and whom we met with her friends at Krækkja yesterday. Maybe there aren't as many people out and about in the mountains at Easter as everybody claims, but on the other hand, we do get to meet the few who are there absolutely all the time.

The mood in this group is also slightly below average. Here the problem is blisters.

Ha! Blisters. We sneer at blisters. Just try skiing with half a boot! We all have blisters.

Well, not me, but I can imagine what it must be like.

WE DISCUSS HOW FAR it might be to the cabin. That's where they're headed too. We all think we can see a pennant or something up ahead. Could it be the cabin? It *must* be the cabin, says one of the friends. Or at least *a* cabin. Nobody would put up a flagpole and raise a pennant out in the middle of nowhere just to tease people.

I really wouldn't be so sure about that.

WE LEAVE THE FRIENDS behind us. They need to rest or argue or change boots or something. Our goal is in sight and we limp onward to the pennant. As we start to get closer, we come to a slightly unexpected downhill. This is a problem. The HLE's broken boot makes it impossible for her to position her skis in the V-shape required to plow down this hill at a manageably slow pace. She'll lose her skis if she tries. She'll have to take them off and walk down, with all the attendant humiliation of falling through the snow. Or she'll just have to shut her eyes and hope for the best. She shuts her eyes and hopes for the best. This is the way the new HLE is. She sets off, without plowing, and picks up a tremendous speed. The rest of us plow down the hill in her wake and watch as the HLE—at breakneck speed and with one loose ski—careens elegantly into the yard in front of a cabin with a pennant that has suddenly appeared, where people sit out in the sun drinking beer and saying "Happy Easter!"

▲

IN RECEPTION OF COURSE we meet a couple we met at both Finse and Krækkja. We chat lightheartedly. It's nice out now.

Then we ask about the chances of a boot repair. The woman in reception answers with a smile that her husband will almost certainly be able to fix it when he gets back. It sounds as if the cabin has its own resident MacGyver. She adds that they have plenty of extra equipment here if it's needed. It seems that a ski race takes place around here once a year. A good many of the participants are somewhat over-keen middle-aged men. Some of the ones we met on the tracks today who were too busy to say "Hi!" probably do this race. At any rate, there's a place nearby where participants who are unhappy with their performance throw away their ski equipment in a rage—not unlike the mountain-biking Swede you may remember from before. Later, somebody from the cabin goes out there and gathers up the discarded equipment, which they can then give away to any guests who might need it. This is the most beautiful display of recycling I've witnessed in a long time.

▲

I LIKE THIS CABIN. The hostess is funny. The cabin is much smaller than the other two cabins we've stayed at. And the hostess and the man who will soon fix the HLE's boot have just taken over the business from the previous generation. We like traditions, us mountain folk.

But we mustn't get too caught up in the conversation. Because today, we must be in time to have a beer by the wall of the cabin before dinner.

Outside, we find our spot, exchange a toast with some jolly Bergen folk and some Americans who are the first foreign tourists we've met since the bewildered Dutch people at Finse. One of them has a blister the size of his foot. It's not a problem, he says.

He's spent too much time in the Norwegian mountains.

We lean back against the wall, squint at the sun, and drink. This is fantastic. And after a couple of minutes it's freezing cold. You forget this from time to time. Either that or it's the delayed effect of the aspic starting to kick in.

And here come the friends we overtook a short while back.

And here, in fact, come Per and Kari from yesterday too.

Right: everybody who's skiing around the Easter mountains this year has now arrived, so dinner can be served.

▲

IT IS, IN FACT, possible that they *are* the only people skiing in the mountains this Easter because here, too—on the third of three attempts—we're given a four-person room all to ourselves. True enough, it's an odd little four-person room, but it's definitely within the bounds of what passes for charming. Or cramped, which is what that actually means. The room is directly under the roof. And to reach it you have to climb up a ladder and go through a small, low door. Or crawl. I know several people who simply wouldn't be able to get through that door, so I take it as a compliment that we've been put there. It's impossible to stand upright in here. We change clothes at ninety-degree angles and clamber down to dinner.

HOLD ON TO YOUR HATS. At dinner, they serve fish! And rice!!

Hello?!

You can tell that a new generation has taken over here, and they are thinking well outside the box. They've diverged from the cabin rule of offering only pork and beef to ensure the exclusion of as many minorities as possible at all times.

We share an extremely pleasant corner table with the group of friends. They're heading to Geilo tomorrow. We are too. Or at least we think we are right until we hear that the last stretch of this route is a downhill ski slope.

Now, we're only going to Geilo to catch the train home. And it's possible to ski to other places in the vicinity where there are also train stations but that don't require you to race down an Alpine ski slope on narrow skis. There is, for example a place called Ustaoset.

That it also *happens* to be half as far away is not a determining factor. The point here is that we must show solidarity with the person in our group who has lousy poles and cracked boots.

And the fact that we have adjusted and shortened our route for the second day in a row just goes to show that we are above the silly macho culture of the mountains, opting for sensible choices instead of making things more unpleasant for ourselves than strictly necessary.

But of course when we learn that one of the friends at the table is going to travel to Geilo by snowmobile tomorrow because of a blister, we crack a dozen or so jokes about it.

That much silly machismo is certainly permissible. This is a vacation after all.

▲

ONCE AGAIN, WE'RE so delighted to have adjusted our route that we order a fair amount of wine. The HLE updates the injury map. The Worrier-in-Chief is the one whose injuries have escalated most since yesterday.

The cabin's resident MacGyver comes to our table and tells us he's fixed the boot. Naturally he is wild-haired, chatty, and pleasant. The boot has been stuck together with superglue and should hold for a while at least, he says. Which is sort of moderately reassuring.

Our hosts inform us besides that a kind of shift change takes place at the cabin every day. After breakfast all the overnight guests set off on their trips. Then it's quiet for an hour or two until all the day guests arrive. These are people who have their own cabins in the area and who drop in at Tuva on their training runs to eat waffles. It seems the waffles here are legendary. Of course they are. It's the fish soup all over again.[3]

"We're not leaving this cabin until we've tasted those waffles," says the Head of Documentation.

▲

WE HAVE A LONG CHAT with Per and Kari. And a short one with the friends. And a short one with the couple we met at Finse and Krækkja and just now at reception. And maybe it's a good thing this is our last evening. All indications are that if we were to continue to yet another cabin tomorrow, we'd meet all the same people once again. And at some point we'd inevitably start talking about something other than mountains and skis and distances and cabins and blisters. And then,

---

[3] Keep up! Or check the chapters called "Indoor Mountains and Popcorn on the Campfire" and "Liquor and Cigarillos."

anything could happen. After all, we have no idea who these people really are. If we start talking about regular stuff, they may turn out to be racists. Or do yoga.

The conversation at the table is already starting to take a dangerous turn toward regular topics between normal people but luckily we're saved in the nick of time.

It's eleven o'clock. The power is shut off.

ANOTHER THING THAT VARIES from cabin to cabin: the temperature. It's either absurdly hot (the fireside lounge at Finse) or absurdly cold (the bedroom at Krækkja). This time we're back to absurdly hot. Because our room is located pretty much directly above the fireplace. And it's roughly two feet beneath the roof, so it warms up quickly. What's more, the outdoor temperature is close to record cold levels, so getting ready for bed in this place involves an expedition with a temperature range of 107 degrees. You go from your bedroom, where it must be 85°F, down a ladder and then outside, where it must be close to -22°F, to the outhouse, whose walls are more holes than walls and where it actually feels colder than outside, and then you have to go outside again to a third building to wash your hands and brush your teeth before returning once again to the main cabin where you go to bed bathed in balmy heat.

Before doing all that, we decide to prolong this final evening a bit and share the last cigarillo.

I WOULDN'T SAY we become melancholy or sentimental as we stand there, but it's pretty nice to share a cigarillo in the darkness and the bitter cold as a blistered American limps by in the background.

GLOSSARY

USEFUL WORDS AND EXPRESSIONS to learn if you're going to the mountains:

- Nice = cold
- Lovely = cold
- Pretty = cold
- Nice and lovely = cold
- Charming = cramped
- Sense of achievement = finally finishing something that's bored you for a long time
- Short = far
- Not far = far
- No problem = problem
- Right around the corner = three miles
- Downhill = uphill
- Hilly = steep
- Not steep = steep
- Meditative = boring
- Airy = straight uphill and lethal

LISTEN TO INEXPERIENCED MOUNTAIN FOLK, PART 3

1. Always take gaffer tape, extra ski boots, superglue, and MacGyver with you.

2. There's a long way left to go. There's always a long way left to go.

3. Always take along plenty of cigarillos or something similar that you like and that isn't appropriate in the mountains. There are many things you can forget to pack for your trip to the mountains without causing a crisis. A surprisingly large number of things can be bought or borrowed at mountain cabins. But you'll have a hard time getting your hands on cigarillos.

4. There's no shame in calling for a snowmobile.

5. There's no shame in adjusting your route, absolutely all the time.

WHITE PEOPLE TALKING ABOUT BLISTERS

Last Leg: Tuva–Ustaoset.
On skis. Six miles.

WE'RE GOING TO sample those legendary waffles. As a last test of the standards of truthfulness in the mountains. So we remain sitting there after breakfast is over. And we remain sitting there when all the others have left.

There go Per and Kari. Bye now. Have a good trip.

And there goes the group of friends. Some of them by snowmobile. Weaklings.

And there goes the couple we met at Finse. And Krækkja. And last night. And at breakfast this morning.

Bye now.

Nice out on the plateau now.

Fantastic when it's like this.

The Seychelles—pah!

Easter's early this year.

Have a good trip.

Green.

AND THEN IT'S JUST US. We have plenty of time. Because today we really *won't* be going far. We'll be going six miles, a lot of it downhill. And not such steep downhills either, our hostess has assured us of that. Not steep at all, just good fun, as she put it.

So we're going to chill and read a bit and wait for those famous waffles. Loaf about by the cabin wall possibly. Maybe even be wild and crazy enough to have one last beer outdoors before we leave.

So that's why we're sitting in the fireside lounge chatting away at ten thirty.

And it's clear that nothing like this has ever happened at a tourist cabin on the Hardanger Plateau before. This is a break with routine. People arrive here in the afternoon, answer questions about thermoses and pack lunches, leave their backpacks in tiny little rooms that are either too cold or too hot, eat dinner with people they met at another cabin yesterday, talk about blisters, go to bed early, get up early, eat breakfast, and leave. People just sitting here, during the daytime, for no reason—that's probably never happened before.

The cabin is supposed to be cleaned now. The cleaning lady comes into the fireside lounge. She stands there for a while looking at us. And then she just walks out again. She's probably called a crisis meeting in the back room.

"There are people here."

"People? Here? Now?"

"Yes."

"What kind of people?"

"Guests, I think."

"Guests? Now? But it's past 10 AM."

"I know."

"What are they doing?"

"Just sitting there."

"Why?"

"How should I know? Chilling or something."

"Chilling?! What kind of a crazy thing is that to do on vacation?"

"I don't know!"

"Are they planning to sit there long?"

"They say they want waffles."

"Waffles? But they've only just had breakfast. The waffles are for the day guests. They won't be here for another hour. We can't let day guests and overnight guests start mingling—everybody knows that, don't they? How on earth would that work out?"

"What shall we do?"

"We've never seen anything like this before. We had four thousand guests in two rooms here one Easter, and we survived the viral outbreak, but nothing as wild as this has ever happened before."

THEY GIVE US WAFFLES. They probably realize it's the only way they're going to get rid of us. The waffles actually *are* very good. Best in the world is a bit of a leap but they are most definitely crispy and very good indeed. Everybody agrees on that. But this may be because we've spent too long in the mountains and have forgotten what ordinary food tastes like. And of course, the cook may have put some aspic in the mixture.

ONE QUITE FUN THING that can happen when you're out skiing on a plateau is that you start humming songs that somehow relate to what you're doing. And I'm not thinking here of the way "The Happy Wanderer" still pops up at regular intervals. There's another reason. During the first break of the day, we talk about what we hum and sing as we ski along in our own world.

"'It's a Long Way to Tipperary,' actually."

"Heavens."

"I know. I'm shocked myself."

"'Over the Hills and Far Away.' "

"Of course!"

"Ever since we left the cabin, I've been singing 'He Ain't Heavy, He's My Brother,' I've no idea why."

"It's probably because it starts off: 'The road is long, with many a winding turn.' "

We look at the tracks ahead of us. Which are long. With many a winding turn. We nod.

And then we hum "He Ain't Heavy, He's My Brother" pensively and in harmony. And not especially beautifully.

"Okay," says the Head of Documentation. "But can anybody explain to me why I'm skiing along singing 'Nearer My God to Thee'?"

We'd rather not think about that.

Especially not the HLE, who's started to get seriously worried about the long downhill that lies ahead. We're supposed to head down into a valley. It must, of necessity, go down at some point. But it isn't so steep—the hostess told us so. And we do, in fact, trust her, even though she's one of the mountain folk. She pretty much told the truth about the waffles, for example. And "pretty much telling the truth" really isn't all that bad by mountain folk standards. The HLE is afraid her boot might fall apart halfway down a steep hill. Not entirely without reason. What we see before us now looks very much like a pretty steep and pretty long downhill slope. One of us quietly hums Bruce Springsteen's "I'm Goin' Down."

But there are a few signs down there; we don't know for sure that we're supposed to go down the steepest part. There are tracks going off in several directions.

There are quite a few people out and about here, so we ask the ones who know the area if the hill down to Ustaoset is steep.

"Not at all, it's nice and gentle," says the first man.

The HLE tells him she has a broken boot.

"Not a problem," says another person.

"I skied down there with broken binding just yesterday," says a third person.

"I do that every day."

"Did I say *one* broken binding? I meant two of course. And I do it every day too. Even in the summer when there isn't any snow."

"Luxury! I ski down this hill four times a day all year round without skis, boots, or bindings."

"Easy. When I was young, we lived in a wooden bathtub without any water, outside, all winter long. Every day we had to get up before we'd gone to bed, clean the wooden bathtub without any water, and go up and down this hill twenty times, naked, and when we got home, what did we get? Breakfast? Far from it. We got a thrashing. If we were lucky!"

"Mm. And you try and tell the young people of today that and they won't believe you."

"They won't—that's the way things are nowadays. Enjoy the rest of your ski."

"You too. Nice out on the plateau now."

"Fantastic when Easter's like this."

"Green."

"The Seychelles can go jump in a lake."

▲

OF COURSE, YOU'LL HAVE GUESSED this long ago and you probably read the glossary that came before this chapter, because you're clever and you read things in the right order and don't jump back and forth in a book at random: It *is* steep. It's very steep. And when we reach the sign, it turns out that, yes, of course, we're supposed to ski down the steepest part. And suddenly somebody comes whizzing down in crouch position at seventy miles an hour.

And yes, the HLE's boot cracks again on the first bend. So much for MacGyver.

▲

WHAT NOW? MAN OR MOUSE? Rick Astley or the Soviet Union?

There's really only one thing the HLE can do. She'll have to take off her skis and walk. Walking in snow is idiotically slow. Especially when you're going down a steep slope where lawyers in suits snug as condoms whizz past because they have to get into shape so they can hurl away their skis in a rage after taking part in a race that means absolutely nothing at all.

And what are the rest of us supposed to do? We're not crazy enough to race straight down. Plowing down in between the tracks isn't an option either because that means you'll risk having a midlife crisis in crouch position crash into you from behind. And *you'll* be the one getting told off.

We decide to zigzag down in the loose snow beside the track. It isn't elegant but at least that means we'll all maintain more or less the same speed as the HLE. We are, and always will be, a supportive bunch.

▲

"WHAT'S THIS? Don't you have the nerve to ski straight down? But it isn't even steep, is it?" somebody says to me in passing. I look up. See a back. Was there something familiar about it?

No.

▲

"DIDN'T I HEAR that you smoke cigarillos out in nature?"

Who said that?

"Ah yes, aren't you the ones who go about making fun of the names in the Norwegian mountains? Wizard's Wiener? Vampire's Vagina? Is that supposed to be funny, eh?"

I turn around—I can't work out who said that.

"You must respect nature."

Now I see him. Or is at a him? Is it the man we met when we took a cigarillo break just before Krækkja? Or is it that woman who gave us a dirty look during our first cigarillo break? Or is it actually the one who told us off in the dinner line at Finse? I think this person looks like all three of them.

"Nature is capricious," he says. "And that hill is not steep. And sixteen miles isn't far."

Then he heads off.

"Nice out on the plateau now. Fantastic when Easter's like this. There's no better place to be. We live in the world's most beautiful country, nobody can say any different, we have . . ."

He fades out.

A MAN COMES walking toward me. He's wearing a sheer mesh tank top on his upper body and nothing whatsoever besides. He's walking along eating a portion of lasagna with potatoes. He stops. Then he stands there and looks at me for a while, chewing, before coming right up to me.

"Old food?" he says, offering me a bit of lasagna with potato.

"No thanks."

"You really ought to try it. It isn't so bad. It helps you forget."

"Forget?"

"I have some aspic in my back pocket if you'd rather have that."

"No thanks."

"A bit of lasagna with potato, a bite of aspic, and the hill isn't steep at all. A little roast pork on top of that and it flattens out completely."

"No thanks."

"Okay. Your call."

He vanishes.

I HAVE TO GET BACK to the track.

I turn around. I can't see the track anywhere. Or the Head of Documentation. Or the HLE or the Worrier-in-Chief. I see a woman with a sled skiing slowly past off in the distance, looking straight at me. Otherwise nothing.

I look behind me, ahead of me, to my right, to my left...

Who's that standing on the edge of the forest staring at me?

I've seen her before.

Is it...? It can't be...

But yes, it's the hostess from the cabin by Galdhøpiggen. The one who said it was a nice hike regardless, even in zero visibility and crappy weather. It's her. She's eating meat and staring at me. She's humming "The Happy Wanderer," I think.

She turns and vanishes into the forest.

Who do I see back there? On the mountainside across the valley? It looks like...Julie Andrews? Dancing with Jim Carrey? And singing "The Happy Wanderer"?

No. That can't be right.

But somebody is singing "The Happy Wanderer"—I can hear it. It's an entire choir. And it's definitely getting louder and louder. I turn and see a long line coming toward me singing. Some of them are taking bites out of a leg of roast pork as they go. In between the singing, they mouth small phrases.

"Nice now."

"Fantastic."

"Good to use your body."

"Doesn't get any better than this."

"Oh no, it isn't far."

I recognize them all. There are Per and Kari. And our friends from yesterday. The one who left on the snowmobile is there with them and is walking. The others stuff food into her mouth.

And there are the oil-rig gang we met before we hiked over Besseggen in the summer. I'm pleased to see them and wave at them. They
don't wave back. I go over to one of them. Ask where they're heading.

"Don't ask questions like that," he says gravely. "Roast pork?"

Then they continue onward.

And there's the woman who lives in Australia. And the one who
turned up at Krækkja after skiing three-and-a-half hours in darkness.
And that guy with the teenage daughter.

And damn it if it isn't the Canadians we met at both Besseggen
and Preikestolen in the summer. Where are they going, all these
people?

It's as if they want something from me. Mr. Canada nods to me,
as if he wants me to come along with him. Mrs. Canada just shrugs.

I follow them. They walk, rhythmically. All of them mutter that
it's fantastic and nice and not steep and not far. Roast pork is passed
around. There is humming.

The road is long.

Do re mi.

⸪

AND THEN THE LANDSCAPE opens up. We come out onto a massive
plain.

⸪

AND THERE THEY ALL ARE. All those friends I've lost to nature over
the years. They're walking around. They're walking around in a circle.
Everybody from the group I came with joins the circle. And then they
continue to go around and around. Everybody greets everybody else
the whole time as if they've never met before. "Hi! Nice," they say.
"Fantastic. Not far. Not steep. Lovely. Doesn't get any better. World's
best waffles. This is the life."

I run over to a person who was at college with me.

"Goodness. I haven't seen you for ages," I say.

"You're wrong," he says. "It wasn't all that long ago. Aspic?"

"Why are you walking around here?" I ask another.

"What do you mean?" he asks. "It doesn't any get better than this."

"Weren't you really funny once?"

"That doesn't sound like me," he says. "Have some of this old confirmation food and come with us."

"But you're going in circles." I say.

"No," replies a person I used to work and party with in the nineties. "We aren't. Sooner or later we'll get to a wooden cabin where white people are talking about blisters. What more does life have to offer than that?"

"Um ... I can think of quite a few things!"

"No you can't. Come with us now."

Everybody in the circle talks to me.

"Come with us. There's absolutely nothing to worry about."

"No problem."

"Shut out life."

"Stop time."

"It isn't far."

"Right over here."

"Fantastic."

"It's only when you come face to face with nature that you realize how small you are."

"Doesn't get any better."

"Love the outdoors."

"Norway wasn't made so you could sit on your ass."

"This is where we are ourselves."

"Why dream when you're living the life everybody else dreams of?"

"Come with us."

"Come with us."

"Come with us."

SOURCES, DIGRESSIONS, AND EXTRA INFORMATION FOR NERDS

THE NUMBER ABOUT Norwegians and hiking at the very beginning of the book comes from Statistics Norway's 2017 survey of living conditions.

And when I write that almost eighty percent of people have gone hiking "in the mountains or the forest" in the past twelve months, that's because the business of mountains or forests was specified in the questions asked in the survey. So if, for example, you go hiking in residential areas, parks, downtown, or lowland nature without any trees in the vicinity, it doesn't count.

THAT'S NOT IT

THE INFORMATION AND JOKES about Stranda's championship adventure in 1983 are drawn from memory, reminiscing with friends, assistance from soccer expert Arne Scheie, the statistics yearbook from 1983, and newspaper articles from the time, many of them conscientiously reproduced on Stranda Football Club's website. The entire match and much of the warm-up are available on YouTube, by the way, for anyone who's really interested.

The information about the increase in outdoor life in my lifetime, and about social differences in outdoor life comes from the survey of living conditions mentioned above. The social differences are, incidentally, particularly dramatic in the case of skiing, maybe because skis cost a lot, although that's not the only reason. Some thirty-three percent of people with secondary education go skiing over the course of a year, which is, quite honestly, a pretty high figure. But the equivalent number for people with post-secondary education is seventy-one percent.

One slightly fun thing that may indicate how much of this is about us simply having more leisure time available is that physical training is not the only activity that has increased in my lifetime. Over the same period, use of cultural resources has also grown pretty sharply. Questions about the cultural resources people had used in the previous twelve months reflected the following development: cinema rose from fifty-eight percent to seventy-two percent between 1991 and 2016; theater and revue from forty-four percent to fifty percent; concerts from forty-eight percent to sixty-two percent; and participation in ballet and dance almost doubled over the same period. In other words, it does not, after all, appear that we can live on nature alone once we've become as civilized as we now are. If I may be permitted to offer anecdotal evidence for this same point (and who's going to stop me?) I'd like to mention Svalbard again. For those of you who don't know it, Svalbard is a Norwegian archipelago that consists almost entirely of nature. Almost no people live on Svalbard, and if you take even a brief walk around beyond its vanishingly few streets, you risk meeting a polar bear. You don't go to Svalbard unless you're rugged and have a soft spot for nature. But even there, people apparently have a need for culture and social gatherings. To a massive extent, in fact. Longyearbyen, Svalbard's largest town by a long margin, has around two thousand inhabitants. At the time of writing, there were sixteen bars and two cultural centers in and around Longyearbyen. That's equivalent to seven hundred cultural centers in Oslo. It's like London having 72,000 pubs and 18,000 theaters. Although that last one's not so far from the truth, so it's not such a good example.

I also found a lot about the development of, and social differences in, outdoor life in the book *Ute!* (*Out!*, Fagbokforlaget, 2016), in particular the chapter written by Kolbjørn Rafoss and Ørnulf Seipel entitled "Outdoor Activities in the Norwegian Population—A Study of Traits of Development and Social Differences in the Period 1990–2013." When it comes to hikes and ski trips in the mountains, these two writers conclude, among other things: "The increased participation and social expansion can therefore be seen as a unique national trait." They also write that increased physical activity since the eighties is not a result of changes in the composition of the population or in lifespan. These are, as they write, "new times."

The research about Norwegians' plans for the fall vacation comes from an Ipsos survey carried out on behalf of the Norwegian Outdoor Council in 2017.

Norway's longest-running reality show is called *71 grader nord* (*71 Degrees North*, the equivalent of *No Boundaries*). The first Norwegian reality series was called *Robinsonekspedisjonen*—our version of *Survivor*, although it's actually Swedish. Both premiered in 1999. *71 grader nord* has both a regular and a celebrity version, the latter often demonstrating that recently retired top athletes are in somewhat better shape than musicians and actors.

As I mention, the origin of the quotation about incest and Morris dancing is disputed. Those credited include Arnold Bax, Thomas

Beecham, and Samuel Johnson. I first heard it in a speech by British polymath Stephen Fry, whom I must admit I trust. He credits Arnold Bax, but hedges it by adding "is reputed to have said." Which actually gets us no further. Indeed barely as far.

THINGS I DON'T UNDERSTAND

HAVE NATURE AND THE OUTDOOR LIFE taken the place of religion over the past thirty to forty years?, I ask in the book. For fun, of course—but I didn't simply pluck this out of thin air. Over time, several surveys have placed Scandinavian countries among the least religious in the world. A survey conducted by Gallup International in sixty-five countries in 2005 ranked Western Europe as the least religious region in the world, and Norway as the least religious country in Western Europe. In January 2018, *The Telegraph* merged three surveys carried out by Worldwide Independent Network/Gallup International in 2008, 2009, and 2015, in which people were asked how religious they felt to produce a ranking of the world's most and least religious countries. Sweden and Norway rank, respectively, fourth and fifth on the list of the least religious countries. In Europe, Sweden and Norway rank number two and three on the same list, beaten only by Estonia, which is, practically speaking, also Scandinavian. And the idea that God had a stronger standing twenty to thirty years ago is demonstrated by Norsk Monitor (Norwegian Monitor), which comprehensively maps Norwegians' worldviews, among other things, and has been carried out every other year since 1985 by Ipsos MMI. In 1985, more than fifty percent answered that they believed in God and just over twenty percent that they did not. In 2015, the situation was totally reversed. Some thirty-nine percent answered that they were not believers, while thirty-seven percent answered that they did believe in God.

Several books are referred to and quoted in this chapter. Here they are:

- William Cecil Slingsby: *Norway: The Northern Playground— Sketches of Climbing and Mountain Exploration in Norway Between 1872 and 1903* (they went in for titles that didn't leave too much to your imagination in those days). David Douglas, 1904.
- Erling Kagge: *Silence: In the Age of Noise*, tr. Becky L. Crook. Pantheon Books, 2018.
- Thomas Thwaites: *GoatMan: How I Took a Holiday From Being Human*. Princeton Architectural Press, 2016.
- Jon Krakauer: *Into the Wild*. Villard, 1996.

The slightly snooty Ibsen quote is, appropriately enough, drawn from the poem "On the Fells."

The statements about human noise are from the Norwegian Broadcasting Corporation (NRK) program *Selskap*, broadcast on NRK2 in September 2015. It's still available on nrk.no in case you're interested.

All the data about what has happened in our lives in the period since everybody started hiking in the mountains are drawn from Statistics Norway. Fling me against the wall and call me Nerdy McNerdface but you can spend weeks on Statistics Norway's website and never get bored.

The world's happiest countries are ranked in the "World Happiness Report," produced by the United Nations Sustainable Development Solutions Network (ugh!). In the 2018 report, the entire Nordic region is in the top ten. The four happiest countries are all Nordic: Finland, Norway, Denmark, and Iceland. Sweden is all the way down in ninth place. Canada comes in at number seven and the United States at number eighteen.

When we in Norway delight in saying that the UN always ranks us as the world's best country we're usually referring to the United Nations Development Programme's Human Development Index, which—strictly speaking—ranks countries according to how developed they are. In this ranking, Switzerland, Canada, and Germany tend to do well, along with the Nordic countries. Probably not because they also happen to be countries where people go hiking in the mountains (except for Denmark) but rather because we're comfortably enough off to have time to do this kind of stuff.

A couple of numbers from Statistics Norway that tell us a bit about the extent to which we've become distanced from nature in our daily lives during my lifetime: In my birth year, 1969, there were over 150,000 agricultural businesses in Norway. In 2010, there were 46,000.

The business about the word "boredom" appearing in the English language at the same time as Englishmen started hiking in Norway is, of course, mostly nonsense. But it isn't totally untrue either. When I read Lars Fr. H. Svendsen's *Kjedsomhetens filosofi* (*A Philosophy of Boredom*), (Universitetsforlaget, 1999), which is a natural choice of reading material when you're supposed to go hiking in the mountains, I came across the detail that the first recorded use of "boredom" in the English language was in the 1870s. Slingsby's first trip to Norway took place in 1872. Just saying.

I've read a great deal about the origin, inspiration for, and launch of the Norwegian Trekking Association in the organization's yearbooks and, for example, the following books:

- Rune Slagstad: *Da fjellet ble dannet* (*When Mountains Were Created*). Dreyer, 2018.

- Per Roger Lauritzen: *Norske fjell og vidder* (*Norwegian Mountains and Plateaus*). Font, 2011.

INDOOR MOUNTAINS AND
POPCORN ON THE CAMPFIRE

I GOT THE CALCULATION showing that the whole world would fit in Østfold County from the fact-based comedy panel show *Brille*. But I've worked it out for myself to be on the safe side. It's true.

I won't tell you the name of the pub I mention in Edinburgh. You don't want to go there.

The calculation about how much you can get for the price of barely a week in Jotunheimen is based on Googling and 2018 prices.

1ST ATTEMPT:
TO JOTUNHEIMEN IN
SEARCH OF SALVATION

IT WAS THE Oslo-based daily newspaper *Aftenposten* that asked its readers to vote for the city's ugliest building in 2008. The clear winner was Galleri Oslo, which houses, among other things, the bus terminal, and which opened its doors at around the same time as the Oslo Plaza, and was heralded as the longest indoor shopping street in the Nordic region. It was important to be the longest and tallest in the Nordic region in those days.

The German original of "The Happy Wanderer" is *"Der fröhliche wanderer,"* also known as *"Mein Vater war ein Wandersmann"* after the first line. The music was written by Friedrich-Wilhelm Möller, and the lyrics by Friedrich Sigismund. There are several Norwegian recordings. Naturally, my favorite is the Søstrene Bjørklund version. There's a very loud and annoying Louis Prima version in English.

"Do-Re-Mi" is of course from *The Sound of Music* by Rodgers and Hammerstein.

The John Irving quote about the sound of someone trying not to make a sound originally appeared in the novel *A Widow for One Year*, in which a fictional children's author writes a book about this. Later, Irving also published a children's book called *A Sound Like Someone Trying Not to Make a Sound*.

The figure for the number of people who hike over Besseggen per year comes from nasjonalparkriket.no, which is also one of the websites that describes the hike as "obligatory for all Norwegians."

I got the figure for the number of overnight stays at Gjendesheim from Gjendesheim's website so you can decide for yourself whether you're willing to trust it.

One of the places you can confirm the fact that you risk falling 1,300 feet from Besseggen is the website of Visit Jotunheimen, which is hardly likely to want to scare people off.

The detail that people have to be helped down from Besseggen fifteen to twenty times a year was provided by the host at Gjendesheim in an interview with *Aftenposten*, among others.

The book containing general advice and tips about outdoor life that began so promisingly is *God tur, håndbook i friluftsliv* (*Have a Good Hike: An Outdoors Handbook*) by Sigri Sandberg (yes, she of the human noise).

I found many old accounts of travel in Norwegian nature in the Norwegian Trekking Association's yearbooks, in several of the books I've already mentioned, and in *Da Norge ble oppdaget* (*When Norway Was Discovered*), edited by Arngeir Berg and Arne Johan Gjermundsen. This is where I found the quotes from both Carter Smith and Fabricius.

The Nietzsche quote is from 1878. So, pretty old.

I read about the doubling in land area used for cabins in the article "Berekraftig eller berre kraftig hytteliv?" ("Sustainable or Just Excessive Cabin Life?") by Carlo Aall in the magazine *Syn og Segn*,

No. 3, 2017. In the same place (it was a special issue about cabins and leisure), I also found the story about the tourism planners in Oppland who thought mountain hotels were the future, in the article "Frå nytte til den modern hytte" ("From Utility to the Modern Cabin") by Håvard Teigen.

The answer to the "Philosophy or yoga?" contest on page 126: Quote no. 2 is Rousseau. The other two are from the article "Yoga naturligvis" ("Yoga Naturally") in *Fjell & vidde*, No. 3, 2016.

The figure for the number of people with power and running water at their cabins comes from a survey Ipsos MMI carried out for *Hytteliv* in 2014.

I took the facts about the not-especially-Norwegian right to roam from Wikipedia and the article "Allemannsrett i andre land" ("The Right to Roam in Other Countries") on allemannsretten.no, a website set up by the lawyer Marianne Reusch, who wrote her PhD on the right to roam, by the way.

The information about how many people visit Preikestolen is from preikestolen.no, so you can decide for yourself whether you're willing to trust it.

I EXPLORE MYSELF AND MY CITY

THE DISCUSSION OF how risky it is to hike to the top of Slogen ran in several local media outlets in northwestern Norway over the summer of 2016. I read about it on the websites of NRK Møre og Romsdal and Sunnmørsposten. The man who started the debate by saying that the Slogen hike was risk-exposed and not suitable for small children is called Jan-Gunnar Hole and he's the head of the Sunnmøre Alpine Rescue Group. Not a guy who's unfamiliar with the dangers of the mountains, in other words.

I read about automation and the like in *Rise of the Robots* by Martin Ford, and in the report entitled "Norway's New Jobs in the Wake of the Digital Revolution" by the Swedish economist Stefan Fölster. Or to be honest, I watched the ten-minute talk he gave about the report's findings. It's on the internet.

2ND ATTEMPT:
TO THE HARDANGER PLATEAU
IN SEARCH OF PEOPLE

ACCORDING TO THE Norwegian Trekking Association's website, the Hardanger Plateau was the most popular mountain area over Easter in both 2017 and 2018. Finsehytta was the most visited cabin in Norway over Easter 2017 and number two in 2018. Krækkja was also in the top five.

The Rick Astley album that topped the charts in the UK and not very many other places in 2016 was *50*, which apparently refers to his age. In other words, he did an Adele, only with much higher numbers.

Scenes from planet Hoth in *The Empire Strikes Back* were filmed in Finse in 1979, which is why nerds continue to travel to Finse for the annual Visit Hoth event. It's not entirely beyond the bounds of probability that you'll meet beings from another galaxy in the snow out on the plateau during this particular event.

It's true that Trollpikken (Troll's Dick) was vandalized in 2017. It was cut off, no less, and the news sped around the world—as if journalists ever needed an excuse to make puns. Trollpikken has since been repaired.

The Stan Ridgway solo album I mentioned is, of course, *The Big Heat*, including high points like "Salesman," "Drive, She Said," and the musical war novella, "Camouflage."

My doctor is Asle T. Johansen and during my work on this book, I've enjoyed reading his book about the South Pole trip, *Til sydpolen 100 år etter* (*To the South Pole 100 Years Later*), (Fri flyt, 2012).

I read about Krækkja's history on UT.no, on the cabin's own website, and on Wikipedia, which largely seem to quote each other.

The cable car the queen opened was Loen Skylift in Nordfjord. Her quote is taken from an article about the issue on nrk.no on May 23, 2017.

Hovden Alpinsenter was the first Norwegian ski center to introduce mandatory helmets in 2017, thereby sparking the debate about this.

I found the information that most Norwegians think it should be illegal to drive boats when you're tipsy in a survey carried out by Kantar TNS Gallup in 2017, which showed that more than seventy percent think the blood alcohol limit should be the same on sea as on the roads.

The quote about living the life everybody else dreams of comes from the book entitled *Kunsten å vandre* (*The Art of Wandering*), edited by Julie Maske and published to mark the 150th anniversary of the Norwegian Trekking Association.

GENERAL RESOURCES

I HAVE ALSO READ a number of other books that have probably given me ideas or confirmed my prejudices. For example:

- Eivind Eidslott: *Helt ute, et skråblikk på fjellfolk, skiturer, turistforeningshytter og løping generelt* (*Far Out: A Sideways Glance at Mountain Folk, Ski Trips, Trekking Association Cabins and Running in General*). Fri flyt, 2014.

- Thomas Espedal: *Tramp: Or the Art of Living a Wild and Poetic Life*, tr. James Anderson. Seagull World Literature, 2010.

- Bjørn Gabrielsen: *Vinterkrigen, nordmenns fåfengte kamp mot den kalde årstid* (*The Winter War: Norwegians' Futile Battle Against the Cold Season*). Gyldendal, 2002. (A very funny book. I've introduced a tiny quote from this book into my own. I did this intentionally and as a tribute.)

- Magnus Helgerud: *Si meg hvor du reiser og jeg skal si deg hvem du er* (*Tell Me Where You Travel and I'll Tell You Who You Are*). Aschehoug, 2018.

- Erlend Loe: *Doppler,* tr. Don Bartlett and Don Shaw. Head of Zeus, 2018. And *Slutten på verden slik vi kjenner den* (*The End of the World as We Know It*). Cappelen Damm, 2015.

- Lars Backe Madsen: *Gullracet, medaljer, makt og mysterier i norsk langrenn* (*The Race for Gold: Medals, Power, and Mysteries in Norwegian Cross-Country Skiing*). Gyldendal, 2017.

- Ian McEwan: *Solar.* Jonathan Cape, 2010. (An unusually funny novel in which, among other things, the protagonist travels to the Arctic to save the world and manages to trap his penis in a zipper while he's getting dressed. I think this scene also provides a slightly sad image of our times.)

- Agnes Ravatn: *Verda er ein skandale, ei bok om livet på landet* (*The World Is a Scandal: A Book About Life in the Countryside*). Samlaget, 2017.

- Peter Wessel Zapffe: *Barske glæder og andre temaer fra et liv under åpen himmel* (*Rugged Pleasures and Other Themes From a Life Beneath the Open Sky*). Cappelen Damm, 2016.

I've also spent a long time here, although it's not something I'd necessarily recommend doing:
- harvest.no
- ut.no
- dnt.no
- fjellforum.no

THANKS TO Arne Flatin, Erland Grev Hesthagen, Tommy Hovde, Jens M. Johansson, Siri Vaggen Kanedal, Berit Susanne Kjølås, Ane Kolberg, Lisbeth Koppang, Morten Lorentzen, Julie Maske, Øyvind Starheim, and other old, new, lost, and found friends I bothered before, during, and after the trips.